THE POLITICS OF
FIELD RESEARCH

THE POLITICS OF FIELD RESEARCH

Sociology beyond Enlightenment

edited by Jaber F. Gubrium and
David Silverman

Ⓢ SAGE Publications
London · Newbury Park · New Delhi

Introduction and editorial material © Jaber F. Gubrium and
David Silverman 1989
Chapter 1 © Roy Turner 1989
Chapter 2 © David Silverman 1989
Chapter 3 © Phil Strong and Robert Dingwall 1989
Chapter 4 © Peter R. Grahame 1989
Chapter 5 © Jaber F. Gubrium 1989
Chapter 6 © Don Slater 1989
Chapter 7 © Lindsay Prior 1989
Chapter 8 © Susan Silbey and Austin Sarat 1989
Chapter 9 © Mary Simms 1989
Chapter 10 © Michael Bloor and Neil McKeganey 1989
Chapter 11 © Peter K. Manning 1989
Chapter 12 © Elim Papadakis 1989

First published 1989

SAGE Publications Ltd
28 Banner Street
London EC1Y 8QE

SAGE Publications Inc
2111 West Hillcrest Drive
Newbury Park, California 91320

SAGE Publications India Pvt Ltd
32, M-Block Market
Greater Kailash – I
New Delhi 110 048

British Library Cataloguing in Publication data

The politics of field research: Sociology beyond
  enlightenment.
  1. Sociology. Field research. Methodology
  I. Gubrium, Jaber F. II. Silverman, David
  301'0723

ISBN 0–8039–8226–7

Library of Congress catalog card number 89–60997

Typeset by Photoprint, Torquay, Devon
Printed in Great Britain by Billing and Sons Ltd, Worcester

Contents

About the Contributors

MICHAEL BLOOR is a senior research sociologist at the Medical Research Council's Medical Sociology Unit, Glasgow University. He is co-author (with Neil McKeganey and Dick Fonkert) of *One Foot in Eden*, a comparative study of therapeutic communities. Currently, he is investigating death certification.

ROBERT DINGWALL is a research fellow at Wolfson College and the Centre for Socio-Legal Studies, University of Oxford. He has published extensively on medicine and law as occupations and organizations. His most recent books are *Divorce Mediation and the Legal Process* (with John Eekelaar) and *An Introduction to the Social History of Nursing* (with Anne Marie Rafferty and Charles Webster). He is currently working on studies of the social organization of asbestosis litigation and of medical negligence.

PETER R. GRAHAME, Assistant Professor of Sociology at Bentley College, Massachusetts, has conducted research on classroom interaction, popular culture, and the interrelations of social criticism and commonsense knowledge. Currently, he is doing comparative studies in the origins of consumerism.

JABER F. GUBRIUM is Professor of Sociology at the University of Florida. He has conducted research on the social organization of care in diverse human service settings. He is the editor of the *Journal of Aging Studies,* author of *Living and Dying at Murray Manor* (1975), *Oldtimers and Alzheimer's* (1986), *Analyzing Field Reality* (1988), and co-author (with James Holstein) of *What is Family? A New Perspective* (1989).

PETER K. MANNING is Professor of Sociology and Psychiatry at Michigan State University and specializes in the interpretive analysis of complex social systems particularly in relation to crime and medicine. His books include *Semiotics and Fieldwork* (1987) and *Symbolic Communication* (1988). Recently, he has researched the regulation of nuclear power production in Britain.

NEIL McKEGANEY is a research fellow at Glasgow University's Social, Paediatric and Obstetric Research Unit. He is co-editor (with Sarah Cunningham-Burley) of *Enter the Sociologist,* a collection of tales from the field, and *Readings in Medical Sociology.* Currently, he is conducting research on intravenous drug use and HIV infection.

ELIM PAPADAKIS is Lecturer in Sociology at the University of New England, Australia and Visiting Fellow at the Australian National University, Canberra. His publications include *The Green Movement in Germany*

(1984) and *The Private Provision of Public Welfare* (with P. Taylor-Gooby, 1987). He is currently researching new social movements and political parties, and public opinion and the welfare state.

LINDSAY PRIOR is Senior Lecturer in Sociology at the University of Ulster (Jordanstown). He has published articles on the sociology of health, illness and medicine and is the author of *The Social Organization of Death* (1989).

AUSTIN SARAT is William Nelson Cromwell Professor of Jurisprudence and Political Science at Amherst College, Massachusetts. His recent publications include 'The New "Formalism" in Disputing and Dispute Processing', *Law and Society Review* 695 (1988) and *Sitting in Judgment: Sentencing White Collar Criminals* (with S. Wheeler and K. Mann, 1988). He is currently researching the ideology of professionalism among solo-practice lawyers.

SUSAN S. SILBEY is Associate Professor of Sociology at Wellesley College where she directs the Technology Studies Program and the Task Force on Racism. Her recent work includes studies of the politics of dispute-processing and legal consciousness among adolescents. Her 'A Sociological Interpretation of the Relationship between Law and Society' appears in *Law and the Ordering of our Life Together* (1989).

DAVID SILVERMAN is Reader in Sociology, University of London Goldsmiths' College and Chairman of London University's Board of Studies in Sociology. His interests range from methodology and discourse analysis to medical sociology. His most recent books are *Qualitative Methodology and Sociology* (1985) and *Communication and Medical Practice: Social Relations in the Clinic* (1987). Currently, he is engaged on two funded studies of counselling people who may be HIV positive.

MARY SIMMS is a sociology graduate of Kingston Polytechnic. Her research interest in social gerontology was first developed during graduate work at the Medical Sociology Unit, Bedford College, London. She has recently completed a study of the community care of the aged at Queen Mary College, London.

DON SLATER, Lecturer in Sociology at Goldsmiths' College, University of London, is the author of *The Political Economy of Advertising* (forthcoming), an investigation of advertising as a commercial practice. His current interest is in theories of consumer culture.

PHIL STRONG has worked in the areas of interaction, occupations, organizations and medicine. His publications include *The Ceremonial Order of the Clinic* (1979) and *New Model Management: Griffiths and the NHS* (with Jane Robinson, 1988). He is currently studying the social history of AIDS at the London School of Hygiene and Tropical Medicine.

ROY TURNER, Professor of Sociology at the University of British Columbia, is the editor of *Ethnomethodology* (1974) and the author of numerous articles on conversation analysis. His ethnographic work has included studies of psychiatric settings and of police work in northern California. Currently, he is engaged in a hermeneutic investigation of the museum.

Introduction

David Silverman and Jaber F. Gubrium

> Power reaches into the very grain of individuals, touches their bodies
> and inserts itself into their actions and attitudes, their discourses,
> learning processes and everyday lives. (Foucault, 1980: 39)

The title of this volume signals both unity and diversity. As far as
unity is concerned, each author engages a deeply political understanding of field research against the commonplace view that
Science, Reason, and enlightened intervention are the straight-
forward hallmarks of Progress in the resolution of social problems.
As the quotation from Foucault conveys, power penetrates the
entire spectrum of concern with human affairs. The contributions
are diverse in the manner by which the political is addressed to go
beyond enlightenment, ranging from commentary on the political
underpinnings of the notion of field as such, to explications of the
political character of field data and policy outcomes – respectively,
politics of, in, and from the field.

The chapters originated at an international conference on the
politics of field research held at Goldsmiths' College, University of
London, jointly organized by Jaber F. Gubrium and David
Silverman. The conference dealt with the political character of
sociological fieldwork and its relation to potential clients and
laypeople. At a time when qualitative field research is becoming
more acceptable to both public and private agencies, policy
proposals are demanded from it. Sociological ethnography now
finds itself also in competition with researchers from other disciplines such as political science and economics. In their varied
manners, the chapters show how recognition of the essentially
political nature of social action is now a necessary feature of social
commentary.

The Enlightenment vision

As Weber pointed out in the early years of this century, all research
is contaminated by the values of the researcher. Only through these
values do certain problems get identified, while conclusions and
implications drawn from a study are, Weber stresses, largely

grounded in the moral and political beliefs of the investigator. Even the commitment to scientific method is, as Weber emphasizes, a value.

Half a century later, Gouldner (1962) showed how Weber had been grossly misinterpreted by positivist sociologists. Because Weber had suggested that purely scientific standards could govern the actual study of a sociological problem, they had used him as the standard-bearer of a value-free sociology. They had conveniently forgotten that Weber had argued that the initial choice of a problem as well as the subsequent attempt to seek practical implications were highly 'value-relevant'.

The 'Minotaur' of a value-free sociology, conjured up by the empiricist misreading of Weber, is effectively destroyed by Gouldner. As Denzin (1970) argues, the myth of value-freedom is shattered not only by the researcher's own commitments but by the social and political environment in which the research is carried out. Grant-giving organizations will seek to channel research in particular directions; there is no neutral money, whether one is speaking about the well-meant initiatives of Research Councils and the National Institutes of Health, or the funding schemes of the pharmaceutical and tobacco industries or the war machine (see Horowitz, 1965). Moreover, organizations that give access to the researcher are likely to want some kind of return in terms of theory-free, usually quantified, 'facts', as well as support for their current goals. Like governments, organizations may also sponsor research merely to buy time and so legitimate inaction. While this makes no demands on researchers, it does constitute them as accomplices in other people's political projects.

Given these constraints, how may the researcher respond? The legacy of the eighteenth-century Enlightenment offers three different paths. Elsewhere, Silverman (1985) has labelled these the roles of the scholar, the state counsellor, and the partisan.

The scholar
The Enlightenment's rejection of traditional beliefs in favour of the dispassionate gaze of Reason and Science formed a space for a version of independent, critical thought. Freed from an absolutist State, rejecting taken-for-granted moral and political assumptions, the scholar was responsible solely to his or her conscience. In Weber's (1946) two famous lectures, 'Science as a Vocation' and 'Politics as a Vocation', he enunciated such liberal principles to a student audience. Despite the patriotic fervour of the time – 1917 – Weber insisted on the primacy of the individual's own conscience as a basis for conferring meaning on the findings of research.

Weber's appeal to the independence of scholarship is fully shared, fifty years later, by Denzin (1970). Denzin rejects any fixed moral standards as the basis for research. He will not accept, for instance, that sociologists cannot conceal themselves or use disguised research techniques. Nor is he prepared to recognize that research must necessarily contribute to society's own self-understanding. By contrast, Denzin's stand is distinctly liberal and individualist, evident in this comment that 'one mandate governs sociological activity – the absolute freedom to pursue one's activities as one sees fit' (1970: 332).

Although Denzin is prepared to recognize a role for the researcher's 'conscience' – for instance, by revealing one's value judgements to research subjects – there remain two major objections to his appeal to the scholar's freedom. First, it fails to attend to the way powerful social forces shape the provision of research access, the funding of research, and the response to research findings. Secondly, appealing to 'conscience' may imply a barren 'decisionist' ethics (Habermas, 1972). For instance, how successful a rebuttal of a colleague or participant's critique of the political implications of your research is it to say that you are merely following your own conscience?

The state counsellor
The Enlightenment did not neglect the social responsibilities of scholarship. If its commitment to Reason protected the independent scholar, its belief in Progress suggested that scholarship could make a significant contribution to the institutions of a benevolent State. Precisely this position has been adopted by Martin Bulmer in his discussion of the function of applied research. The role of Bulmer's (1982) 'Enlightenment model' is to provide knowledge of alternative possibilities and problems to administrators.

Bulmer begins by rejecting two other models of applied research. Empiricism fails because it assumes that facts are theory-neutral. Instead of mobilizing the insights of social science, it simply reflects the administrative view that research is a neutral tool for the collection of useful facts. Equally, Bulmer rejects what he calls an 'engineering model' of research where administrators define problems or where researchers are confined to the evaluation of existing policies. Instead, his preferred 'Enlightenment model' would allow researchers to reconceptualize the problems which policy makers define for themselves.

The limitations of such a model derive from its reduction of the role of social research to that of a state counsellor. Elsewhere, Silverman (1985) has argued that the principal appeal of such

'Enlightenment' is that it preserves the autonomy of researchers in their dealings with state apparatuses. However, this professional freedom is, to some extent, a fraud, for it never questions the role of research as the supplier of concepts and information to the powers-that-be. Precisely because it represents applied research as the handmaiden of the state, the 'Enlightenment model' offers a purely bureaucratic model of politics.

A case in point is the famous Project Camelot (Horowitz, 1965). This was a study funded in 1963 by the Pentagon with a budget of six million dollars. Its purported aim was to gather data on the causes of revolutions in the Third World. However, when it became clear that such research was to be used as a basis for counter-insurgency, a storm of protest arose and it was withdrawn. Horowitz points out that many social scientists had been prepared to overlook the source of the money when offered such enormous research funding. Presumably, they might have defended themselves as seeking merely to spread enlightenment rather than to engage in political or social engineering. However, this in no way settled the moral issue over whether social scientists should have this kind of relationship to a government agency. Conceived in terms of counter-insurgency, Bulmer's preferred 'Enlightenment model' takes on an altogether more sinister tone.

If the scholar unrealistically seeks to stand apart from the world, the state counsellor is in danger of co-optation to the state apparatus. Perhaps, as Howard Becker (1967) has implied, the problem with this is not that it takes sides but that it takes the *wrong* side.

The partisan
Becker's enduring concern with the moral underside of law and the 'moral entrepreneurs' who promulgate it informs us that in a socially differentiated world, we cannot hope to produce a singular and uniform depiction of reality. We must take sides, as he puts it, and it might as well be the side of the so-called underdog, whose experience and realm are rarely understood on their 'own' terms.

Still, Becker's partisan position, which has informed a broad range of ethnography in the American context, especially studies of deviance, has a sinister tone of its own. It centres its enlightenment on the experience of outsiders, presumably as a way of making visible to all, and notably to the powers-that-be, the natively sensible, yet stereotyped and neglected worlds of those at the margins of society. At the same time, its focus on the underdog hides from us what we might call the 'discourse of exclusion' or the language and activity shared by all engaged in deviance as a social project. The point is that if we were to witness and document the rhetoric of moral entrepreneurs in relation to the codes and lived worlds of outsiders as deviants, we would find that a common sense of the real and unreal underpins their ostensibly separate domains of experience (see Pollner, 1974). We would find that Becker's laudable intention of making visible the netherworld of daily living – to presumably let its members speak for themselves – is, in practice, an incitement to all to speak the language of insiders, outsiders, inclusion, and exclusion. The realization would bring us to Foucault's vision of power and knowledge.

Beyond Enlightenment: Foucault's vision

Foucault's (1980) discussion of the 'capillary' form of existence of mechanisms of power is profoundly discomfiting to *all* versions of Enlightenment thought we have been discussing. Although, as we have noted, 'scholars', 'state counsellors', and 'partisans' have serious differences with one another, they are common inheritors of the system of thought that has dominated the West for the last two centuries. Their disputes are grounded in the familiar polarities of theory/practice, fact/value, reason/emotion, science/ideology, and society/individual.

Foucault deconstructs these polarities not just by an intervention in the history of ideas but by revealing the very practices and technologies which deploy such representations. This constitutes five challenges to the Enlightenment thinker: an onward march of Progress can no longer be assumed; politics is not reducible to the practices of the State, for power does not arise in any central point; power is seen in an incitement to speak as much as in censorship, repression, or exclusion; the human sciences are not free-floating critical apparatuses but are inside mechanisms of power; and, finally, the 'free individual' is a construction of power/knowledge, not its antithesis. We will briefly review each of these arguments before touching upon their consequences for the politics of field research.

1 *Progress* The three different versions of the theory/practice debate that we have considered derive from an idea at its zenith in the nineteenth century – the idea of Progress. Thus 'scholars' see scientific truth as cumulative and steadily enlightening, 'state counsellors' hold out the hope of a state apparatus enlightened by scientific input, while 'partisans' ally themselves with progressive interests or the proletariat. In line with an era which unites Nietzsche's re-evaluation of morals with Einstein's theory of relativity, Foucault is less optimistic. His 'genealogies' reveal no

straight line of progress. Systems of punishment appear more enlightened, for instance, but also deploy more subtle forms of power (see Foucault, 1977).

2 *The State* A common thread also unites our three versions of scientific practice. They all define themselves in relation to the State or its apparatuses – either for it (counsellors), against it (partisans), or apart from it (scholars). Yet Foucault reveals a micropolitics of power which operates 'within the social body rather than from above it' (Foucault, 1980: 39). Power does not arise from any central point: the State, the law, or the forces of order are only the terminal forms that power takes. Moreover, there is no single, unitary strategy. Sexuality, for instance, cannot be defined simply in terms of repression or limitation; different sexual politics are deployed with each sex, different age groups, and social classes (see Foucault, 1979). Each deployment may arise from a range of sites. As Foucault argues:

> Power is not located in the State apparatus . . . nothing in society will be changed if the mechanisms of power that function outside, below, and alongside the State apparatuses, on a much more minute and everyday level are not also changed. (1980: 60)

3 *Power* The Enlightenment vision saw power in the force of a negation which repressed or posed limits and hence had to be overturned. Its model was essentially juridical. This model of law reduced 'all the modes of domination, submission, and subjugation . . . to an effect of obedience' (Foucault, 1979: 85). Everything positive about power was neglected both in terms of its strategic resourcefulness and in its ability to give voice as well as to censor. Moreover, because power was seen as external to social relations – moulding them, shaping them, determining them – we failed to understand how the workings of power were immanent, not external. For instance, the issue is not how power shapes sexuality but rather how power is implicated in putting 'sexuality', as a system of representations and practices, into discourse. So, for Foucault, the old (Enlightenment) model of law, prohibition, and sovereignty must give way to a new model of a multiple, mobile field of force relations where effects of truth are produced.

4 *The human sciences* Our three earlier approaches did not doubt the likelihood of the benevolent impact of the human sciences, whether in the service of the scholar, state counsellor, or partisan. By contrast, Foucault helps us to understand how the discourses of the 'social' and the 'psyche' are not simply 'true' or 'false' but have effects of 'truth' or 'falsity' when employed in particular institutional sites. Ironically, the human sciences have

achieved their desired impact as 'humanizing' influences by cultivating 'behaviours and beliefs, tastes, desires and needs as seemingly naturally occurring qualities and properties embodied in the psychic and physical reality [or 'truth'] of the human subject' (Smart, 1985: 160). Concerned with the person behind the act, the human sciences have participated in the surveillance, training, and normalization of individuals. With their help, prisons, clinics, and schools have enhanced the utility of individuals by judging and surveying them, as well as encouraging them, as 'free subjects', to survey themselves.

'Discipline' has thus come to take on a double meaning. Scientific 'disciplines' constitute fields of knowledge within a tactical struggle over the politics of truth. In turn, with their help, within a range of institutional settings, bodies, spaces, and time are disciplined and ordered. Through the homogenizing, normalizing techniques of the human sciences, an order is being brought about in which bodies will be healthy, secure and productive. This 'bio-power' is seen most clearly in the explosion of discourses on sexuality documented by Foucault – demography, biology, medicine, psychiatry, psychology, ethics, pedagogy. A science of sexuality, through its commitment to exhaustive, delicious enquiry has, Foucault (1979) argues, developed a new form of the confessional. Here scientifically acceptable observations (the questionnaire; the examination) replace 'sin' with the equally powerful language of the normal and the pathological. Sexuality is held to be latent and hence in need of being prized out and interpreted by an expert. So the human sciences take the place of religion, as the confession ceases to be a test but is instead constituted as data, to be evaluated by a discourse of truth.

5 *The free individual* Foucault's project deconstructs 'progress', 'science', 'the past', and most notably, 'Man'. He remarked that his final works were concerned not so much with power but with the very constitution of subjects within discourses and technologies. *Discipline and Punish* and *The History of Sexuality*, Volume I, show how the everyday discourses of punishment and sexuality provide models through which people learn to recognize themselves as subjects (for example, as sexual subjects). In turn, the supposedly reforming human sciences offer the representations and practices which sustain this subjectification of the body.

So Foucault teaches us not only that the human sciences are implicated in power/knowledge but that they help to construct the very 'free individual' who is supposed to be the autonomous creature to whom science speaks. Even attempts to reject scientific or professional guidance, as for instance in the self-help group, involve subjects whose 'confessions' can do no other than express subjectivities formed within science's normalizing gaze. Consequently, the humanistic thrust of the Enlightenment is implicated in power/knowledge. The chastening message from Foucault is that power does not inhere in the intentions or interests of human subjects but in discourses which, although neither true or false in themselves, produce effects of truth.

Having moved 'beyond Enlightenment', there is a danger that Foucault's analysis may be disabling for practice. In an interview towards the end of his life, Foucault certainly disclaimed any emancipatory role for the human sciences. To the suggestion that social workers had been 'anaesthetized' by the 'implacable logic' of his *Discipline and Punish*, he replied that the problem of prisons is not one for social workers, but for the prisoners themselves. Rather than tell people what is to be done, his project is:

> Precisely to bring it about that they no longer know what to do, so that the acts, gestures, discourses which up until then had seemed to go without saying become problematic, difficult, dangerous. This effect is intentional. (Foucault, 1981: 12)

So Foucault seeks to destroy the image of the benevolent human scientist who passes on knowledge to a grateful participant. Instead, the ball is thrown back in the court of the subject who acts:

> What is to be done ought not to be determined from above by reformers be they prophetic or legislative, but by a long work of comings and goings, of exchanges, reflections, trials, different analyses. (1981: 12–13)

Where, then, are we left when we have conducted our Foucauldian genealogies, having examined power as a network of relations and analysed the incitement to speak, as well as repression and censorship? Two possibilities suggest themselves. First, Foucault reminds us that the workings of power create multiple points of resistance – we are not dealing with an unchallengeable Leviathan. Secondly, since effects of truth are intra-discursive (there is no appeal to a non-discursive 'outside'), power is not contested by proposing new, more truthful discourses (the Enlightenment dream). Instead, resistance operates by entering into and re-articulating elements which are present in existing discourses. This difficult challenge animates the chapters of this book.

The politics of field research

Following on these themes and considerations, the chapters are organized into three sections, according to their emphasis of the politics of field research. The first part, entitled 'Politics *of* the Field', deals with the broad political and philosophical surroundings

of the concepts of social research, field, and field of study. Roy
Turner, in his chapter, 'Deconstructing the Field', argues that the
'field' is a product of disciplinary technologies used to examine
individuals and groups. Turner suggests that the fieldworker can
occupy three spaces or analytic sites: (1) detachment from the
lifeworld in order to develop a commentary on its underlying reality
by way of reasoning that is separate from 'prejudice', (2) the post-
Foucauldian inquirer who aims not to discover who we are, but to
refute who we are; and (3) drawing on Gadamer, aiming to know
oneself rather than to refute who we are, while treating 'prejudice'
as a condition of knowledge. David Silverman's chapter, 'The
Impossible Dreams of Reformism and Romanticism', adopts
Turner's second space and argues that prevailing versions of
practice are derived from Enlightenment or Romantic visions which
respectively privileged the reasoning or feeling subject. As an
alternative, Silverman explores the political potential of practices
which seek to re-articulate existing discourses. Conversely, Phil
Strong's and Robert Dingwall's chapter 'Romantics and Stoics',
rejects what the authors see as the anarchistic impulses of recent
French and German thought, and argues that the British researcher,
for one, could learn from local traditions, in particular political
economy and English empiricism. They call for a 'modest' Enlightenment vision drawing upon Zeno's stoicism in the pursuit of wisdom,
balance, and civic duty. Finally, Peter Grahame, in 'The Construction of a Sociological Consumer', provides a case study of an
American movement to establish a field of research, one 'prejudiced' by the then-current language of market expansion, consumer
ignorance, and scientific accountability. Grahame argues that what
ultimately came to be an objective analytic space was rooted in
market relations.

The second part, entitled 'Politics *in* the Field', concerns the
political character of particular fields of data, the chapters of which
variously illustrate how 'facts' can be deconstructed into diverse
categories of power/knowledge. Jaber Gubrium's chapter, 'Local
Cultures and Service Policy', suggests that organizational 'troubles'
are situationally and temporally embedded. He argues that by
analysing participants' 'reality work', field researchers can reveal
the political character of facts, obscured by global pictures of
troubles. In a chapter entitled 'Corridors of Power', Don Slater
shows how social science research has avoided systematic study of
the economics and microsociology of the advertising industry.
Unlike Foucault's chosen areas, his chapter is not about the 'mad,
bad, and ill'. Advertising depends on a model of a rational,
sovereign, amoral subject, and, as such, can only be judged by the

means it uses to achieve its ends in the context of its version of the 'consumer' in the 'marketplace' of a capitalist economy's way of mediating between production and consumption.

Lindsay Prior's chapter, 'Evaluation Research and Quality Assurance', criticizes the objective pretensions of work dependent on purely behaviouristic models and on managerial interests. For Prior, behaviour must be reinserted into meaningful contexts and discursive practices which constitute subjects. In their chapter, 'Reconstituting the Sociology of Law', Susan Silbey and Austin Sarat demonstrate that the sociology of law has commonly spoken *for* the State as much as speaking *to* it. By refocusing away from the State, Silbey and Sarat argue for a sociology of law grounded in daily 'legal' experiences, located in the micropolitics of the normative world between the law and actual interactions.

The third and final set of chapters, in the part entitled 'Politics *from* the Field', addresses the implications for policy and political action of the relation between 'objective' yet political facts on the one hand, and the desire to affect those facts, on the other. Taking up Prior's critique of a dependence on purely managerial interests, Mary Simms' chapter, 'Social Research and the Rationalization of Care' shows how social science research has been used to legitimate the presentation of the status of the aged. Goffman's analysis of 'total institutions', for instance, suited a government bent on cutting the public sector. Such official legitimations enter into the public accounts of staff in the caring professions. A more optimistic possibility is suggested by Mick Bloor and Neil McKeganey in their chapter, 'Ethnography addressing the Practitioner'. They argue that fieldwork could address practitioners, as distinct from policy makers, to promote 'therapy' by encouraging residents in treatment in therapeutic communities to make one another responsible for staying in treatment. Peter Manning's chapter, 'Studying Policies in the Field', shows how processes of defining technical problems and violations in Britain's Nuclear Installations Inspectorate can be seen as a 'semiotics of policy'. Manning shows how the discourse-in-practice of Inspectorate personnel works to define policy at diverse points *in* the very field to which policy ostensibly is to be applied. Elim Papadakis' chapter, 'Intervention in New Social Movements', is concerned with interventions by social researchers into contemporary social movements. Data from interventions in the anti-nuclear protest in France and in new social movements in West Germany are used to illustrate the relationship between both individual activists and organizations, and Foucauldian and modernist accounts of social change. Papadakis argues that the dichotomy that is frequently evoked between these two accounts does not preclude their complementarity in practice.

The analytic/political relevance of 'of/in/from'

Before we turn directly to the individual chapters, here is a final comment on how to read their division of labour. From the book's organization into three sections – politics of, in, and from the field – it could very well be inferred that the political issues *of* the field can be separated from those deconstructed *in* the data gathered there and, in turn, *from* those encountered in the public presentation of research. The analytic relevance of this would be that the researcher could, say, solve the political problems *of* the field and take pleasure in being able, having settled these matters, to move on to tackle separately the other two kinds of political problem. For example, having acknowledged the politics surrounding the establishment of a field of study or a discipline, one might safely limit one's attention to more local issues of the social construction of facts. The political consequence of the separation would bring us close to a politics of Enlightenment in that, having acknowledged and dealt with the politics of facts, one could leave that aside in the pursuit of public policy. The separation itself – whether for analytic or political purposes – would warrant rational intervention, in which one might systematically deal with matters political, each in their own proper turn.

In contrast, the chapters in this book, in their own ways, take issue with the separation. If the etiquette of readability were not so important, each chapter would, in the course of conveying its particulars, comment on its rhetorical placement in the series of messages that constitute the book as a whole. Each would make explicit its textual 'siting' as a very part of communicating a critical message that attempts to go beyond Enlightenment. In other words, each would tell us, in Barthes' (1968) apt phrase, that it was not 'writing degree zero': as if to give the reader the impression that its own grounds somehow were unabashedly foundational. Two papers, those by Strong and Dingwall and by Turner, come furthest forward in informing us that it is always some foundation – whether tradition, 'home', or national political culture – that, hopefully critically, issues our discourse. At the same time, as Silverman's chapter infers, that information should not overshadow the Foucauldian insight that, in practice, tradition, home, or culture also provide us with the imaginative apparatus to recognize foundations as of our own making.

Thus, the analytic/political relevance of politics of, in, and from the field should rightfully be written 'of/in/from' to signify – like Foucault's phrasing 'power/knowledge' – that the separation is a communicative etiquette. While a separation of sorts is conveyed, we simultaneously are reminded that the separation is more shorthand and convenience than reality. Of/in/from means to read that we cannot safely and honestly treat facts as constitutively political and, then, do an about-face and straightforwardly enlighten those concerned of what can be done based on them. What must be available is a space for those concerned, say, with an aging policy or disturbed children or legal matters, to re-achieve on their own what the politics of field research shows they are doing otherwise.

The analytic/political relevance of the chapters of this book, then, is that they are as much about possibilities as they are about facts. To place slash marks between of/in/from urges the reader not only to attend to messages about how we can proceed to go beyond Enlightenment, but reminds him or her, too, that going beyond it is as much a possibility as what is surpassed – the incitement of critical, not rational freedom, as it were. Thus the politics of field research is neither analytic nor political alone, but inexorably analytic/political.

References

Barthes, R. (1968) *Writing Degree Zero*. New York: Hill and Wang.
Becker, H. (1967) 'Whose Side are we on?', *Social Problems*, 14: 239–48.
Bulmer, M. (1982) *The Uses of Social Research*. London: Allen and Unwin.
Denzin, N. (1970) *The Research Act in Sociology*. London: Butterworth.
Foucault, M. (1977) *Discipline and Punish*. Harmondsworth: Penguin.
Foucault, M. (1979) *The History of Sexuality*, Volume I. Harmondsworth: Penguin.
Foucault, M. (1980) *Power/Knowledge*, ed. C. Gordon. New York: Pantheon.
Foucault, M. (1981) 'Questions of Method', *Ideology and Consciousness*, 8: 13–14.
Gouldner, A. (1962) 'Anti-Minotaur: The Myth of a Value-free Sociology', *Social Problems*, 9: 199–213.
Habermas, J. (1972) *Knowledge and Human Interests*. London: Heinemann.
Horowitz, I. (1965) 'The Life and Death of Project Camelot', *Transaction*, 3–7: 44–7.
Pollner, M. (1974) 'Sociological and Commonsense Models of the Labelling Process', in R. Turner (ed.), *Ethnomethodology*. Harmondsworth: Penguin.
Silverman, D. (1985) *Qualitative Methodology and Sociology*. Aldershot: Gower.
Smart, B. (1985) *Michel Foucault*. London: Tavistock.
Weber, M. (1946) 'Science as a Vocation', in H. Gerth and C.W. Mills (eds), *From Max Weber*. New York: Oxford University Press.

PART ONE
POLITICS OF THE FIELD

1
Deconstructing the Field

Roy Turner

[The ethnographer] whether he wants to or not – and this does not depend on a decision on his part . . . accepts into his discourse the premises of ethnocentrism at the very moment when he denounces them. This necessity is irreducible; it is not a historical contingency . . . this does not mean that all the ways of giving in to it are of equal pertinence. (Derrida, 1978: 282)

the connected critic . . . does not wish the natives well, he seeks the success of their common enterprise. (Walzer, 1987: 39)

The interpreter does not dispense with his prejudices. He puts them at risk. (Weinsheimer, 1987: 115)

Ethnographers who have read Foucault lose their innocence. The pre-Foucauldian ethnographer could easily understand himself as one who resisted ethnocentrism, detaching himself from the prejudices of everyday life and treating the lifeworld as the site of scientific inquiry. But to read, for example, that 'the appropriate application of correct punishment required an object who was fixed as an individual and known in great detail', and that this motivated 'an important step in the growth of the sciences of society' (Dreyfus and Rabinow, 1986: 149) is to be made uncomfortably aware that one's 'science' was conceived in suspicious circumstances, and its birth attended by concerns which cast doubts on its purity. Following this line of thought, 'the field' can be conceived of as a space – better, an attitude – which, far from being neutral or inert, is itself the product of 'disciplinary technologies'. Prisons, schools, hospitals, clinics can no longer be treated as self-limiting sites available for scientific inquiries into their everyday life, but are to be understood as 'only the clearly articulated expressions of more generalized practices of disciplining both individuals and populations' (1986: 153). Sociological inquiry itself can easily be located here as one more source or validation of the distribution of categories which function to 'control', that is, to punish, cure, rehabilitate or recuperate individuals and populations. 'The field', then, is no longer that unselfconscious designation of a place where the life of the other can be objectively investigated, but becomes assimilated to disciplinary technology. It constitutes, shall we say, an attitude towards their 'clients' needed by agents of social control, a framing of the life of actual or potential subjects, a point of view which will force an intersection of the interests of the inquirer and the life of the subject.

The post-Foucauldian ethnographer may still choose to continue with his inquiries as before, but now he can hardly deny that to associate himself with 'policy' is to align himself with a complex history which he does not know, with practices which have come to seem natural and inevitable, despite their origin in the pragmatic concerns of a society that conceives of itself as authorised to shape and discipline its membership. The very idea of 'the field', put into this perspective, is tainted by its political history.

Is the ethnographer condemned, then, either to acknowledge his complicity with the forces of social control or to leave 'the field'? Or does Foucault's own practice as a historian of practices prepare an escape from this bleak pair of choices? One possible response to the Foucauldian thrust is to concede the discrediting of the enlightenment model of inquiry, but to argue that the prospect Foucault himself offers us displays its own limits with respect to what is possible by way of action in the lifeworld. It is true, such an argument might run, that 'we' are shaped by cultural practices and that our lives are lived within confines laid down not by nature but by the disciplines, but to say this is to say nothing more than that throughout history 'we' have only known ourselves and our lives through inhabiting a tradition.

Foucault has sketched for us the genealogy of our practices, he has reminded us of the nexus of power and knowledge, he has surfaced 'disciplinary technologies' and proclaimed their character as the capillaries of power; but it is easy in all of this to lose sight of a question that the Enlightenment, in all its naïveté, never forgot, namely the question of pertinence. Knowledge, for the Enlightenment, intended progress or improvement, it 'pertained' to the social world in that it made promises that knowledge would liberate men from the ills which had plagued history. The social sciences, under the influence of the Enlightenment, have mostly ignored the relationship between knowledge and power – Foucault's attraction is to have understood this – and have mechanically aligned themselves with policy as their version of pertinence, as though it were self-evident that institutional and bureaucratic goal-setting and implementation were simple instruments of progress and liberation. This has included incorporating 'the field' into the social-scientific framework as the place where knowledge will replace ignorance and ethnocentrism. But Derrida is surely right when he tells us that '[the ethnographer] whether he wants to or not – and this does not depend on a decision on his part . . . accepts into his discourse the premises of ethnocentrism at the very moment when he denounces them' (1978: 208). In the following pages I shall want to say something about ethnocentrism from this point of view, a point of view which, it seems to me, endorses Foucault's account of power's inevitable connection with the production of knowledge. But Derrida suggests a further step – though he does not clarify what he might mean – when he adds that the 'necessity' of accepting ethnocentrism 'does not mean that all ways of giving in to it are of equal pertinence' (1978: 208). If we accept this, then we face the further question: How shall we distinguish between and evaluate alternative notions of what is pertinent?

Much of what I shall have to say here constitutes an attempt to answer that question. After some preliminary theoretical discussion I shall turn to a consideration of some of my own early fieldwork on former mental patients. I shall want to argue there that what readily comes into view is the sheer act of social designation, the procedure of naming a population under the auspices of the disciplinary interests that Foucault has made us so aware of. Nevertheless, as I shall also try to show, a simple uncovering of the channels through which disciplinary attention flows still leaves much to be said on the subject of pertinence. This is something I shall address towards the end of this chapter.

Field and lifeworld

To develop the idea of 'the field' it is necessary to talk about various ways in which 'the field' may be related to the lifeworld. We can think of the ethnographic inquirer as one who detaches himself from the lifeworld and dwells on the distinction between its appearances, available to all, and the 'reality' which his analytic powers will disclose. The Enlightenment inquirer who takes the attitude of 'the field' to the medical clinic in the interests of 'policy', and who is free from the pragmatic constraints which clinic decisions, operations and procedures impose on staff, nevertheless at the same time accepts as part of the framing of his project the mandate which provides for the legitimacy of clinic life and practice. (At most he is critical of staff from within such an acceptance: what staff do may need to be 'improved', precisely so as to better implement policy.) Such an inquirer is keenly aware of the discrepancies his project reveals between what appears and what could (and should) be; only (his) knowledge, allied with power, can cross this gap or erase this discrepancy. From this point of view, 'the field' is the place where reason will make its appearance to combat the prejudice and ethnocentrism of the lifeworld. So far, such an inquirer argues, the lifeworld has been dominated by that ragbag of prejudice and super-stition which we can call the tradition (and against which Descartes railed when he told us that the ancients built on 'sand and mud'). It is against the tradition that science must make headway, and to make headway it must enter and observe the lifeworld with an atti-tude detached from commonsense thinking. Inquiries originating in 'the field' will generate knowledge that will transform the lifeworld.

The post-Foucauldian inquirer understands the working of the tradition more precisely and more analytically, and of course for him the Enlightenment itself has now become a part of that tradi-tion. For him the tradition is constituted of *practices*, which repeatedly inscribe themselves upon the lifeworld. When such an inquirer ventures into the clinic, for example, he is concerned to describe and analyse the disciplinary practices which ground what observably takes place, to show, via an account of their genealogy, that their rationality is of quite a different order than can be glossed by the Enlightenment understanding of policy and progress. Hence, for the genealogical inquirer also the tradition is unsatisfactory, but he is unable to turn to Truth and Reason for relief, since they too are through-and-through practice. As formulated by the Enlighten-ment they have become part of the problem, and are no part of the solution. The post-Foucauldian inquirer, then, hears the voice of the modern world as the articulation of disciplinary technology, a voice which addresses us as occupants of categories and bearers of names, categories and names which allocate us to a space structured by power/knowledge. Consequently, 'the field' is no longer that simple place where the inquirer loyally serves policy on behalf of the reign of Truth and Reason, but has become a place where scepticism is nourished and where we learn of the malformations of the lifeworld – it is this knowledge which we need in order to resist the oppression of history and the tradition, so as – in Foucault's words – to 'liberate us both from the state and from the type of individualization which is linked to the state' (1980: 216).

Lifeworld, field, habitation

I have suggested so far that to address 'the field' is to engage some particular understanding of the connections between lifeworld, knowledge and tradition, and I have characterized two such understandings, that of the Enlightenment and that of Foucault. Foucault has certainly liberated us from the belief that the disciplines which enjoy the blessing of Enlightenment thinking are 'natural', and has given us a sophisticated awareness of the subtle and complex history of the institutional framework of the lifeworld we inhabit. He has provided us with an analysis of the forces that produce 'the field' – both the lie of the land itself, and the shaping of the eye that surveys it – but he shows less interest in how this conception of a world subject to inquiry also involves a conception of the lifeworld as the domain of action, and our possible relation to it. How to proceed, if this is how things are? What is Foucault's conception of the place from which he speaks as a site for possible action?

Dreyfus and Rabinow characterize Foucault's understanding of the place from which he speaks as follows:

> The practitioner of interpretive analytics realizes that he himself is produced by what he is studying; consequently he can never get outside it. The genealogist sees that cultural practices are more basic than any theory and that the seriousness of theory can only be understood as part of a society's on-going history. The archaeological step back that Foucault takes in order to see the strangeness of our society's practices does not mean that he considers these practices meaningless. Since we share cultural practices with others, and since these practices have made us what we are, we have, perforce, some common footing from which to proceed, to understand, to act. But the foothold is no longer one which is universal, guaranteed, verified, or grounded. (1986: 125)

Thus, cultural practices have the status for Foucault that prejudice has for the Enlightenment. Both practices and prejudice are treated as 'more basic than any theory', in Dreyfus' and Rabinow's words, which is to say that theory must treat them as the place to begin, since the bad news is that they were there first. Hence 'the seriousness of theory can only be understood as part of a society's on-going history'. Clearly 'history' here is not to be read as the fall of events but rather as the narrative through which a society attempts to understand itself and its collective life. Whereas the Enlightenment needed to theorize a way of escaping from the prejudice which it found preceded it, Foucault's account of practices implicates the theorist inextricably – such a theorist 'realizes that he himself is produced by what he is studying . . . he can never get outside it'. Dreyfus and Rabinow underline the way Foucault's position differs significantly from the Enlightenment: the 'foothold' we have is 'no longer one which is universal, guaranteed, verified, or grounded'.

Nevertheless, there is a puzzle here. The Foucauldian position acknowledges that 'since these practices have made us what we are, we have, perforce, some common footing from which to proceed, to understand, to act', yet it is hard to derive from Foucault any account of just how 'we' might 'proceed . . . understand . . . act'. We can locate a friendly suggestion in Gadamer's dictum that, in the moral realm 'the knower is not standing over against a situation that he merely observes, but . . . is directly affected by what he sees. It is something he has to do' (Gadamer, 1986: 280). If this is so, then we can ask Foucault, given his version of the social world, 'What is it he has to do?' One answer Foucault might give to Gadamer's question is his laconic 'maybe the target nowadays is not to discover what we are, but to refuse what we are' (Foucault, 1983: 216). Foucauldian inquiry seems to disclose a formation of the self which is unpalatable, and which calls for negation as a rational response. The self so viewed is a contingent product of cultural practices, a shaky foundation that the self wishes to repudiate. Yet where else can it stand?

To find a way of responding to this question it is useful to recast the complaint of both the Enlightenment and Foucault concerning the prejudicial nature they attribute to the tradition (and a fortiori ethnocentrism) as, in Weinsheimer's nice phrasing, the quality of being 'subjective accident' (1987: 176). (Foucault parts with the Enlightenment in not concluding that these accidents are 'finally or at least ideally remediable' [Weinsheimer, 1987: 176].) What Weinsheimer's phrase draws attention to is the desire for a history and a narrative in which what is important is not contingent or accidental but is grounded in the absolute or the certain – call it God, Science, Reason or whatever. For the Enlightenment, clearly, the problem of the tradition just was its accidental character, its appearance as a shambles of institutionalized prejudice, waiting for the advent of an engineer who would banish the contingent and the prejudiced and replace them with foundations on which any man could build.[1] Just as clearly, Foucault will have none of this. In Foucault's implied narrative the story tells of the collective's slow realization that its cherished account of the steady advance of Reason is false: now the Enlightenment, far from being the true beginning of Man's real history, is itself one of those accidents, those ruptures which direct prejudice along a track new and different, but having no steadier foundations.

Despite the power and sophistication of his analysis, though, Foucault seems not to offer us a way of responding to our situatedness other than to repudiate it. An alternative approach to the collective's self-understanding – and hence of its notions of research and 'the field' – can be located in both Michael Walzer (1987) and H.G. Gadamer (1986).[2] It is not that Walzer or Gadamer have to refute Foucault, but that they offer the prospect of a more fruitful way to respond to situatedness. Walzer, for example, in discussing the social critic's relation to the moral world of the society in which he lives, tells us 'we do not have to discover [this] moral world', because 'we have always lived there'. 'We do not have to invent it', he continues,

> because it has already been invented – though not in accordance with any philosophical method. No design procedure has governed its design, and the result no doubt is disorganized and uncertain. It is also very dense: the moral world has a lived-in quality, like a home occupied by a single family over many generations, with unplanned additions here and there, and all the available space filled with memory-laden objects and artifacts. (1987: 20)

What I find of value here is the way in which Walzer in effect rotates on its axis the idea of prejudice – commonsense thought – as subjective accident, so as to throw an entirely different light on it. For Walzer, the tradition gives us a moral world with a 'lived-in quality'; it is like home, with 'all the available space filled with memory-laden objects and artefacts'. What Walzer suggests, then, is that despite the fact that it has a history of the kind Foucault uncovers, the lifeworld *is* nevertheless a habitation: we might say that precisely the skill or art which the idea of 'home' calls upon is the ability to transform the contingent into the worthwhile. Home, in short, is (like 'the field') an attitude; the attitude which grasps what is at hand in order to make of it something liveable. When this attitude confronts the ethos it sees not simply an arbitrary aggregation of beliefs, norms and cultural artefacts which make an unreasonable claim on the member, but rather the resources for *bricolage*, for the work of making something that shall express the life of the inhabitant. Thus, while it may be true that our modern world is both veined with power and shaped by the history of its practices, this makes it no different from any human life, but simply sets the limits within which any worthwhile life is to be made.

I have tried to show that we can locate a way to understand alternative theorizings of 'the field' by delineating the character of the ethnographer as a social actor whose conduct embodies a moral relation to the social world. The Enlightenment inquirer goes to the field as an agent of knowledge, certainty and control, with the aim of reforming and revising the lifeworld on behalf of his fellow men.

His more sophisticated Foucauldian successor understands that our encounters with the configurations of power/knowledge constantly transform the readings we make of our circumstances, and that these readings are not paths to either certainty or mastery. The controlling belief here is that our inquiries yield us a place from which to resist as we face an oppressed and oppressive lifeworld. Finally, Walzer's 'connected critic' shares with Foucault the belief that certainty and mastery are not to be had, but is committed to the belief that to reject our 'memory-laden objects and artefacts' on the grounds that they entered our lives as 'accidents', or else to 'refuse what we are', is to render ourselves homeless by an act of will. (This is a risk Foucault seems prepared to take.)

Pertinence

But where is 'the field' in all of this? As I have already suggested, if we understand 'the field' as a complex attitude dependent on our understanding of the relationship between knowledge and lifeworld, then Enlightenment and post-Foucauldian inquirers will have quite different notions of the aims and procedures of research into the lifeworld. An inquirer influenced by Walzer and Gadamer will, like the post-Foucauldian, also reject the reformist Enlightenment model. Since he begins with the conviction that the most important thing about the lifeworld is that it is home, he will need to think of 'the field' as the site where inquiry can fruitfully illuminate the nature of the place where we live. What is most provocative about the attitude the connected critic takes to the field is its re-evaluation of prejudice and ethnocentrism. It is through this re-evaluation, however, that we can best clarify the idea of pertinence.

Derrida begins the provocation by insisting that ethnocentrism is inescapable in the discourse of the ethnographer, a provocation which lies in the fact that ethnocentrism is for the ethnographer a cardinal sin: it is just the taken-for-granted, traditional, prejudice-ridden thought of his own society that he must lay aside in order to qualify *as* ethnographer and to validate his investigative space *as* 'the field'. Derrida's context is his reminder that any attempt to extricate ourselves from 'metaphysics' is dependent on just that 'metaphysics', since it necessarily supplies the only language we have for the act of extrication. Its application to ethnocentrism will tell us, for example, that the very desire to leave behind our own 'values' which marks the inquirer is integral to a set of understandings which he possesses by virtue of his origin in modern society. The very terms in which he formulates the difference of the 'target' culture from his own – 'kinship', 'property', 'myth' – are *his* language. Thus a typical example of the ethnographer's 'accept[ing]' into his discourse the premises of ethnocentrism at the very moment when he denounces them' is to be found in a popular sociology text, where the authors tell us that it is ethnocentric to say 'Orientals are inscrutable', whereas 'Labour productivity is lower in Guatemala than in the United States' is a 'simple statement of fact' (Horton and Hunt, 1976: 55) – as though the notion of and an interest in labour productivity was free of a highly specific historical context. Ethnocentrism need not possess this naïveté. An ethnocentrism that knows itself, that is mindful of its pervasiveness and permanence, can clarify our relation to the lifeworld we inhabit. Paradoxically, such a re-centred ethnocentrism makes more demands on the inquirer than the more naïve version which occupies the textbooks (and which standardly presents the author as himself free of the taint).

Once we introduce pertinence, as Derrida does, we come to see that this is criterial for *how* we think about ethnocentrism and prejudice. Yet Derrida's own speaking about ethnocentrism here, though surely true, lacks power in that it is silent as to its understanding of how the ethnographer needs to proceed. Walzer's and Gadamer's emphasis on the lifeworld as habitation, in contrast, gives a strong motivation for a kindlier assessment of prejudice and ethnocentrism than is customary, in that they locate traditional thought as the very material out of which a life must be made, and hence open the way for questions of a better or worse life. Clearly there is no intention on either author's part of rubber-stamping 'prejudice' in the vulgar sense of crassness and thoughtless contempt for the different; Walzer's whole interest is in responsible *criticism* of action within the lifeworld, and Gadamer (paraphrased by Weinsheimer) has it that 'the interpreter . . . puts [his preju-dices] at risk' (Weinsheimer, 1987: 208). What is powerful in both Walzer and Gadamer is the sense that they are concerned with making a difference: to understand 'the field' through their eyes will transform the interpretive framework by which the ethnographer finds pertinence in his encounters. To cite Walzer's dictum, 'the connected critic . . . does not wish the natives well, he seeks the success of their common enterprise' (1987: 39). A strong way to read this, I suggest, is not to treat the idea of the 'common enterprise' too concretely, but to receive it as a reference to the sharing of the moral world which inquirer and subject jointly inhabit. Thus it is significant that Walzer characterises his 'connected critic' as one who 'earns his authority, or fails to do so, by arguing with his fellows' (1987: 39). In other words, the connected critic refuses to appear as expert or outsider, preferring instead to speak to his fellows persuasively (and to run the risk of failure). It is this which marks their enterprise as common and thus appears as the kind of discourse appropriate to those who share a habitation. How we might understand this, and what it might look like, I shall try to show by turning to a discussion of my own fieldwork with former mental patients.

Encountering former mental patients: deconstructing the field

Some years ago I undertook to do fieldwork on the 'problems' of former mental patients, under the auspices of an interest in Goffman's formulation of stigma (1963). Beginning the fieldwork presented a serious practical difficulty: how and where would I find former mental patients? (The problem of what I would observe when I found them was at first in abeyance.) The obvious first move seemed to be to locate a much more accessible population, namely professionals engaged one way or another with servicing, monitoring or treating the population I wanted to see. I went about this in various ways. I made contact with a friendly and helpful social worker in a bureau of mental health (in Northern California), who gave me introductions to other professionals strategically placed. I tracked down a social club with weekly meetings for former mental patients, where I served as a volunteer. I also served as a volunteer for several months in a day psychiatric hospital. All of these contacts sooner or later led me to interviews with former mental patients, interviews which I tape-recorded and transcribed. Thus I ended up with a set of observational notes and a collection of transcribed interviews.

That former mental patients were 'hard to find' was not a problem of the same order as the difficulty in finding, say, Tibetan Buddhists or Amazonian Indians. It wasn't that they were remote, or few – they were many, and they were close by. The difficulty was that they didn't want to be known and available to me. However much *I* thought that the professionals and their disciplinary frame of mind were as much part of my data as anything that former mental patients told me, *they* clearly saw me as one more professional, as part of a 'team'. My difficulty in finding them was not independent of what would come into focus once I had made contact (as I assume it would have been with Tibetan Buddhists or Amazonian Indians), but was the very stuff of their understanding of what it meant to be a former mental patient.

Time and time again former mental patients told me of their common and recurrent troubles: old employers did not want them back; new employers were suspicious of the time they could not account for; neighbours were distant, and were thought to be deliberately so; friends might simply vanish, acquaintances snub them on the street; family would frequently maintain a formidable silence, and show no interest in the former mental patient's hospital experiences.[3] At the time I did the research I glossed these troubles as problems with 'resuming', wanting to capture the situation in which one who has been absent from customary scenes needs to do interactional work to resume old relationships (Turner, 1968).[4] But precisely the problem for the former mental patient was that a willingness to do such work seemed irrelevant, since the other frequently showed signs of an unwillingness to restore the relationship to its previous state.

Former mental patients in effect provided their own analysis of this situation. As they repeatedly expressed it, it was not a condition of health or illness which caused them problems, it was the sheer fact of their having spent time in a mental hospital. More precisely, it was the 'knowability' of this fact: insofar as it was unknown to and could be concealed from significant others, there simply was no such status as 'former mental patient' – to insist on it would be to give in to mere logic, as one might label others as 'former chevrolet owners', or 'former students'. The status 'former mental patient' for its incumbent was purely artefactual. Former mental patients spoke as though they lived in a reversed panopticon, situated in a centre surrounded by a community of viewers. When others knew 'who' they were, there was a problem. Hence it was clear to them that the knowledge others might possess was the root of their difficulties, and concealment the handiest solution.[5]

What can I make of this today, with my interest in deconstructing the field? To begin, I note that the former mental patient's view of his social fate seems to recapitulate or echo the Enlightenment version of history, namely that the 'prejudice' he suffers is subjective accident. The former mental patient reasons as follows. He has a plight that is sheerly social in origin. He knows that there are other plights which cause unhappiness and suffering, but he understands them to be constructed very differently from his own. For example, his plight is not – like illness – from nature, and hence does not suggest a kind of relief for which he can appeal to the assistance of his fellow men. Neither is his plight like poverty, to be understood as an undesirable effect of the life the collective chooses to live, and therefore intelligible as something that the collective could remedy by positive intervention. Whereas poverty can be understood as an unintended consequence of collective life, the former mental patient's plight just is that the collective designedly gives him its attention. As the former mental patient understands it, there is not *first* a problem, and then a collective response to it; there is *only* the problem which the collective attention itself creates. In short, the former mental patient understands his plight as sheer social creation, the pure result of an act of designation. We could even say that, as I portray him, he possesses a folk version of Foucault – he sees discipline and designation at work in his situation, he sees a combination of knowledge and power. More importantly, he also sees injustice in the arbitrariness of the collective act.

What 'the field' discloses then, is that the former mental patient's 'problem', in his own analysis, comes down to *designation*, and that for us designation is intelligible as the result of a Foucauldian history. But of course the former mental patient's account is unreflectively ethnocentric – his concern is not to inquire into the place of designation within the general social text. Yet clearly his is not a unique 'problem'. Perhaps the most illuminating discussion of designation is Sartre's account of how the 'democrat' analyses the situation of the Jew (1948). The Sartrean democrat understands the characterization 'Jew' as indeed sheer designation, for in his mind the Jew is simply Man. Thus the democrat can only see the fact of Jewishness – that is, the Jew's attachment to what appears to be only a designation – as depriving the Jew of being man-in-general, and he thinks that the Jew will be 'free' if he is relieved of his particularity. The democrat cannot see this particularity as the reality and richness of a way of life which springs from and nourishes a tradition, a habitation.[6]

But what of the former mental patient? As Wittgenstein once said, going to the heart of designation as a social process, 'what is or is not a cow is for the public to decide'. I take the application here to be that indeed 'the public' does decide, it decides that there truly are 'former mental patients' and it allocates persons to this category without asking their leave. Such designation is no less effective because we can show it has a Foucauldian genealogy. But we can scarcely ask the former mental patient to treat his place as the basis of a social identity, as Sartre's Jew does. The former mental patient would be mistaken if he acted as though *his* designation offered any nourishing particularity, since in fact his is a place that is hollow: it has no roots, no tradition, no substance, no resources, no essence.

If we seek help in analysing the issue of designation from an earlier, that is, Enlightenment, perspective, we find that such an attitude towards what 'the field' encounters simply regards the categories in use as the proper and necessary framework for inquiry, and certainly does not treat the field experience as the site for self-query. A Foucauldian, as I have noted, will understand the originating categories as themselves products, and in this sense will liberate our conception of the former mental patient from the perspective which has such a grip on our understanding of the consequences of mental illness. Yet this still leaves the former mental patient with his lifeworld problem, and it leaves the ethnographer unclear about a desirable formulation of that problem.

At this point I want to re-introduce my modified connected critic: the inquirer willing to formulate 'the field' in such a way as to avoid both the positivism of the window and the nihilism of the mirror. The connected critic is frankly ethnocentric in the sense that his concerns are those he shares with the community. How then does he differ from the former mental patient? In that the model inquirer of this persuasion holds not that 'the field' must be formulated free of ethnocentrism – Derrida is surely right: it cannot be – but that the inquirer himself only truly becomes properly centred in his own tradition through the process of using 'the field' to clarify what he necessarily takes to it, he resembles Weinsheimer's interpreter, who 'does not dispense with his prejudices. He puts them at risk' (1987: 208). This he can only do by using his readings of 'the field' to uncover the assumptions he shares with the subjects in locating the intelligibility of their situations. Once uncovered, these assumptions must be voiced; the aim is not to proclaim them as definitive or as 'findings' but to make them available for conversational response (by himself and others). In this respect, the work of the ethnographer also resembles that of the historian, if we conceive of the latter as a parallel inquirer whose interest in the past is to make new sense of the present; it 'transports us not to another world but to our own . . . the fact that we do indeed need to be transported to our own world . . . suggests that we are no more present to our own world than to any other. That immediacy too is a task to be achieved through mediation' (1987: 115). This suggests that the difference between our lifeworld and 'the field' is not that one is present, therefore clear, and the other remote and opaque: the real problem of ethnocentrism isn't simply that the conventional ethnographer applies unreflectively his own understandings to others, but that he applies unreflectively in the field standards about which he is *all along* unreflective.

Here then there is the potential conflict between two ethnocentric assertions, in which power is usually decisive when the Enlightenment ethnographer constitutes 'the field' as a space where expertise yields incorrigible descriptions of the life of the other. The inquirer who is willing to be 'transported to our own world' – call him the connected critic – will not produce the former mental patient as uniquely determined by the particularities of his 'plight' but will argue that whatever account the former mental patient gives of his plight *must* be made up of the materials with which the general cultural narratives are written. There are no other materials. Hence the inquirer has the opportunity to clarify these materials – which are his, as much as they are his subjects'.

What becomes available in the material at hand, I suggest, is the necessity of gaining a perspective on designation other than the one we have so far considered, for while the designated status 'former mental patient' belongs to Foucauldian genealogy, what the former mental patient elects to *make* of it does not: *this* emphatically is not for the public to decide.[7] The connected critic who is prepared to argue with his fellows – that is, to risk his prejudices – will point out that the former mental patient has no monopoly on designation as a social fate. What surfaces here is the force of a cultural narrative in which names, categories and social identities are allocated, a narrative which does not yield us the right to name ourselves. This is the unlikely material out of which lives are made, and though any given place in the narrative may seem to its occupant to be accidental, *that* there is a place – that there are particular places – is central to what it signifies to be social.

The inquirer needs, of course, to understand the former patient's understanding, but he does not need either to ratify it or to make it his own. We might say that it is the inquirer's task to interrupt the prevailing narrative – in this case the narrative that tells us of the residues of mental illness, of the need for aftercare, etc; but then we must add that this interruption is not in the service of an analysis outside the tradition (as Derrida has rightly said) but displays its pertinence by not only clarifying the materials of the tradition (as Foucault does) but also by raising the question of their potential for making life choices intelligible. The product of this interruption of the common narrative will itself be a narrative, and hence itself susceptible of interruption or deconstruction, for unlike the Enlightenment it does not proceed on the premise that the desirable is a concrete state of affairs to be described and realized, but prefers to think that it operates (in Wittgenstein's phrase) within a language game to 'assemble a series of reminders'.

These reminders are directed to the collectivity as it seeks self-understanding and as it goes about choosing one kind of life as better than another. Going 'beyond Enlightenment' is not a technical progress, then, but a move in the direction of clarifying the life that the inquirer himself represents as he enters 'the field'. Hence the pertinence of 'the field' is to be established on every occasion of its employment. To take this seriously is to ask the inquirer to resist the temptation to treat the particularities of 'his' subjects as distinctive and definitive – this is arguably the most ethnocentric act of all, in that it segregates the subjects from the moral community they share with the ethnographer. It is to treat the conditions under which identity is forged and lived as though they were strict determinants of who we are. The connected critic does not, of course, like the Sartrean democrat, urge that we think of the former mental patient as man-in-general, but resists the easy conclusion that there is only one way in which one could *be* a former mental patient. In not denying the misfortune of occupying the status he does not assert that there is no possibility for the occupant of making a better rather than a worse life. Nevertheless, the connected critic will disappoint the inquirer who simply accepts the Enlightenment definition of 'problems', who goes to 'the field' confident that he can devise concrete organizational action which shall (eventually) remedy what his subjects tell him is wrong.

In a sense the whole of this present discussion of the idea of 'the field' *is* the deconstruction it seeks. I do not mean this to be cryptic or abstruse; it is simply a reminder that the present writing can be brought under the same scrutiny it proposes. From this point of view one could argue that the ethnographer who chooses to study the lives of former mental patients cannot help but validate their plight, and hence himself recapitulate the framework in which the point of fieldwork is melioration. Yet if the inquirer decides to resist the pathos of the former mental patient who turns a designation into a social identity, he risks the charge of callousness, of wilfully ignoring the obvious, that is, that the pertinence of such a study is its potential for 'remedy'. In the material at hand the ethnographer has used the concrete materials of 'the field' as a way to look at the lives of former mental patients and has come away from it to talk of such things as the (general) problems of resuming relationships, the social fact of designation, and the theoretical foundations of the notion – shared by former mental patients with the Enlightenment – that insofar as fate and history are understood to produce our lives as unjust, then the undesirable features of a life are best thought of as 'subjective accident'. This has required that the ethnographer offer an alternative version of pertinence, namely that what needs to be seen is what the former mental patient shares with his fellows, what in his plight is written in the common language (and makes reference to both the necessity and the possibility of making a habitation out of whatever materials the lifeworld provides). Finally, this particular deconstruction of 'the field' has suggested that the ethnographer does not (cannot) cease to be ethnocentric as he confronts the lifeworld of the other, but that *his* obligation is to put his prejudices at risk, even such deeply seated prejudices as that the inquirer is a kind of social physician, diagnosing troubles and inventing remedies. It goes without saying that such an exercise in deconstruction itself has the status of 'arguing with one's fellows', and hence invites the reader, not to reiterate the platitudes of sociological fieldwork, but to continue and develop the argument.

Notes

1   The imagery here echoes Descartes, of course. Cf. 'those ancient cities which, originally mere villages, have become in the course of time great towns, are usually badly constructed in comparison with those which are regularly laid out on a plain by a surveyor who is free to follow his own ideas' (1969: 113). Descartes liked to think of the reconstruction of knowledge as the work of a single mind, capable of ridding itself of its opinions.

2   Walzer and Gadamer begin from quite different theoretical perspectives and interests. I have borrowed from both what I have found useful in the construction of an alternative model inquirer.

3   This is clearly a generalized description. My claim is not that it was never otherwise with former mental patients, but that typically when it was otherwise it would be so noted – for example, 'nobody stopped talking to me' – as though the speaker saw himself as an exception to these known and expected troubles.

4   For other accounts of the lives of former mental patients see Freeman and Simmons (1963), Cockerham (1981) and Gallagher (1987).

5   Goffman uses the terms 'discredited' and 'discreditable' to make the distinction between what is known and what could be known (1963: 41–42). He also speaks of the fact of hospitalization as the cause of the patient's (social) troubles: 'the psychiatric view of a person becomes significant only insofar as this view alters his social fate – an alteration which seems to become fundamental in our society when, and only when, the person is put through the process of hospitalization' (1961: 128).

6   This is not the place to enter into the complexities of what it is to be a Jew. I am certainly not claiming that it is no more than a designation. All I need argue here is that in the second-world-war context of Sartre's writing, whatever else it signified 'Jew' was a designation as I use the term. Sartre's democrat says, 'There are no Jews' (1948: 57); the democrat 'reproaches [the Jew] with wilfully *considering himself* a Jew' (1948: 58, original emphasis). From the point of view of the Sartrean democrat, then, Jews ought to resist taking the designation seriously.

7   Stephen Karatheodoris (1982) has helped me in thinking about the ideas of 'making something' of a disadvantaged position.

References

Blum, Alan (1982) 'Victim, Patient, Client, Pariah: Steps in the Self-understanding of the Experience of Suffering and Affliction', *Reflections: Canadian Journal of Visual Impairment*, 1: 64–82.

Cockerham, William C. (1981) 'The Post-patient Experience' in *Sociology of Mental Disorder*. New Jersey: Prentice Hall.

Derrida, Jacques (1978) *Writing and Difference*. London: Routledge and Kegan Paul.

Descartes, René (1969) *Discourse on the Method*, in Margaret D. Wilson (ed.), *The Essential Descartes*. New York: Mentor Books.

Dreyfus, H. and Rabinow, P. (1986) 'What is Maturity? Habermas and Foucault on "What is Enlightenment?"' in D. Hoy (ed.), *Foucault: A Critical Reader*. Oxford: Basil Blackwell.

Foucault, M. (1980) *Power/Knowledge*, ed. C. Gordon. New York: Pantheon.

Freeman, Howard E. and Simmons, Ozzie G. (1963) *The Mental Patient Comes Home*. New York: Wiley.

Gadamer, H.-G. (1986) *Truth and Method*. New York: Crossroad.

Gallagher, Bernard J. (1987) 'Life as an Ex-mental Patient', in *The Sociology of Mental Illness*. New Jersey: Prentice Hall.

Goffman, Erving, (1961) *Asylums*. Garden City, NY: Anchor Books, Doubleday.

Goffman, Erving (1963) *Stigma*. New Jersey: Prentice Hall.

Horton, Paul B. and Hunt, Chester L. (1976) *Sociology*. New York: McGraw Hill.

Karatheodoris, Stephen (1982) 'Blindness, Illusion and the Need for an Image of Sight'. Mimeo.

Sartre, J.-P. (1948) *Anti-Semite and Jew*. New York: Schocken. (First published 1940.)

Turner, Roy (1968) 'Talk and Troubles', unpublished PhD, dissertation, University of California, Berkeley.

Walzer, Michael (1987) *Interpretation and Social Criticism*. Cambridge, MA: Harvard University Press.

Weinsheimer, Joel C. (1987) *Gadamer's Hermeneutics*. New Haven: Yale University Press.

2

The Impossible Dreams of Reformism and Romanticism

David Silverman

Contrary to the view of medical sociology, the person does not dissolve the activity of power as he or she begins to speak about what is important. (Arney and Bergen, 1984: 5)

Using Foucault's arguments about the non-repressive, productive character of power, Arney and Bergen reveal how many programmes which aim to resist the effects of power are caught within power's web. For instance, the reformist aspirations of medical sociology may conceal its incorporation within the workings of medical power. So the reformers may be pushing at an open door. Beyond the door, medical knowledge and hence power: 'not only allows the patient to speak as an experiencing person, but needs, demands and incites him to speak' (1984: 46).

However, although this chapter begins with a focus on medicine, my intention is to raise much more general issues about the relation between what Foucault calls the 'human sciences' and practice. Two questions will emerge. First, what are the roots in the history of ideas of current reformist thinking? Secondly, can the alternative Foucauldian method be anything other than disabling to resistance to the status quo? In answering the first question, I will attempt to bring out the impossible dream of reformism and show its basis in pre-twentieth-century thought. Yet, if first Nietzsche and then Foucault have taught us to look askance at conventional moral assumptions, together with a belief in progress through knowledge, do they leave us trapped in a vicious circle where knowledge is always incorporated within the workings of power, and intellectuals who seek to apply knowledge to produce change are inevitably élitist?

'Communication' in medicine

Medicine transformed the patient's personality from something that at best was irrelevant to medical work and at worse interfered with it, into something that could be used to improve medical work. The management of the subjective aspects of illness complemented the management and treatment of the traditional objective aspects of disease. (Arney and Bergen, 1984: 69)

The complementarity between the reformist thrust of the human sciences and current professional models of good practice is shown very clearly in medicine. We can observe this in the ways in which medical schools are incorporating what psychologists and sociologists insist are issues of communication between practitioners trained in clinical decision making and patients committed to a 'lay perspective'.

Two recent newspaper reports show the direction of change. At Glasgow University, we learn, 'communication skills' will become a required course for medical students, examined together with more traditional 'medical' subjects. Here is how the views about this change of the Professor of General Practice are reported:

I think there's a realization that there has been too much stress put on the high science of medicine, and not enough on responding to patients' expectations, and involving them in their own health care. A lot of teachers feel that when medical students graduate, they are extremely bad at communication – they tend to ask questions and not listen. (*The Times Higher Education Supplement*, 26 September, 1987)

In another report, nine days later, we find that the Universities of Cambridge, Leicester and Manchester have also pioneered schemes to improve the teaching of communication with patients. At Cambridge, a 'teacher of doctor–patient communication skills' is quoted as follows:

When patients are dissatisfied with treatment, their complaints generally fall into two categories: either that doctors do not listen or that they do not tell them anything. There is a school of thought that says, 'What do patients know about it? We have no need to give them much information'. But when people get upset and angry it is almost always because of a lack of communication, either about symptoms or when bad news is badly handled. This can not only delay recovery but make life much more difficult for the doctor as well. (*The Sunday Times*, 4 October, 1987)

It is important to note that these teachers are fully in line with current social science research. From Byrne and Long (1976) we learn about 'patient-centred' medicine. Mishler (1984) tells us about more 'democratic' forms of the consultation in which the contexts of the patient's experience are explored. Calnan (1987) reveals the 'lay perspective' as the essential context for understanding illness beliefs and behaviour.[1]

One way to step back from this union of social science with 'progressive' practice is to pose the following three questions:

1   Who are the subjects who 'communicate'? There seems to be an assumption here that patients have raw 'experiences' and 'authentic' inner selves. Yet we do not need to have read Wittgenstein's (1968) critique of 'private' language to recognize that our understandings are grounded in communal languages, in public discourses. Perceived in this way, the 'lay perspective', conceived as the authentic expression of the patient's experience, is a nonsense – scientific and medical discourses enter into everybody's conceptions of health.[2]

2   Is there a language which is more 'true' or more 'authentic' than others? My own research on medical settings has revealed the double-binds and power plays which may arise precisely in the context of 'patient-centred medicine' or ostensibly 'democratic' consultation formats.[3] Should then we seek a more 'authentic' language or recognize that ways of speaking have no intrinsic value and develop a meaning only in the ways in which they are articulated with each other in specific social settings and conversational sequences?

3   As already suggested, how far is 'communication' necessarily a threat to the workings of power? Do the close interweavings of social science and 'enlightened' medicine imply benevolent progress? If patients are being encouraged to speak and doctors to listen, has this done any more than 'fabricate a subjective being' who surveys itself (Armstrong, 1987: 71)?

A little later on, I will respond to some of the rather depressing implications of these questions. For the moment, I want to pose a question with an easier answer. Where did this liberal theory and practice emerge?

In answering this question, I ask readers to bear with me over three tricky issues. First, the emphasis below on the history of ideas may be misleading: traditions of thought are always embedded in specific institutions, practices and technologies. Second, this is a very hasty sketch of two traditions, a mere caricature which also totally ignores other traditions.[4] Finally, for no logical reason at all, I will introduce these traditions via a brief excursion into styles of music.

The 'Classical' and 'Romantic' styles

In the eighteenth century, music was approached very differently from today. The current distinction between arts (including music) and sciences seems to have been foreign to that period. According to Enlightenment conceptions, music was a matter of 'objective' judgments of taste. In Mozart's time, the highest praise of a musical work was to say that it was 'scientific'. This was because the same logic or reason that was perceived to underlie science was seen to be at work in the arts. Hence assessment of a piece of music could be objective without any reference to or conception of the subjective response of composer or audience.

In an acclaimed study of the 'Classical style', associated with Mozart and Haydn, Charles Rosen (1976) brings out the appeal to logic and form. Before 1770, the late baroque style was forced to choose between dramatic surprise and formal perfection. After that date there was created 'a style in which a dramatic effect seemed at once surprising and *logically motivated*, in which the expressive and the elegant could join hands' (Rosen, 1976: 44, my emphasis). Here the sense of what one heard was seen to be motivated by the logic of the relationship between forms, without any appeal to the 'emotional' response of the audience. Musical wit thus became a play on forms – Rosen tells us that 'a wealth of double-meaning (became) a part of every composition' (1976: 96). Unlike baroque music, which had used ornamentation and decoration to conceal structure and form, the classical style decorated its music in order 'to emphasize structure, to articulate it, and to sharpen the spectator's sense of it' (1976: 107).

With its confident belief in rationality and progress, achieved by a universal and autonomous science, the Enlightenment believed that reason and logic could be the measure of all things. In this context, the 'Classical style' need not refer to anything outside itself. The audience would achieve satisfaction by perceiving the 'scientific' organization of forms, guided by the tutelage of experts.[5]

Conversely, the Romantic style made room for the 'subjective' response of both composer and audience. Music became an expression of our inner natures or a response to outer nature – for an early example of this, think of Beethoven's Pastoral Symphony. Such 'programme music', typical of this style, sought to evoke a response precisely by appealing to parallels between the music and what lay outside in the exterior world or in the interior conscious-ness of the participants. Instead of an exercise in logic or 'science', Romantic music became 'a spiritual rite, communicating directly with the initiate's soul'.[6]

The nineteenth century believed it had discovered the individual. In fact, it had discovered an individual suffused with subjective emotions and experiences. As Rosen shows, the operas of the sixteenth and seventeenth centuries were equally concerned with the differences between individuals but this was seen in the context of a view of human personality rooted in the 'humours'. A different version of drama was present in the opera of the Classical style:

> In comparison to the individualised characters of the sixteenth and seventeenth century stages, the personages of the eighteenth century are almost blanks; their reactions can be controlled and manipulated by the intelligent rascal and the clever valet. (Rosen, 1976: 314)

In its emphasis on situation rather than character, the opera of the Classical period was proto-sociological. However, it was a particular kind of sociology, based on a belief in the ability of experts to control the world through their exercise of reason. To fully understand its basis and to grasp its implications for practice, we must put the Classical style in the context of what I will call Enlightenment Reformism.

Enlightenment Reformism

What was involved in the turn of European thought expressed in the eighteenth-century Enlightenment? Let me attempt a brief summary. Although a caricature of many different positions, it will suffice for our purposes.[7]

1   Thought could no longer ground itself in the revealed truths of metaphysics and religion.
2   The intellectual's gaze shifted away from abstract contemplation to the political, historical world in which we live.
3   This world is best surveyed by a universal, autonomous science.
4   The employment of this science will lead to progress, rationality and Enlightenment.

At first sight, this programme looks to be some way removed from the views on reforming medical education discussed earlier. These share a criticism of the way in which medical practice, in becoming something like a universal, autonomous science, had excluded the patient's non-scientific gaze from its field of vision. For instance, the Professor of General Practice, as we saw, wants to de-emphasize what he calls 'the high science of medicine'.

However, these are surface differences from the Enlightenment model. It is not the benevolence of the scientific gaze that is fundamentally criticized here but a too narrow definition of its parameters. These reformers want to incorporate the mind as well as the body within medicine's gaze. The human sciences are to provide medicine with knowledge of 'patients' expectations' and how these are to be satisfied by better techniques of communication. The employment of this knowledge and of proper communication techniques will lead to progress in the form of better patient management in which patients recover more quickly and 'life' is 'much (less) difficult for the doctor'.

So the reformers of medical education are wedded to the Enlightenment vision of progress through the application of reason. But they are not alone. As Table 1 illustrates, this faith in the power of reason in the hands of scientific and professional 'experts' extends beyond medicine into contemporary sociology and the media.

Table 1   *Enlightenment reformism: reason and progress*

Medicine	Sociology	Media
Patient-centred medicine to replace doctor-centred medicine	Variable analysis leading to social engineering	The appeal to respected experts to explain events
	'Distorted' communication to be replaced by an 'ideal speech situation'	

The entry of the human sciences into medicine parallels how Bulmer (1982) has characterized the appropriate relation between science and practice. While Popper (1972) had called for 'piecemeal social engineering' based on variable analysis, Bulmer seeks a dialogue between researchers and policy-makers. Here researchers supply concepts and information to practitioners, while preserving their professional independence. Interestingly, Bulmer terms his preferred approach 'the Enlightenment model'. The faith in (expert) reason which the Enlightenment vision encouraged also has a home in non-empiricist versions of social science. As I have remarked elsewhere, Habermas' (1972) notion of an 'emancipatory' interest, geared to the revelation of 'systematically distorted' communication may reduce the subject to a mere patient in the gaze of the philosopher–doctor (Silverman, 1985: 185).

Habermas' theoretical model of an 'ideal speech situation' and Bulmer's more concrete model of expert–practitioner interchange both express an era in which the intellectual's gaze has moved away from abstract contemplation of metaphysics to the political world about us. In an age dominated by new forms of information-technology, this gaze is in much demand by the media. Whether the current disaster is natural, economic or political, the appropriate expert is always on hand to present the 'lowdown' on the event.[8]

What is revealed by these family resemblances across a wide range of practices? It is mainly that the self-understanding of this Enlightenment vision is inadequate. First, that reason or science is

not as autonomous as it supposes. Lay and professional understandings interweave. The media reveal underlying truths through the
pronouncements of experts, and scientific and medical discourses
enter into everybody's conceptions of themselves – think of the
content of the advice pages of popular magazines or the appeal of
series of questions (often purportedly designed by psychologists)
whose answers reveal how you really 'are'.

The second, related flaw of this vision arises in its touching faith
in the possibility of reason transcending language(s) in order to
reveal underlying realities. Wedded to (what Foucault would call)
its 'discourse of truth', it does not perceive that its research-based
'reforms' do not institute a new regime of truth – they merely
substitute one discourse for another. For instance, as Armstrong
(1984) has noted, the 'patient-view' was constituted by medicine
first as an aid to history-taking and then as the voice of an
experiencing subject. In both cases, however, we are dealing with
discourses which fabricate the patient. History looks more like the
succession and re-articulation of discourses with no intrinsic value
than a progress towards reason and truth.

If Enlightenment reformism works by substituting one discourse
for another in the name of Reason, Romanticism seeks to avoid the
rule of Reason by escaping discourse altogether in order to
apprehend a more 'authentic' realm of 'feelings' and 'experiences'.
We have already seen the Romantic style at work in music. Let us
observe it at work in medical practice.

Romanticism in the cleft-palate clinic

The following transcript is taken from a recording of a consultation
in an outpatient clinic in a hospital in Brisbane, Australia. Simon,
the patient, is aged 18. He has had his lip and palate repaired as an
infant. The issue now is that he feels his lower jaw sticks out and
says that he wants cosmetic surgery to repair it.

> *Doctor*:   Do you really worry at all about your appearance?
> *Simon*:   Oh, I really notice it but I, um, if it could be improved I'd
> like to get it done. I really worry about it.
> *Doctor*:   *Really?*
> *Simon*:   Yeah.
> *Doctor*:   Not really but *really?*
> *Simon*:   But *really*, yes.
> *Doctor*:   And why is it, what about your appearance is it that you
> worry about?[9]

This Australian doctor's questions about Simon's 'worries' mirror
tens of consultations I have observed in British clinics treating

teenage cleft-palate patients. Such paediatric practice was in the forefront of medicine's discovery of the experiencing subject. When wedded here to the prospect of cosmetic surgery, the doctor feels compelled to explore his patient's 'feelings'.

Unfortunately, this Romantic quest for authentic experience is unattainable. Neither Simon's expression of his 'worries' nor the doctor's interpretation of this expression are transparent: both are grounded in discourses (of the self, of medicine, etc.). For instance, the inarticulate response by most teenagers to this line of questioning is routinely interpreted in another clinic as expressing a lack of 'concern' about appearance. But Simon's own articulacy contains the seeds of a further problem for this doctor.

We have already seen how Simon's initial response is not regarded as sufficient, and two further questions are asked about his choice of the word 'really'. The basis for this interrogation is revealed after Simon leaves.

> *Doctor*: It's very difficult to assess, isn't it? Because he's pretty sophis-
> ticated in some of his comments and it's, er, it's just the, you know,
> continuously sunny nature that's troubling me a little bit about the
> problem as to whether it should be done.

Simon's 'continuously sunny nature' troubles the doctor presumably because of a version of its lack of fit with the trauma that should accompany deep discontent about one's appearance. This actually creates a double-bind for patients because the looked-for trauma may be seen to produce inarticulacy which itself does not lead to surgery. More important for our present purposes is that the Romantic thrust of the doctor's first question turns out to exist side-by-side with a Reason which seeks to look behind mere feelings. The doctor's speculation about Simon's 'motives' turns out to have an economic basis – he is worried that Simon is abusing the free health-care service in order to get time off work. So Romanticism, despite its claims, grounds itself in available discourses of the patient as experiencing subject and of the doctor as the interpreter of psychopathology and the guardian of scarce health resources.

Romanticism and authenticity

The Romantic thrust is not so easily disposed of as the foregoing analysis might suggest. As before, let us examine its place in the discourses of both the human sciences and of media representations (Table 2). Sociology is one of the human sciences associated with the drive towards a patient-centred medicine, revealed in the cleft-palate clinic to have Romantic as well as Enlightenment roots. As a

Table 2   *Romanticism: the authenticity of experience*

Medicine	Sociology	Media
Inciting patients to speak (patient-centred medicine)	Approaches which stress the primacy of 'experience' or 'perception'	'How did you feel?' (the authenticity of the personal narrative)
The cleft-palate clinic (the centrality and 'difficulty' of interpreting feelings)		The 'holy family' (in conflict with 'expert' accounts?)

child of the Enlightenment, sociology's flirtation with Romantic motifs was a long while in coming. Perhaps provocatively, I would suggest that we see these motifs at work in certain versions of feminism and of phenomenological sociology which privilege 'experience' and 'perception' over the construction of subjects in discourses. Like the cleft-palate doctor, such sociologists use interviews to document 'authentic' experiences. Like him, they can only 'interpret' what they hear by appealing to available discourses.

Nevertheless, such Romantic sociologies are very much in tune with one aspect of media representations. In this era of the chat-show and the news interview at the site of some disaster, the media's question is the same as the sociologist's: 'How did you (it) feel?' I would argue that some form of this enquiry is the central cultural concern of the moment. Whether the subject has experienced an earthquake or traffic accident, won or lost a sporting event or is just a celebrity, we want to hear everything. It is as if the personal narrative has an immediacy and authenticity which guarantees its importance and demands our attention.

Such narratives are much in the news as I write – in the context of 'child abuse' cases, parents tell their 'own' stories; against the background of the 'crisis' in the British National Health Service, parents are interviewed about what it feels like to have their childrens' heart operations delayed. In both cases, these accounts are compelling: their authenticity and our commitment to the truth and immediacy of 'family' experience feed off one another and challenge 'expert' accounts of clinical or economic 'evidence'.

Driven by its urge to attain 'authentic' expression of our inner-nature, Romanticism offers the impossible dream of transcending the discourses that we speak/speak us. The 'personal' statements, so loved by the TV interviewer, attain their power precisely from the public language that feeds them. Even as we think we are hearing the most authentic, 'personal' account, the same old stories are ringing in our ears. As Propp (1968) recognized, folktales derive their force from simple, repetitious structures. It is not just the similarity of story-form that undoes the Romantic thrust. For the very content of our stories feeds off the truths that are dispensed via the media by the human sciences. Our accounts of the 'good life', while having a personalized format, derive from these scientific and professional knowledges. Through them, we understand 'the truth about desire, about vitamins, about humanity or society' (Hacking, 1986: 239). So the Enlightenment motif of objective knowledges penetrates Romanticism's desire for authenticity. The figure that catches this movement best is perhaps the emergence of counselling throughout many areas of experience from marital discord to HIV infection. Here we speak authentically to experts. In this exchange we learn 'what we are like, what our experience is, how things are with us' (Taylor, 1986: 78).

Both Enlightenment Reformism and Romanticism would have us believe that they speak a discourse of truth. Like the other great nineteenth-century philosophy, Materialism, their essentialism is revealed in their claim to have access to an underlying reality of things independently of language and context. As I show below, there are, however, competing traditions which hold out the prospect of a productive, non-essentialist form of analysis. If we reject the certainties of other approaches, this still leaves a fundamental political question, with which I shall later conclude, about the dangers of a cosy relativism. At least the optimistic philosophies of the past believed in progress. Must the postmodernism of the late twentieth century be a mere intellectual game?

The sociology of context

If we reject essentialism, we must recognize that the discourses of the human sciences have no single meaning. Thus sociology, for instance, is not essentially tied into a prevailing cultural apparatus – although any sociological knowledge always has that potential.

There is one sociological tradition, in particular, which seems to threaten Romanticism's pretensions to give us a glimpse of inner experience. Almost fifty years ago, C. Wright Mills (1940) emphasized that 'motives' derived from 'vocabularies' and that our task was to understand the context and the means through which motive was attributed. Such a context can be a limited institutional setting but it usually has a wider political significance. Let us look briefly at a few examples.

Gubrium and Buckholdt's (1982) ethnography of a rehabilitation unit reveal that patient 'progress' has no essential meaning. Staff would present progress to a patient in terms of 'learning a good attitude'. In case-notes and official records, where the patient would be defined as passive, progress would be defined in relation to effective medical treatment. Finally, families of patients might be exposed to two different vocabularies of 'progress'. Where the patient was doing well, the explanation was medical treatment. Where there was little change or even failure, it was all due to the patient 'attitude'. This 'organizational embeddedness' of interpretation does not mean that the staff were relativists or sophists; their attempts to sort out what everything meant in specific contexts coexisted with a belief in the factual character of social structure and personality.

The importance of context in practical decision making extends beyond a particular work setting. For instance, Gubrium and Buckholdt show that the content of paperwork at the unit was shaped by the need to satisfy insurance companies in the context of fee-for-service medicine. The current situation of welfare service in Britain – in particular the rationalization of public provision – provides another example of how professionals make sense of their actions in a wider political context.

What is particularly striking here is how a liberal ideology of 'choice' can go hand in hand with the rationalization of care. In this volume, Mary Simms shows how the community care for the aged, based on the liberal language of 'consumer freedom' is used by community nurses and social workers to justify cuts in state care and to legitimate the private sector. Similarly, David Nelken (1987) argues that the increasing use of 'contracts' by social workers is legitimated in terms of limiting intervention in the lives of clients. Yet, in the context of rationalization, it serves two unspoken ends. Hard-pressed social workers now need to spend less time with clients because they have a limited, contractual relationship. Moreover, they can justify their continued employment by showing the quantified 'results' of their labour in the form of contracts written and kept.

So 'choice' and 'freedom of contract' are neither good nor bad in themselves. Sociology can reveal that such discourses have no meaning apart from the way in which they are articulated in a given historical and institutional context.[10]

Language and social practices

> *Bird* – wish you were one, saying with a sigh: 'Oh for a pair of wings'. This shows a poetic soul.

Celebrities – find out the smallest details of their lives so that you can run them down. (Flaubert, 1976: 295, 297)

As Flaubert's 'Dictionary of Received Ideas' reveals, not everybody in the nineteenth century was taken in by Romanticism's desire for authenticity. If Flaubert shows the culturally specific language at work here, it was early twentieth-century thinkers who were to illuminate the linguistic practice at work in claims to depict how things really are.

Saussure's (1974) emphasis on the 'arbitrariness' of the sign knocked off court attempts to privilege 'scientific facts' or 'personal experience'. For Saussure, signs derive their meaning only in relation to other signs. So analysis must first understand the internal economy of signs. Similarly, Wittgenstein (1968) rejected any appeal to an essential, underlying reality behind language. For him, words develop their meaning in use and what lies behind them is only these uses. Usage constitutes a substantial reality. To attempt to compete with ordinary language(s) by erecting a new (more scientific or authentic) language was, for the later Wittgenstein, a worthless move into 'metalanguage'.

Foucault starts off from these perspectives. There are no certainties from which analysis can proceed. 'Man', 'the past' or 'progress' are not beginning points but constructions which need to be pieced together. Foucault's contribution was to show how these constructions involved institutional as well as linguistic practice.

Instead of choosing one side or another of the subject/object dichotomy, Foucault's later studies show how human beings are constructed as subjects in the Church's or psychiatrist's 'confessional' or as objects in Bentham's prison panopticon (Foucault, 1977 and 1979). The homogenizing techniques of prisons, armies and schools involve disciplines in two senses: the disciplining of time, bodies and spaces and scientific disciplines which constitute fields of knowledge of how bodies and minds function. Such techniques and sciences work with 'bio-power'. They aim to secure an order in which people will be 'healthy, secure and productive' (Dreyfus and Rabinow, 1986: 116).

This intertwining of power and knowledge in multiple ways provides Foucault with two tactics. First, refuse to accept that the twentieth-century turn to language explains everything. As Rajchman (1985) has argued, while many of Foucault's contemporaries, like Barthes and Derrida had focused on writing and the play of texts (intertextuality), Foucault was concerned with a range of textual and non-textual practices. In the latter's studies of documentation and surveillance, the issue is not language but power. The problem of other approaches is their degree of formalism which conceals the specificity and institutional bases of different practices – for example the discovery of the interior of the body by anatomy, the panopticon, the alliance between medicine and the mother. So Foucault moves beyond a play of signifiers in (usually literary) texts to the site of texts in specific social practices: 'rather than deconstructing texts to reveal their attempt to conceal their self-reference to their own textuality, Foucault uses texts as clues to other social practices' (Dreyfus and Rabinow, 1986: 114).

Foucault's second tactic emerges from this focus on specifics. There is no whole object out there. Contrary to Enlightenment wisdom, with its off-shoots in Marxism and in non-Marxist structural sociologies, 'society' is no single entity with a single logic. So we should not look for a logic of the 'totality', only what Laclau and Mouffe (1985) have called 'totalizing practices' as a version of such a logic is constructed upon a particular site. It follows that what 'the social' means is not essentially fixed in one way or another: '[there is] no single underlying principle constituting the whole field of differences' (Laclau and Mouffe, 1985: 111). But this lack of any essential meaning gives us our research task – to understand how 'discourses of the social' operate in particular institutional settings. Based on a range of different strategies, we have seen how 'the social' comes to be formulated in 'community care' and in social work. Earlier, I examined how the education of medical students was stressing 'patient expectations'. What all three instances, with their different histories, reveal is 'a series of methods, techniques and practices which have effected a particular form of social cohesion' (Smart, 1986: 159). Each encourages a particular 'regime of truth' by encouraging 'behaviours and beliefs, tastes, desires and needs as seemingly naturally occurring qualities and properties embodied in the psychic and physical reality (or 'truth') of the human subject' (1986: 160).

Political implications

Foucault's work contains an unsettling political message. While it allows us to uncover the essentialisms of the past, it seems to discourage the forms of political action that come so readily if, for instance, you are wedded to the reality of 'reason' or 'emotion'. Four aspects of this discouraging message can be distinguished.

1   There is no 'discourse of truth'. No universal intellectuals or universal classes (the proletariat) can provide us with enlightenment. Knowledge is always implicated in power. The discoveries of the human sciences take their place in institutional practices with both intended and unintended consequences. So theories of

communication can provide further bases for patient management and the surveillance of populations, while economic theories of 'choice' can be used to justify cuts in public services.

2 Different struggles have different logics. There is no single meaning of 'the social'. Indeed, as Laclau and Mouffe (1985: 96) argue, the complexity of modern societies involves a growing proliferation of discourses of 'the social'. No single discourse (for example, 'socialism') can fix all these differences for there is no single subject (for example, the 'working class') constituted by each of these discourses – we are variously men, women, black, white, workers, consumers, shareholders, unemployed, and so on.

3 It is not just a matter of (changing) discourse. We are dealing with technologies of power as well as ideologies of power. Discipline and bio-power seem to be engrained in current social processes. Can the human sciences, for instance, do anything other than survey populations while embedded in circuits of professional and practitioner power?

4 In any event, should intellectuals be aiming to change situations for others? Foucault puts his finger on the élitist assumptions at the heart of Enlightenment Reformism:

> What is to be done ought not to be determined from above by reformers, be they prophetic or legislative, but by a long work of comings and goings, of exchanges, reflections, trials, different analyses . . . the problem is one for the subject who acts. (Foucault, 1981: 12–13)

Foucault gets us neatly off the hook, in one sense. However, there are political practices consonant with these arguments which do not involve a mere retreat to academe. First, Foucault's own work with the inmates of prisons implies how the analyses of the intellectual can be part of the exchanges and reflections through which 'the subject who acts' comes to decide. Secondly, we can learn, as Foucault has done, from post-modernism's 'playfulness'. Derrida (1976) has shown us that there is no transcendental or privileged signified (for example, 'reason' or 'emotion'), only a play of substitutions or differences. When faced with an apparently privileged polarity, however, there is no way out by creating a new way of speaking – hence Wittgenstein's critique of metalanguages. Instead, Derrida opts to choose the unfashionable side of the polarity. The aim is not to privilege this side but, by this unexpected turn, to unsettle the polarity itself.

Such a tactic of 'reversal' is employed to good effect in Foucault's (1979) refusal to accept the fashionable view that the politics of sexuality revolves around the polarity of (bad) repression versus (good) 'openness'. If Foucault makes us start to think that at least repression is an open, challengeable form of power, unlike the apparently liberating voices of the human sciences, it is not because he favours repression. As he has commented:

> It is necessary to pass over to the other side – the other side from the 'good' side – in order to free oneself from those mechanisms which made two sides appear, in order to dissolve the false unity of this other side whose part one has taken. (1977 interview with Foucault, quoted by Dews, 1984)

The politics of articulation

Foucault and Derrida take us back to Saussure's insight: signs derive their meaning only in relation to other signs. If the polarities that pervade Western thought have no fixed meaning, we are forced to turn away from the history of ideas to the politics of the sign. The issue becomes: how, in particular contexts, is the relationship between signs articulated and what interventions might re-order that articulation?[11]

I have discussed elsewhere (Silverman, 1985: 62–8) Laclau's employment of this approach in his discussion of the politics of the Italian Left. Their populist politics worked precisely by the re-articulation of existing political languages. Today we see populism being used to great effect by the Thatcherite Right – notice particularly the successful re-articulation into a right-wing strategy of the language of 'freedom' and 'choice'.[12] As the British Labour Party is slowly realizing, a successful counter-strategy must begin by de-coupling and rearticulating this vocabulary, rather than by merely continuing to speak an élitist metalanguage with no cash-value outside a circle of the party faithful.

I want to conclude by returning to the medical settings with which I began. The discussion of the politics of articulation provides a way of getting a fresh grip on the argument about 'communication' in medicine. The fashionable polarity here is between (good) patient-centred practice and (bad) doctor-centred practice. Earlier, I tried to disentangle the ways in which this current fashion reworked the polarity between reason and authenticity present in eighteenth- and nineteenth-century music and, more generally, in the Enlightenment and Romantic traditions. Now we are in a position to suggest a form of intervention into this debate about medical practice. Foucault's strategy of 'reversal' gives us a clue: 'it is necessary to pass over to the other side'. A call for 'doctor-centred' medicine from within social science might unsettle the conventional wisdoms upon which the debate proceeds.

This would be deeply upsetting to 'liberal' practitioners who have turned to social science as an ally in their battle with their 'conservative' colleagues. However, it could be justified in terms of the increasing evidence of the ways in which, in certain contexts, the entry of medicine into discourses of the social and of the psyche creates a series of double-binds absent from traditional medical practice.[13] More importantly, it might just dissolve the new certainties which the glib use of the word 'communication' threatens to install into medical education.

Ultimately, however, as Foucault writes, 'the problem is one for the subject who acts'. How far is the politics of articulation merely a game for intellectuals? This suspicion of the intellectual auspices of Derrida's 'play of substitutions' or of Barthes' 'play of signifiers' in Paris fashions is widespread and partly justified. Using a brief extract from a transcript of a clinic consultation, I will try to demonstrate the presence of the politics of articulation in everyday practice.[14]

The transcript below is taken from a clinic for adolescent diabetics run by a paediatrician in a new town some thirty miles from London. Elsewhere, I have shown how a central problem for medical staff here is the conflict between their desire to give 'autonomy' to patients whom they see as 'young adults' and their professional responsibility to monitor 'objective' data about their patients' blood-glucose and to give proper advice (Silverman, 1987: 205–32).

A similar conflict appears to arise in how the relations between these young people and their parents are conceptualized. Mrs A is the mother (M) of June, a 16-year-old diabetic patient seen at the clinic. June usually asks to be seen without her mother. While June is being given a blood test outside, a health visitor has asked the doctor if he could 'have a word' with Mrs A. Having explained her worries about her daughter's bad record of testing her own blood and poor diet, the doctor (D) intervenes:

1 *D*: It sounds as if generally you're having a difficult time.
2 *M*: Her temper is vile.
3 *D*: She with you and you with her?
4 *M*: Yes. And her control of the diabetes is gone, her temper then takes control of her. She's going through a very languid stage (?). She won't do anything unless you push her.

Mrs A seems to hear the doctor's comment at 3 as a charge that she has breached an autonomy norm. If June is 'having a difficult time' with her mother, it might be that this is because Mrs A is failing to respect her daughter's autonomy and nagging her. Notice, at 4, how Mrs A acknowledges her agreement with the doctor's observation but then launches into a depiction of June's present temperament ('going through a very languid stage') which justifies her 'pushing' as proper parental responsibility rather than nagging. After all, if June does not behave as a young adult (that is, responsibly) towards her diabetes, then it is proper that her mother should take charge.

However, in this no-win situation, parents like doctors can take 'responsibility' too far. This possibility seems to be opened up by the next exchange:

5   D: So you're finding you're having to push her quite a lot?
6   M: No well I don't. I just leave her now.
7   D: Huh mm . . .
8   M: I've come to a compromise. If she says something (?) I need to get it under control. I say, 'That's up to you'.

Faced with the doctor's attempt to make her 'pushing' accountable, Mrs A now emphasizes her commitment to the autonomy norm: 'I just leave her now . . . I say, "That's up to you" '. However, Mrs A's very presence today indicates some sort of appeal to the responsibility norm and demands some account of where her daughter is going wrong.

Mrs A now develops this account in a description of her worries about her daughter's diet. However, the doctor's next intervention seems to be heard as a charge of her *irresponsibility* as a mother:

9   D: So there's no real consistency to her diet? It's sort of . . .
10   M: No well I keep it as consistent as I can at home but . . .
11   D: Yes.
12   M: But I wouldn't put it past her having chips but they all do don't they? I can't watch her every (?). She knows the consequences.

Contrary to her stance at 6 and 8, Mrs A now asserts the responsibility norm (at 10). However, this is now laid side by side with a recognition of the intellectual autonomy of her daughter ('she knows the consequences') and her practical autonomy ('I can't watch her every . . .').

Where are the politics of articulation in all this? We can find an answer to this by asking another question: who is Mrs A? At one moment, she seems to be a very responsible, even nagging, mother who watches her daughter's every move. At another moment, she seems to be prepared to stand back to such an extent that some people might say that she was irresponsible towards her daughter.

The point is that Mrs A is not intrinsically 'nagging' or 'irresponsible', 'liberal' or 'responsible'. These polarities come to make sense in the ways in which they are deployed in particular contexts. The diabetic clinic is a very powerful context in which this vocabulary can be deployed as a charge or as a defence by and against doctors and parents. In response to this, Mrs A skilfully builds a defence of herself which 'squares the circle' of the polarities of responsibility and autonomy.

Mrs A's replies offer a practical critique of the Reason of the Enlightenment – her position is 'illogical' but it works (in terms of providing an effective response to the 'charges' available in the doctor's comments). It also demolishes Romanticism's version of the 'authentic' subject. So Mrs A avoids the intellectual's mistake of inventing new languages. Instead, she intervenes in and rearticulates an existing language. To paraphrase Foucault: Mrs A doesn't find herself, she *invents* herself.

Notes

This chapter is a revised version of a talk given at the Sociology of Medicine Conference, University of York, September 1987. I am most grateful for the comments on an earlier draft made by David Armstrong and Anssi Perakyla.

1 I have explored these 'liberal' versions of the medical consultation elsewhere (Silverman, 1987: 192–204).

2 Indeed, as I suggest later, there are no 'subjects' outside a multiplicity of discourses: 'All experience depends on precise discursive conditions . . . subjects therefore cannot be the origin of social relations – not even in the limited sense of being endowed with powers that render an experience possible' (Laclau and Mouffe, 1985: 115).

3 I am particularly thinking of the 'democratic' format of consultations with the parents of Down's Syndrome children with congenital heart disease. This coincides neatly with the execution of a clinic policy of surgical non-intervention on such children (Silverman, 1987: 136–57).

4 In particular, I am thinking of Materialism.

5 This is not to imply that this was the only kind of music written in this period. Composers were only too aware of their need to satisfy audiences with less discrimination. My impression is that this demanding standard was generally complied with more in chamber music than in other musical forms.

6 This comment is made by John Carey in a context of a discussion of romantic literature but, I believe, it is equally applicable to music (book review, *The Sunday Times*, 31 January 1988). David Armstrong (personal correspondence) has rightly pointed out that, when we talk about such styles, we invoke the present not the past.

7 For further discussion see Foucault (1981) and Dreyfus and Rabinow (1986).

8 As I later argue, even experts can be downgraded when confronted by 'authentic' accounts of experience.

9 This consultation is discussed at greater length elsewhere (Silverman, 1987: 179–86).

10 As I later argue, such an approach to discourse suggests a disconcerting conclusion about programmes for medical education which privilege 'patient-centred' medicine.

11 I use 'sign' for simplicity rather than the proper term 'signifier'.

12 For an elegant discussion of articulation in terms of the logics of 'equivalence' and 'difference' see Laclau and Mouffe (1985: 176–93).

13 Further examples could be taken from the role of languages of the psyche in

48   David Silverman

cleft-palate clinics (see Silverman, 1987: 158–90). Again, Armstrong implies the creative side of 'double-binds' – they constitute a subject which reflects on itself in the context of the 'contradictions' offered.

14   This transcript is discussed at greater length in Silverman (1987: 243–9).

References

Armstrong, D. (1984) 'The Patient's View', *Social Science and Medicine*, 18 (9): 737–44.

Armstrong, D. (1987) 'Bodies of Knowledge', in G. Scambler (ed.), *Sociological Theory and Medical Sociology*. London: Tavistock.

Arney, W. and Bergen, B. (1984) *Medicine and the Management of Living*. Chicago: Chicago University Press.

Bulmer, M. (1982) *The Uses of Social Research*. London: Allen & Unwin.

Byrne, P. and Long, B. (1976) *Doctors Talking to Patients*. London: DHSS.

Calnan, M. (1987) *Health and Illness: The Lay Perspective*. London: Tavistock.

Derrida, J. (1976) *Of Grammatology*. Baltimore: Johns Hopkins Press.

Dews, P. (1984) Comment in *New Left Review*, 144: 91.

Dreyfus, H. and Rabinow, P. (1986) 'What is Maturity? Habermas and Foucault on "What is Enlightenment?" ', in Hoy, 1986: 109–22.

Flaubert, G. (1976) 'Dictionary of Received Ideas', in *Bouvard and Pécuchet*. Harmondsworth: Penguin.

Foucault, M. (1977) *Discipline and Punish*. London: Tavistock.

Foucault, M. (1979) *The History of Sexuality*, Volume 1. London: Allen Lane.

Foucault, M. (1981) 'Questions of Method', *Ideology and Consciousness*, 8: 13–14.

Gubrium, J. and Buckholdt, D. (1982) *Describing Care*. Cambridge: Oelgeschlager, Gunn and Hain.

Habermas, J. (1972) *Knowledge and Human Interests*. London: Heinemann.

Hacking, I. (1986) 'Self-Improvement', in Hoy, 1986: 235–40.

Hoy, D. (ed.) (1986) *Foucault: A Critical Reader*. Oxford: Basil Blackwell.

Laclau, E. and Mouffe, C. (1985) *Hegemony and Socialist Strategy*. London: Verso.

Mills, C.W. (1940) 'Situated Actions and Vocabularies of Motive', *American Sociological Review*, 5: 904–13.

Mishler, E. (1984) *The Discourse of Medicine: Dialectics of Medical Interviews*. Norwood, NJ: Ablex.

Nelken, D. (1987) 'Social Work Contracts and Social Control', in R. Matthews (ed.), *Reconstructing Crime, Law and Justice*. London: Sage.

Popper, K. (1972) *The Logic of Scientific Discovery*. London: Hutchinson.

Propp, V. (1968) *Morphology of the Folktale*. Austin: Texas University Press.

Rajchman, J. (1985) *Michel Foucault: The Freedom of Philosophy*. New York: Columbia University Press.

Rosen C. (1976) *The Classical Style: Haydn, Beethoven, Mozart*. London: Faber & Faber.

Saussure, F. (1974) *Course in General Linguistics*. London: Fontana.

Silverman, D. (1985) *Qualitative Methodology and Sociology*. Aldershot: Gower.

Silverman, D. (1987) *Communication and Medical Practice*. London: Sage.

Smart, B. (1986) 'The Politics of Truth and the Problem of Hegemony', in Hoy, 1986: 157–74.

Taylor, C. (1986) 'Foucault on Freedom and Truth', in Hoy, 1986: 69–102.

Wittgenstein, L. (1968) *Philosophical Investigations*. Oxford: Blackwell.

3

Romantics and Stoics

Phil Strong and Robert Dingwall

The Sea of Faith
Was once, too, at the full and round earth's shore
Lay like the folds of a bright girdle furl'd.
But now I only hear
Its melancholy, long, withdrawing roar,
Retreating to the breath
Of the night-wind, down the vast edges drear
And naked shingles of the world.
(Matthew Arnold, *Dover Beach*, 1867)

Beyond Enlightenment? – the title challenges us all with the need to say what creed might now replace our Sea of Faith as we stand on our own 'darkling plain . . . where ignorant armies clash by night'. To the extent that sociology can itself be said to be a creation of the Enlightenment, the local crisis of confidence which provokes this question is one with implications for the whole discipline. Our response is divided into two broad sections. One treats the current condition of British sociology as a case study in the consequences of Romanticism. The other sets out our own thoughts on the future and on the desirability of an infusion of stoic doctrines.

The death of Romanticism

In his contribution to this book, David Silverman offers one diagnosis for the contemporary ills of sociology. The essay concentrates on the case of Britain, but its message has implications for a wider audience. The crisis in British sociology has its own local characteristics but its fundamental nature is far from unique. Throughout sociology there has been a general collapse of the discipline's reformist ambitions with the loss of faith in the virtue of Reason. The relativist revolution of the twentieth century has overturned the Enlightenment utopia of a world ordered by an idealized rationality. With that, or so it is argued, has gone the possibility of an objective social science. There is no Archimedean point from which we may presume to lever the universe, to engineer social betterment. Indeed the very concept of progress has itself been called into question. Who has any standing to define what is a good or moral action?

Silverman concentrates much of his fire on the modern Romantics' claim to have resolved this problem. If there is no external standard to which we can appeal, they suggest that we might, instead, turn inwards to consult our hearts. As he notes, this is a motif which is prevalent in certain versions of feminism and phenomenology: indeed, we might add, it can be found in most types of underdog sociology which celebrate experience and empathy over reason and system. But, as he goes on to show, these accounts are vulnerable to much the same sorts of criticism as Enlightenment Reformism. If our humanity is constructed through discourse, then there can be no such thing as an immanent human nature to which we can appeal to judge the particularities of a time and place. Thus Silverman reaches his bleak conclusions. There is no 'discourse of truth'. All discourse is an embodiment of power. Intellectuals have no status to promote change for others.

What, then, can we do? One answer might lie in Foucault's celebration of the virtues of play and of permanent opposition. But this stance is itself profoundly Romantic. It reflects that movement's advocacy of personal creativity, the unconscious mind, the unseen power of community, the waywardness of history and the sheer difference of one culture from another. In the Romantic scheme the scholar is the court jester or the resident cynic, arguing for capitalism in Poland or for communism in the United States. But, and this qualification goes to the heart of the whole analysis, this role is crucially dependent upon the existence of a society which perceives some virtue in the encouragement and material sponsorship of opposition. Where a regime believes that it has solved all the problems of human organization the usual fate of jesters and cynics is at best ostracism and at worst imprisonment. Moreover, there is a further paradox in that, in a tolerant society, the logic of the Romantic position is that the sociologist should argue for intolerance.

Sociology owes a great debt to Romanticism. Its emphasis on the virtues of community and on the scope for individual world building stems in some measure from a Romantic heritage. So too does a good deal of the discipline's genuine moral commitment to the creation of a better world. But the virtues of Romanticism need to be countered by a frank recognition of its vices: the substitution of evangelical zeal for scholarship, the lust for experience over reflection, the elevation of the personal above the communal.

Our analysis differs from Silverman's in two fundamental

respects. First, as we have already hinted, we would want to give greater weight to the material circumstances of sociological production. The influence of Foucault tends to lead to an Idealist version of history. But sociology is not just a current of ideas: it is also people's work (Payne et al., 1981). As such, it is as vulnerable as printing or stevedoring to changes in the relations of production and as much an object of study for the sociology of occupations as for the sociology of knowledge. Having proposed an alternative diagnosis, we would prescribe an alternative therapy. In particular, we shall take issue with the view that there is no world beyond that of discourse from which moral statements can be inferred. We reach this conclusion from a firm belief in the enduring relevance of the Anglo-American empirical and theoretical tradition in sociology. Paradoxically, while the discipline in both Britain and the USA has swung towards European theory over the past decade, both countries – and, indeed, most of the rest of the world – have seen a vast resurgence of neoclassical economics, the central intellectual product of the Anglo-Saxon tradition. If sociology is to find a serious place in the modern world, it needs to rediscover the tools forged by earlier generations of Anglo-American social scientists in their confrontation with utilitarianism, and their demonstration of its limits.

The organizational context of British sociology

The next two sections of this chapter are a case study of the situation we know best, that of sociology in Britain. It is always tricky to draw general lessons from a single case, but it can be done if something is known about its relative location. Briefly, in the period from the 1960s to the 1980s, the British university system led an extraordinarily privileged existence. Although they received a massive injection of state funding, universities enjoyed a huge degree of practical independence and, for the most part, modelled themselves on an Oxbridge ideal. The expansion of state funding was not matched by any concomitant increase in control until the late 1980s. Indeed, the great municipal universities founded by the Victorians actually became less oriented to local interests and practical concerns. State funding had the paradoxical effect of allowing, at least for a short time, all universities to aspire to the freedom long enjoyed by the few. Modern British sociology was born into this unique context of unparalleled affluence and academic freedom.

Both quantitative and qualitative traditions in British sociology have their roots in the late nineteenth century. The discipline, however, did not develop a substantial material base until the 1960s.[1] This expansion left the dominant mode of sociological production essentially untouched. Like most areas of British academic life outside the natural sciences, sociology was a cottage industry. The production process was dominated by people whose primary function was teaching. Academics developed a strongly syndicalist outlook on their organizational life. This is the typical doctrine of the skilled craftsman, a worldview which stresses equality, democracy and individual autonomy within the ranks of the brotherhood and an attitude of some disdain or indifference to those outside. Like the medieval craftsman with his Saint Monday, work-discipline was negligible. These producers had life tenure, were accountable to no one and did pretty much as they pleased. Individuals laboured only so much as to achieve whatever personal goals they might set for themselves.

In the 1980s, however, British academic production has begun to experience an infusion of the industrial disciplines which have swept through the manufacturing sector since the mid-nineteenth century. As in other service industries, the combination of changing technology and economic recession has transformed the relations of production. Government has begun to exert a degree of control to match its financial contribution. The demand for accountability has stimulated corporatist reorganizations in higher education and the research councils designed to centralize control over the production of graduates and of new knowledge in the hands of generalist managers. There have been large-scale redundancies, and a major reorganization of the productive plant is now in progress. The cottage industry is giving way to the market-oriented knowledge factory with its mission to respond to external client demands rather than producer interests. Societal relevance, financial discipline and productivity have been elevated as concerns at least equal to those of scholarship.

What has been the impact of these changes on the social sciences? The most obvious perhaps is the radical shift that has occurred in the balance of power. Utilitarian economics, the intellectual basis of industrial reorganization, dominated British social science until the 1940s, and the rise of what was called social administration under the sponsorship of the Welfare State. In the 1980s, the balance of power has changed again. Academic economists have re-established formidable stakes in areas like law and health care and their more polemically minded neoclassical colleagues have achieved a significant political influence. Social administration has lost the pre-eminence it once enjoyed under Labour governments and is searching anxiously for a new role. Sociology, the most popular subject for the most gifted students of the 1960s, has been reduced to the butt of public ridicule while other social sciences, most notably geography, anthropology and business studies, pick over its rags for those which will still serve a useful market. Even social administration or its new simulacrum, social policy, casts covetous eyes on the legacy of field research in human service organizations (Glennerster, 1988).

At a more domestic level, however, the impact is less clear-cut. On the one hand, there are those who clearly hope that it will all go away eventually, a position which seems unrealistic in the light of the international movement towards greater social control of higher education. On the other, there are still those who see the attack as some kind of vindication, that sociology really is the sort of threat to capitalism that they thought it was in 1968. In our view, however, the net effect of either indifference or blind antagonism may well simply be to ensure that virtually nothing of the discipline will survive the next few decades. This is not to say that sociological ideas will be extinct: they will have been appropriated by other disciplines who have come more readily to terms with the new environment. But once the material base for sociology has been destroyed, the discipline itself faces a bleak future.

There are senses, certainly, in which we have been victims of our own success. Sociologists have made an important contribution to debunking many of the more inflated claims of other professions. But should we then be surprised if the suspicion of expertise which we have helped to foster is turned back on us? We have been quick to condemn the imperialism of biologists, psychiatrists and doctors while refusing to acknowledge the colonial programme which is embedded in any strong version of social constructionism (Strong, 1979a). We have received large sums of public money. What have we offered in return? We have flocked to expose the exercise of power, as if that were in itself a sin, or smirked at the way all organizations blunder. We have been less ready to accept the responsibility of helping to see that power is used wisely or of getting organizations to run more effectively.

In short, while some of what has happened to British sociology and British sociologists may seem immoral, cruel and unnecessary, other parts seem inevitable and some even justifiable. We do not have high hopes that these changes will simply be reversed by some future government. No system of higher education dependent upon massive injections of tax-raised money can sustain indefinitely for all its employees the autonomy and privileges enjoyed when academics were a small leisure class living on its endowments, private incomes and the fees of élite students. It is in the recognition of this constraint that the international implications of this chapter emerge.

The question arises then of what positive suggestions we could make about the reshaping of the discipline in a way that might contribute to its survival and development under these new conditions. We take them as given because it is not in our power as sociologists to affect them. As citizens, we might campaign for higher public expenditure and a freer reign for social inquiry. But, as members of an occupation, the material conditions of the market for our labour are matters over which we can only exert a limited influence. What we can change, however, is our own professional culture, a move which modern organization theory regards as a prerequisite of any successful enterprise attempting to adapt to new conditions. Thus, we begin by appraising the intellectual tools available to British sociology and their capacity to respond to the present crisis.

British sociology and the Triumph motor-cycle

The 1960s were a period not only of massive expansion in employment opportunities in academic sociology but also of great intellectual ferment. The indigenous tradition of sociological theorizing was swamped by successive waves of foreign imports. Indeed, its obliteration was so complete that Perry Anderson (1969), in his celebrated essay, 'Components of the National Culture', could pose as a major question why Britain, alone of major Western societies, never produced a classical sociology. This was, in his view, created only with the influx of Central European refugees from Fascism in the 1930s and 1940s.

But this statement is true only to the extent that British sociology did not develop in the Continental mould as a liberal response to Marxism. That debate was imported, as Anderson notes, by white émigrés at a time when Marxism was enjoying a temporary fashion among British intellectuals. But Britain had its own sociology which had developed in competition with a quite different opponent, utilitarian economics. An understanding of that debate is crucial to understanding the place of the social sciences in our national culture.

Like sociology, economics is a creation of the Enlightenment, in this case, though, of Scotland rather than France. As we have noted, it became the dominant mode of social theorizing throughout Britain in the nineteenth century and remains the most powerful and strongly institutionalized of the social sciences to the present day. Nineteenth-century economics was, however, a more complex phenomenon than is generally recognized. This comes through most clearly in the original writings of Adam Smith and a number of his successors.

Nowadays Smith is known almost exclusively for *An Enquiry into the Nature and Causes of the Wealth of Nations*, first published in 1776. This is based on the last part of a course of lectures given at the University of Glasgow in the 1750s. It was, however, preceded in that series by the substance of a less well-known work, *The Theory of Moral Sentiments*, first published in 1759 and substantially revised in 1761 and 1790. The earlier revisions are largely the result of philosophical criticism, but the later ones clearly reflect some of the response to *Wealth of Nations*. For Smith, they are part of one and the same project, to discuss not merely expediency and the workings of self-interest but also the extent to which these are necessarily tempered by considerations of ethics, equity or justice.

Wealth of Nations is an exploration of ways in which self-interest can promote public good. In a famous passage, Smith writes:

> As every individual, therefore, endeavours as much as he can both to employ his capital in the support of domestic industry, and so to direct that industry that its produce may be of the greatest value; every individual necessarily labours to render the annual revenue of the society as great as he can. He generally, indeed, neither intends to promote the public interest, nor knows how much he is promoting it . . . he is . . . led by an invisible hand to promote an end which was no part of his intention. (1976: I, 477)

But, throughout the book, there are also numerous reminders that self-interest alone is not an adequate basis for social organization. Smith, for example, observes that merchants and manufacturers have an inevitable tendency to try to establish combinations or cartels 'to widen the market and narrow the competition'. Here, self-interest leads to monopoly profits, 'an absurd tax upon the rest of their fellow-citizens'. The trading classes achieve this by taking advantage of the generosity and simplicity of the country gentry, whose integrity should be the countervailing political power to their acuity (1976: I, 278). Similarly, Smith points several times to the need to foster trust and confidence in social relations as the basis for the division of labour. Dingwall and Fenn (1987) have recently shown the importance of this in understanding Smith's exemption of the professions from his usual critique of monopolies but he makes the same point in other contexts. The principal clerk who supervises some manufacturing enterprise for the owner is rewarded in proportion to the trust reposed in him, not merely on the basis of his labour and skill, for instance (1976: I, 55). Put in somewhat more modern terms, the general thrust of Smith's work as a whole is that market relations cannot be sustained in isolation from a framework of values which does not derive from the market itself. This remained a potent theme in ninteenth-century economic writing. As Parsons (1968: 151) pointed out, Alfred Marshall envisaged a dual mission for social science: a study of wealth, its creation and distribution; and a study of human character. Like Smith, he repeatedly emphasizes that a market economy can only survive and prosper in an environment which is regulated by strong ethical principles, 'uprightness and mutual confidence are necessary conditions for the growth of wealth'.

But, in the course of the nineteenth century, the vision was narrowed by the radical hedonism of utilitarianism and by the impact of Darwinian evolutionary thought. The reservations of Smith and Marshall gave way to the uncritical celebration of markets as a social equivalent of natural selection in which only the fit would and, indeed, should survive. This position is forcefully represented in the work of Herbert Spencer.

Spencer's star has been in decline for more than half a century. Indeed, Parsons began *The Structure of Social Action* in 1937 with a quote from Crane Brinton: 'Who now reads Spencer? It is difficult for us to realize how great a stir he once made in the world . . .'. Yet, he is perhaps the leading theorist of the *laissez-faire* society and, as Parsons and Brinton both recognized, was a thinker whose radical doctrines provoked the elaboration of much Anglo-American sociology both by their supporters and by those who found them scientifically unsatisfactory and ethically unacceptable. He was the European writer most frequently cited by Ward, Giddings and Small and a significant influence on Ross, Sumner and Cooley (Hinkle, 1980: 51). Much British sociology from Beatrice Webb to T.H. Marshall was directed at his atomistic individualism. His intellectual impact on the second half of the nineteenth century alone gives the lie to Anderson's dismissal of British sociology.

But for most contemporary sociologists, Parsons's study was the final despatch of the positivist–utilitarian tradition which Spencer represented. Insofar as we still mention it at all in our teaching, it is to dismiss it as a canon of error. While this is a classically 'Kuhnian' way of proceeding – ignoring the discarded paradigms of the past – it also has the disadvantage of cutting us off from our own national social-scientific culture. For, while sociology may have dismissed utilitarianism, economics did not. Instead, it discarded the moral dimensions of Smith's teaching and continued to elaborate on the evolutionary lines adopted by Spencer. In abandoning that debate in favour of the European debates with Marxism, British sociology found itself engaged in an activity which was often irrelevant to local conditions. With the increasing problems encountered by Keynesian economic planning and social democracy and the resurgence of radical utilitarianism, we have found ourselves with nothing but slogans with which to chatter defiance at the changing times. Like the Triumph motor-cycle company, we have ignored our national market in favour of producing for ourselves and a handful of enthusiasts. We risk the same fate.

A Stoic social science?

If part of our programme, then, is more Spencer and less Marx, it should not be thought that we are advocating Spencerian doctrines. They remain as unsatisfactory as they ever were. What is important is that we understand why. Smith himself stopped short of the full-hearted endorsement which his successors gave the free market as a principle of social organization. He did so under the influence of Stoicism, a philosophy which had a great influence on nineteenth-century social theory and is now almost completely ignored. Yet this is the logical check on Romanticism and as such must have a part to play in any reconstructed sociology.

The Stoic school of philosophy was founded around 300 BC in Athens by Zeno, a Cypriot immigrant, and elaborated into a system of thought by his successors, Cleanthes and Chrysippus, over the next fifty or sixty years.[2] It seems to have remained largely a minority interest in Greece but came to exert considerable influence over the Roman aristocracy and on early Christian writers. The last generally acknowledged Stoic author was the Emperor Marcus Aurelius, who died in AD 180. Inevitably, over a period of 500 years, the approach changed and developed in ways which we shall not attempt to detail here. At its heart, however, Stoicism was the first theory of social constructionism.

Zeno described the acquisition of knowledge as a four-step process. The human mind was constantly exposed to a stream of *impressions*. But these impressions were only absorbed and became a basis for action as the result of a deliberate act of *assent*. This, in turn, was subject to the exercise of reason in determining whether it should become a matter of *conviction*. Finally, by comparing the present conviction with past experiences and the evidence of others, it might become a matter of *knowledge*.

It is important to emphasize that the Stoics did not argue that human beings did not *feel* unassented impressions. If a Stoic were being tortured, he would still experience pain: the point is that he would not permit that pain to become the basis of an unworthy action. Two other details are also worth noting at this juncture. The first is that this was a thoroughly social theory. Stoics held that infants were born with the capacity to receive impressions and the potential for reason but that neither of these were innately formed in particular ways. They drew an analogy with a blank sheet of paper which is the foundation for writing and has a potential for being written on but which may be marked in many different ways. The infant is similarly shaped by his or her experience of the world. The second observation is that Stoicism makes no discrimination between the capacities of men and women or slaves and the freeborn. Although it is a private creed which challenges existing social arrangements by example rather than by action, Stoicism does not acknowledge any fundamental qualitative differences in human nature: everyone has the same potential for living a moral life.

Unlike modern social constructionists but in common with other philosophies of the period, Stoicism had an enduring concern with the attempt to define what would constitute morally acceptable conduct in everyday life. It is this element that we see as particularly crucial for understanding the potential of modern constructionist theory to propose social policies which rest upon something more than the prejudices of their author.

The display of reason was central to the Stoic ethic. It was reason that distinguished humans from beasts or plants. Only in exhibiting the powers of correct reasoning could men and women display their true nature. Indeed, early Stoicism drew a very hard line under good or virtuous actions which were explicitly informed by moral reasoning and dismissed all other acts as vicious. Later writers modified this to acknowledge the existence of a class of indifferent or appropriate acts which were not in themselves of any great moral significance but still provided an opportunity to display one's moral competence. How was correct reasoning recognized and, more importantly, what counted as correct?

The Stoics' predecessor, Aristotle, had treated meaning as the product of the author of an act. Although Stoicism does not adopt a fully interactionist theory of meaning which locates this primarily in the response of others, they acknowledged that acts could have unintended meanings. A speaker could utter words with a meaning that he had not entertained, and discovered only through the reaction of hearers. Thus virtue, for the Stoic, was not purely an inner state but something constructed in the course of social relations.

At the same time, virtue was not purely a matter of negotiation. The good life was defined as one lived in harmony with the immanent nature of the universe. This statement requires some elaboration. First, this immanent nature is not manifest: it is something which can only be discovered by systematic and disciplined inquiry. Stoics, then, put great emphasis on scholarship and learning, not as ends in themselves but as means to the goal of virtuous living. Secondly, human virtue lay in a life lived in accord with the immanent nature of humans. The emphasis on reason noted above derived from this. Perhaps more important was the stress on the social dimension of human nature. The community of all humans was founded upon their shared capacity to reason. But the use of this reason could be turned to specify the conditions necessary to the perpetuation of our common existence.

The 'wise man' was the idealized hero of the Stoic system. (It is one of the minor ironies of classical scholarship that, despite the abundant evidence of the Stoics' acceptance of the equal humanity of women, commentators almost invariably translate *phronimos* as 'wise *man*' when it would probably be more authentic to render it with a gender-neutral term.) He had so refined and disciplined his own self that he was incapable of a wrong action. Early Stoicism was highly critical of ordinary human failures to achieve this status. Just as with its stringent attitude to good and evil which refused to acknowledge any shades of grey, either one was wise or one was worthless. From Chrysippus onwards, however, this austere doctrine was modified. In real life very few, if any, people could ever properly be described as wise. But anybody could become a seeker after truth, attempting to follow such rules or precepts as scholarship had been able to establish as principles for right living in the hope that these would eventually become so internalized as to govern action without further reflection. The wise man was not a rule follower, although he might be a rule maker. His wisdom came from an understanding of his own nature and the requirements of social relations which was so thorough as to lead his reasoning unerringly to right assents. If one could give right assent only by means of a rule, one was following others' teaching, not realizing one's own nature. The exact point of transition is not very clearly explained in accounts of Stoic writing and seems to have been something of a weakness in the system. What it does do, however, is to focus attention on the sincerity of action. Rule following on its own merely establishes the actor as someone who knows the rules and who may therefore break them, manipulate them or fail to apply them correctly. Right actions, that is to say those that flow from the actor's own natural reason, portray the actor as someone who is an *inherently* moral person.

How can we characterize the wise human being? He or she is a person of moderate emotions: someone who takes a proper delight in pleasure, wealth and sexual relations without being consumed by greed, covetousness or lust; someone with a due sense of self-preservation but who will not hesitate to lay down their life if it seems fitting to do so, either in the interests of society as a whole or as the ultimate moral example. Health is to be preferred over sickness, but not to the point of obsession. Disease is a natural phenomenon and its afflictions must be accepted without complaint, although the rational person will always seek to avoid them as far as possible.

The ideal Stoic has a keen sense of civic duty. Men and women with the opportunity to do so should involve themselves in public life. The rich should delight in paying taxes as a symbol of their obligations to others. The powerful should exercise their authority only with kindness in token of the source of that power in the deference of others. The wise should formulate laws and precepts for those less gifted but should always seek to persuade others to comply rather than coerce them. A Stoic offers his or her life as a model, a moral example to be freely chosen, not a straightjacket into which others must be forced.

Even in this summary form, it should be clear that the Stoics' thinking on society and human relations should be of more than antiquarian interest to modern sociology. In particular, as Macintyre (1967: 106) pointed out, the Stoics were among the first to seek a foundation in the material world for the definition of moral behaviour. Perhaps more strongly than Macintyre, we would emphasize the way in which Stoic thought regards certain aspects of human relations as quasi-material phenomena, that there are certain prerequisites for our existence as social beings from which a system of proper behaviour may be inferred. This was certainly the way in which Stoicism influenced Adam Smith.

The Theory of Moral Sentiments is Smith's attempt to set out those values in the form of an ethical theory based in Stoicism. Its stance initially appears to be dramatically at odds with that of *Wealth of Nations*. What are we to make of a statement like this?

> to feel much for others and little for ourselves . . . to restrain our selfish and to indulge our benevolent affections, constitutes the perfection of human nature . . . (1976: 25)

As the editors of the Clarendon edition show, however, passages like this contradict *Wealth of Nations* only to the extent that self-interest is identified with selfishness and hedonism. For the Stoic, the wise person has a proper sense of self-preservation and self-love, but he or she also acknowledges the force of social obligations. In the same way both *Moral Sentiments* and *Wealth of Nations* stress the importance of character development: the pursuit of wealth is an opportunity, but not the only opportunity, to display personal industry, frugality and self-control.

Smith also took from Stoicism an emphasis on social relations as the basis of moral development. The opinion of others is an important factor in our self-evaluation:

> We suppose ourselves to be the spectators of our own behaviour and to endeavour to imagine what effect it would, in this light, produce on us. This is the only looking-glass by which we can in some measure, with the eyes of other people, scrutinize the propriety of our own conduct. (1976: 112)[3]

At the same time it is still subject to the test of a more fundamental principle:

> One individual must never prefer himself so much even to any other individual, as to hurt or injure that other, in order to benefit himself, though the benefit to the one should be much greater than the hurt or injury to the other . . . by this unjust preference he renders himself the proper object of the indignation and contempt of mankind; as well as of the punishment which that contempt and indignation must naturally dispose them to inflict, for having thus violated *one of those sacred rules, upon the tolerable observation of which depend the whole security and peace of human society*. (1976: 138, emphasis added)

This natural foundation for law, in what a later generation might call the functional prerequisites of social existence, forms the basis of Smith's ethical system. There are those rules or conventions which are merely temporary agreements between men and women in a particular time and place, and those which represent the conditions which make society possible at all.

It is the attempt to identify these latter that seems to us the distinctive task of the social sciences. Indeed, it is the key to understanding Small's (1907: 77) observation that sociology could be seen as the true heir to Smith's vision of a comprehensive study of social relations, while economics had become merely 'the mystery of the craft of the capitaliser'. In so doing, of course, much of what we take for granted in an everyday sense may well be revealed as of ephemeral significance. But, in concentrating on the transient in human existence, we find ourselves in competition with other writers on society who may well be better equipped for the task (Strong, 1983). To the extent that we can identify the necessary conditions for social organization, however, we may also establish a basis for the evaluation of particular acts in the extent to which they contribute to or detract from that possibility.

The decline of interest in the Stoics is itself a significant marker of the rise of Romanticism throughout the humanities. A hundred years ago, the *Meditations* of Marcus Aurelius would have been an essential part of the learning of any scholar or, indeed, any member of the educated élite. Beatrice Webb, for example, uses Stoic ideas to criticize Spencer. Behaviourism, she argues, is only possible in sciences which do not deal with human character and mind. Her words might have been written by Zeno the Cypriot.

> But when we come to analyse human intelligence, the subjective is prior to the objective element. The elements which build up these complex existences which we call feelings, ideas and acts of will, can only be discovered and examined within our own consciousness. By a long and involved series of inferences, the conclusion of which recommends itself to our faith by its congruity with all other experience, and by its confirmation through correct anticipation, we assert that these elements exist in other minds. (Webb, 1946: 140)

A reappraisal of Stoicism would offer not merely an array of new philosophical tools but also an alternative ethic for sociology. As Worsley (1974: 2–3) remarked in a Presidential Address to the British Sociological Association, certain ideas do not decline while their material base survives. Utilitarian economics is one such. If we want to preserve our material base we cannot afford to disregard it and to deny ourselves the resources to argue against its crabbed and destructive vision of human social relations. At the same time this is not an era for gestural politics. The Stoic ideal is not an evangelist but an explorer or a seeker after truth. It is not a question of right talking or right preaching but of right living and right doing. In the final section of this paper we turn to offer some thoughts on the translation of this ethic into a practice. What does a Stoic social science *do*?

A scientific programme

Given these considerations, how can we formulate the object of social science? Two core tasks suggest themselves. The first is the definition of universals in human nature and human social organization. Here, in Stoic vein, we part company decisively with the relativism of the strong social constructionist programme. As we have explained elsewhere (Dingwall, 1977; Strong, 1979b, 1982; see also Goldschmidt, 1966), we believe that sociologists have been too quick to disregard the material limits to human action. The occasional excesses of pop sociobiology have obscured the serious relevance of studies in human ecology and primate ethology. And, to use a favourite analogy, heaven help the aircraft passengers with a social constructionist pilot who defines away the mountain in their flight path. As Isaiah Berlin (1988: 14) has recently written,

'Intercommunication between cultures in time and space is only possible because what makes men human is common to them, and acts as a bridge between them'.

At the same time, our capacity for natural language has allowed us to transcend many of the simple material limitations that confine most species to well-defined ecological niches. The second part of the study of humanity is, then, the analysis of the extraordinary historical and cultural variety of the forms of social organization which we have been able to generate over some millions of years (Strong and McPherson, 1982).

What sort of generalizations does such a programme produce? The laws of human nature are unlikely to resemble the laws of classical physics. Instead, as Macintyre has argued, we are more likely to end up with something like the maxims of Machiavelli or the aphorisms of the Stoics – generalizations which are more or less true but which are always vulnerable to exceptions. It seems inherently unlikely that any creature that can modify the factors which determine it so successfully can ever totally be pinned down in the sort of calculus that describes the movement of a billiard ball.

Many of these maxims are just lying around waiting to be picked up. Human beings are good observers of their own behaviour. As Cooley (1964) and Mead (1962) pointed out, this is an important life-skill. However, their formulations do tend to be rather unsystematic, occasionally contradictory and lacking in rigorous empirical support. These are all areas where our specialist training should be able to offer some improvement. The difficulty, of course, may well be persuading people who do not share our canons of evidence.

This problem is well-nigh insoluble. Electrons do not seem to care much about physics, one way or the other, but human beings already have a lot of beliefs about their world to which they are strongly attached. In social science, one cannot rely on the traditional Kuhnian solution – the death of the old guard – because the avant-garde are just as likely to hold the same beliefs. Nor can one employ the most powerful technique of natural science, controlled experiment, for more than a very limited range of questions. It seems that social scientists may be doomed to endure the fate of Cassandra, the maker of true prophecies cursed never to be believed.

This need not, however, induce a state of gloom. A more creative response is to insist on the Baconian pace of science – a joint enterprise engaged on the slow, painstaking pursuit of slippery truths. It embraces the dignity of the Stoics and their reluctance to betray their moral principles for transient, secular ends. Of course, individual scientists are ordinary human beings with their own interests and fallibilities. In this sense, the pursuit of science may be a Stoic ideal, one whose achievement may always be just beyond the reach of ordinary mortals. Nevertheless, one should not deny the power of aspiration. The attempt to discipline ourselves in pursuit of a worthy goal may still bring real improvements in our human condition.

The Stoic programme also raises the question of what science is *for*. How does it contribute to the collective wisdom of the community? How can it promote virtuous living, in the sense of a mode of existence which is an expression rather than a perversion of human nature and society?

It is a commonplace of organizational literature that experts are very hard to control. Doctors like to do the things they are interested in, regardless of their cost or actual benefit. Computing departments prefer to write their own programs, which take years to develop and which only they can understand, rather than buy in packages from outside. So it is with academics. Given half a chance we do our own thing – basic science. We would not, of course, want to be too critical of this. The unplanned pursuit of knowledge is precisely what generates novelty and innovation.[4] Thirty years ago – at least in Britain – field research was very poorly understood. Now we have a large and relatively sophisticated workforce trained mostly through basic research. At the same time, however, we have been slow to consider the social returns on this investment. How can it be made to contribute to the improvement of our society?

The answer to this is not to be found from within our discipline. It lies rather in an understanding of the nature of the market for knowledge. What does a modern society require and where might we have a comparative advantage? An open society which values the capacity for change and development that will enable it to adapt to a rapidly changing environment needs to keep its institutions and policies under constant review and evaluation from the point of view both of their internal processes and of their outcomes. Currently, most of the public demand in this country is for outcome evaluations. What outputs do you get for a given basket of inputs? This demand reflects the force of the utilitarian tradition in British social analysis which recognizes no intervening influences between individuals and the incentives of the market or the penalites of performance indicators. However, it is clear from the USA and from the private sector here, that there is also a substantial role for process evaluation. The business community, at least, recognizes that, to achieve the optimal use of resources, the link between inputs and outputs cannot simply be treated as some kind of 'black box'. Unless we are clear what human beings are doing in between, the chances of influencing their behaviour by simple manipulations of rewards and sanctions are limited. This has received tacit recognition in the growth of policy analysis and cultural studies of organizations, which often draw directly on qualitative sociology. It is also reflected in the attempt to re-establish institutional economics, itself once a significant partner of Chicago sociology, in the transactional school inspired by Williamson (1975). To the extent that process evaluation is an expanding market, it is clearly one we should be seeking to enter.

Evaluation itself is an activity with several dimensions. We would distinguish four: equality, humanity, efficiency, and effectiveness. Sociology is traditionally strong on the first two of these and we would not wish to see that change. Indeed, a Stoic view of human nature demands the assessment of any act for the extent to which it respects or degrades another.

But sociology has always been suspicious of a worldly concern for efficiency and effectiveness, the stock in trade of the manager or policy maker. In this it shares the British academic disdain for the *homme d'affaires*. If you look up the word 'management' in Raymond Williams's book, *Keywords* (1976: 156–8), for instance, his main concern seems to be that it derives from an old Italian term for training horses. In true romantic fashion, Williams manages to imply that this might be just about acceptable for the beasts but certainly not for human beings. The sociological literature on the National Health Service, to give an example nearer to home, almost invariably uses 'managerialism' as a term of abuse. It is only acceptable to be on the side of the sick and under-privileged.

But a Stoic social science would recognize that this denies the common humanity of managers who see their task precisely as providing better care. Part of the problem is our reluctance to accept the basic tenet of economics, that we live in a world of finite resources. Unlike many of the axioms of that discipline, this makes a pretty fair degree of empirical sense and is a good example of the sort of universal statement that Stoicism has no difficulty in accepting. It is certainly more realistic than the romantic sociological assumptions of boundless growth which may be used to provide equal shares for all. One of the challenges to all human social organizations, then, is to consider how scarce resources may be allocated. Savings made through greater efficiency potentially mean more services for all – including more equal and more humane services. It may be, in the present circumstances, that those savings are simply being clawed back for distribution in tax cuts, but that is a different matter. In modern health care, for example, there is no article of faith that says the wasteful expenditure of national resources on unproductive employees or extravagant therapies must be defended at all costs. Of course, 'efficiency' can be a code for all kinds of unpleasant and inhumane practices, but often it simply means ensuring that an organization does not order vast quantities of stock that it does not need, or that things get to the right place at the right time.

The main sociological contribution to studies of efficiency may, however, lie in our skills in dealing with the question of effectiveness. Chicago-inspired sociology must make us the brand leaders in understanding why organizations do not work. What we have been less successful at is in turning this analysis to the more positive task of making them operate more effectively, except perhaps where this has been expressed as synonymous with more equality or more humanity. Yet effectiveness is central to real efficiency. Is there any point in having a wonderful health service which is consuming vast resources on ineffective treatments? However kind the staff are, is it really humane to subject patients to therapies which do not work? What is the point of guaranteeing equal access to useless interventions? As a leading management theorist has put it, in a commercial context, 'Efficiency is doing things right; effectiveness is doing the right things' (Drucker, 1979: 44). Qualitative sociology urgently needs to consider what it can contribute here.

For all this to be possible, a new orientation is necessary. At the moment most of us concentrate on trying to do sociology all the time. The good ethnographer wanders around for months or even years looking for the problem or the formulation of the problem that will tie all the various observations together. The issues which prove central to this are those which we have been trained to notice through years of reading within our discipline, although, characteristically, that reading has been of a series of disconnected wanderings rather than of a seriously cumulative literature. Certain events intrigue us, reminding us of half-forgotten anecdotes told by some other fieldworker. We mull over them and eventually produce an analytic description for our colleagues. We may have solved our self-devised intellectual puzzle, but too often we have forgotten the real practical problems of the people we have been studying.

So we need to develop a quite distinct genre of work – the policy ethnography. Its techniques will be similar to those of conventional ethnography but its objective will be very different. Fieldwork and analysis will be driven by policy questions rather than by the interests of the discipline. In the process, however, we suspect that the demands on basic research will also change. Specifically, for it to be used as a resource to support more-focused policy studies, ethnography itself may need to become a much more systematic enterprise. In particular, basic research needs to be more concerned with the general properties of social institutions than the constant celebration of their uniqueness. Of the major post-war writers on qualitative sociology, perhaps only Erving Goffman and Anselm Strauss have fully grasped this. Where others told one-off stories, they sought to systematize and classify. What we need is a body of propositions which are sufficiently well defined that we do not have to start over from scratch every time we are confronted with a new site, but which enable us to move rapidly to at least a provisional classification which will pass muster for the cruder demands of a policy audience.

This chapter has been written out of our sense of the crisis of sociology in our own country. Nevertheless, we suspect that its analysis may have wider relevance, for utilitarianism is an intellectual force throughout the contemporary world. If we are to engage fully with it we need a much stronger sense of history than is commonly found in much sociological debate. Peacock's satirical novels, published at the beginning of the nineteenth century, display many of the characteristics of these modern controversies. Unlike one of his more naïve characters, however, we believe that certain arguments may be eternal:

> The sentimental against the rational, the intuitive against the inductive, the ornamental against the useful, the intense against the tranquil, the romantic against the classical; these are great and interesting controversies which I would like, before I die, to see satisfactorily settled.

We do not come with a call to cast out romanticism. But we do hope to have drawn attention to the neglect of its proper antagonist. Our proposal is that there is a continuing place in modern sociology for Stoic influence. Without this balance any nation's sociology risks the lingering fate of all romantic dreamers.

Notes

1 This is not intended to denigrate the work done at the London School of Economics and the University of Liverpool, or of the various departments which developed in the 1950s offering external degrees of the University of London. It is simply to observe that they were a numerically small component of a small system of higher education.

2 The account which follows draws on Rist (1969), Sandbach (1975), Arnold (1911) and Marcus Aurelius (1964).

3 The imagery of the mirror recurs in social constructionist theories of the self. Cooley (1964: 184) uses words almost identical to those of Smith:

Each to each a looking glass
Reflects the other that doth pass

More recently, of course, Strauss uses the same image in his title, *Mirrors and Masks* (1977), to capture the main elements of the dialectic between self and society.

4   One of the more obvious absurdities of a government which claims some inspiration from the writings of F.A. Hayek is the attempt to impose central planning on all scientific research when, as he shows quite convincingly, such control is anathema to innovation.

References

Anderson, Perry (1969) 'Components of the National Culture', in Alexander Cockburn and Robin Blackburn (eds), *Student Power: Problems, Diagnosis, Action*. Harmondsworth: Penguin. pp. 214–84.

Arnold, E.V. (1911) *Roman Stoicism*. Cambridge: Cambridge University Press.

Berlin, Isaiah (1988) 'On the Pursuit of the Ideal', *New York Review of Books*, 17 March: 11–18.

Cooley, Charles H. (1964) *Human Nature and the Social Order*. New York: Schocken. (First published 1902.)

Dingwall, Robert (1977) *Aspects of Illness*. London: Martin Robertson.

Dingwall, Robert and Fenn, Paul (1987) 'A Respectable Profession? Sociological and Economic Perspectives on the Regulation of Professional Services', *International Review of Law and Economics*, 7: 51–64.

Drucker, Peter (1979) *Management*. London: Pan.

Glennerster, Howard (1988) 'Requiem for the Social Administration Association', *Journal of Social Policy*, 17: 83–4.

Goldschmidt, Walter (1966) *Comparative Functionalism: An Essay in Anthropological Theory*. Cambridge, MA: Harvard University Press.

Hayek, Friedrich A. (1960) *The Constitution of Liberty*. London: Routledge & Kegan Paul.

Hinkle, Roscoe (1980) *Founding Theory of American Sociology 1881–1915*. London: Routledge and Kegan Paul.

Macintyre, Alasdair (1967) *A Short History of Ethics*. London: Routledge & Kegan Paul.

Macintyre, Alasdair (1981) *After Virtue*. London: Duckworth.

Marcus Aurelius (1964) *Meditations*, tr. M. Staniforth. Harmondsworth: Penguin.

Mead, George H. (1962) *Mind, Self and Society*. Chicago: University of Chicago Press. (First published 1934.)

Parsons, Talcott (1968) *The Structure of Social Action*. New York: Free Press. (First published 1937.)

Payne, Geoff, Dingwall, Robert, Payne, Judy and Carter, Michael P. (1981) *Sociology and Social Research*. London: Routledge & Kegan Paul.

Rist, J.M. (1969) *Stoic Philosophy*. Cambridge: Cambridge University Press.

Sandbach, F.H. (1975) *The Stoics*. London: Chatto & Windus.

Small, Albion (1907) *Adam Smith and Modern Sociology*. Chicago: University of Chicago Press.

Smith, Adam (1976) *An Enquiry into the Nature and Causes of the Wealth of Nations*. Chicago: University of Chicago Press. (Reprint of 1904 edition. First published 1776.)

Smith, Adam (1976) *The Theory of Moral Sentiments*. Oxford: Clarendon Press. (First published 1759.)

Strauss, Anselm (1977) *Mirrors and Masks*. London: Martin Robertson. (First published 1969.)

Strong, P.M. (1979a) 'Sociological Imperialism and the Profession of Medicine', *Social Science and Medicine*, 13A: 199–215.

Strong, P.M. (1979b) 'Materialism and Medical Interaction: A Critique of "Medicine, Superstructure and Micropolitics",' *Social Science and Medicine*, 13A: 613–19.

Strong, P.M. (1982) 'Materialism and Microsociology – a Reply to Michele Barrett', *Sociology of Health and Illness*, 4: 98–101.

Strong, P.M. (1983) 'The Rivals: An Essay on the Sociological Trades', in Robert Dingwall and Philip Lewis (eds), *The Sociology of the Professions: Lawyers, Doctors and Others*. London: Macmillan. pp. 59–77.

Strong, P.M. and McPherson, K. (1982) 'Natural Science and Medicine, Social Science and Medicine: Some Methodological Controversies', *Social Science and Medicine*, 16: 643–57.

Webb, Beatrice (1946) *My Apprenticeship*. London: Longman. (First published 1929.)

Williams, Raymond (1976) *Keywords*. London: Fontana.

Williamson, Oliver (1975) *Markets and Hierarchies, Analysis and Antitrust Implications: A Study of the Economics of Internal Organization*. New York: Free Press.

Worsley, Peter (1974) 'The State of Theory and the Status of Theory', *Sociology*, 8: 1–18.

4

The Construction of a
Sociological Consumer

Peter R. Grahame

The currently fashionable term 'the consumer society' permits commentators to gather into a single discursive body a diversity of tendencies associated with modern Western societies. In effect, the projection of such a unity glosses over the varied social circumstances under which specific knowledges of consumption have been assembled during different periods. If we can now speak of a consumer society, is it not because we already assume the centrality of consumption in our lives, whether this is presented positively as the ever-widening democratization of a glassy opulence or negatively as mass acquiescence to a system of domination based on a calculated proliferation of false needs? And has this very assumption not been already secured through a succession of half-forgotten discourses which preceded contemporary discussions, establishing and elaborating the terms within which talk about consumers could proceed? And finally – to borrow a phrase from Foucault – is the contemporary critique of consumption not 'part of the same historical network as the thing it denounces (and doubtless misrepresents)' by placing it under the rubric of the consumer society (Foucault, 1980: 10)?

Two roads are open to those who would like to resist the blurring together of social analysis and cultural criticism which pervades contemporary thinking about consumption. On the one side, they can join those who, with Habermas, would lay bare the normative foundations of all of our efforts to produce significant discourses on topics such as consumerism, individualism, and so on. The laudable telos of this analytical labour would be the drawing out of the emancipatory potentials lurking within the variously distorted portrayals of consumer life with which we are confronted. On the other side are those who will find this strategy perhaps admirable in its commitment to promoting enlightenment, but lacking a sense of historical specificity or of the lived circumstances of everyday life: does the retreat into a foundational discourse not avoid contact with the deeply practical conditions within which the present diversity of commentaries has been assembled?

In recent years, Foucault has emerged as one major figure whose work demonstrates the viability of a second road. In his treatments of a number of institutions, one can glimpse a mode of inquiry which does not depend on either cultural criticism or foundational analyses. Central to this work is an exploration of relationships between forms of knowledge and uses of language. Foucault once used the expression 'historical pragmatics' to describe this kind of inquiry.[1] I take this to imply an alternative to the 'universal pragmatics' developed by Habermas (Habermas, 1979): if the latter aims to unfold what is involved in every use of language (universal and unavoidable presuppositions), the former undertakes an empirically informed recovery of historically specific uses of language (discursive practices). This second road suggests to me the prospect of developing an analysis of consumption which focuses on the coupling of knowledge and action through forms of writing and speaking which in some way make 'the consumer' central. In the present chapter, I attempt to make some progress along this second road without, I hope, abandoning sensitivity to the kinds of concerns which travellers along the first road gloss as 'emancipation'. The specific focus of my inquiry is the construction of a sociological consumer, particularly in the writings of Robert S. Lynd.

During the early 1930s, Lynd was one of a number of prominent intellectuals who were drawn into the effort to articulate the new problem of consumption. Lynd's interest in the consumer coincided with a strong wave of public concern with consumption as a social problem. His writings on consumption can be seen under two aspects. On the one hand, he contributed, along with other writers like Stuart Chase, to the promulgation of a view of consumer troubles which suggested new forms of activism. He thus played a prominent role in dramatizing the practical dimensions of the problem. On the other hand, he also played a seminal role in establishing 'the consumer' as a topic for serious sociological analysis, wresting this category from the restrictive treatment accorded it in economics.[2]

Post-World War II studies of consumer society have virtually ignored the groundwork laid by Lynd. Critical analyses of consumer culture have tended to depict consumers as the all-too-willing victims of a manipulative system based on an ever-expanding regime of false needs (Horkheimer and Adorno, 1972; Ewen, 1976; Lasch, 1979; Jamieson, 1983). The result has been a one-sided caricature which portrays the consumer as a judgemental dope (Garfinkel, 1967) caught in the grips of an all-pervasive dominant ideology (Abercrombie et al., 1980; Grahame, 1985). Reliance on this caricature, as well as an excessive preoccupation with advertising (Schudson, 1984), has helped to stunt the development of consumption as a field of sociological investigation. A more promising approach might involve the development of research strategies which focus on specific social practices (in addition to advertising) which were associated with the constitution of modern forms of consumption. For example, instead of relying on the typifications of consumer life found in contemporary literature, we might consider the period of Lynd's involvements as a moment when 'the consumer', as a category, was being assembled into an object of social-scientific analysis, public policy, and movement-based activism.

In this chapter, that process of assembly is studied in the light of the proposal that the modern world of consumption is, to a massive extent, a textually mediated world. This is evident both in the realm of common sense, through our everyday experience of media texts, and in the domain of academic research, through the burgeoning critical literature which takes these texts as objects of analysis. Semiotic analyses have been especially prominent recently (Williamson, 1978; Dyer, 1982; compare Leiss et al., 1986), yet as Anthony Giddens has pointed out, this has too often tended towards a focus on the texts in themselves rather than as components of the constitution of social practices (Giddens, 1987). Accordingly, Giddens recommends an approach which would examine texts with respect to their uses and embeddedness in broader forms of social organization. I see in this a call to steer research on textual pragmatics – an area opened up so suggestively by Foucault – in a more specifically sociological direction. One demonstration of how research of this kind might be developed is available in the work of Dorothy E. Smith. In a succession of studies, Smith has focused on various aspects of what she terms 'textually mediated social organization' (D.E. Smith, 1984; 1987). A major theme of this work is the role played by official documents in organizing social relations (for example between school and family, professionals and clients, or industries and government training programmes). More generally, Smith has sought to develop a perspective which examines how, in contemporary social formations, texts function as constituents of particular kinds of social practices.

The present study aims at an extension of the approach outlined above to an investigation of textually mediated practices which were associated with the construction of consumption as a social problem. It examines concerns about consumer illiteracy which were articulated within the consumer discourse which coalesced in the United States between roughly 1925 and 1939. The focus is on responses to these concerns which were shaped in relation to two kinds of activist writing about consumption. Lynd's conception of consumer 'illiteracy' forms the main theme; its counterpoint is Stuart Chase's appropriation of this label for a purpose distinct from Lynd's. It should be noted that the current study is not intended as a portrait of Lynd as a consumer activist (on this, see M.C. Smith, 1979) or as an assessment of the whole corpus of his life work (on this, see Fox, 1983). In the next section, I examine the new form of consumer advocacy which Chase and his collaborator, Frederick J. Schlink, were initiating in the mid-1920s. This account forms the backdrop for a subsequent discussion of the conception and measures advocated by Lynd.

The advent of scientific purchasing

In a crucial sense, the modern consumer movement can be dated from a broadside delivered by Chase and Schlink in *The New Republic* at the end of 1925. In a pair of articles entitled 'A Few Billions for Consumers', they articulated links between (1) the development of scientific specifications and the standardization of commodities, (2) the lack of resources for decision of unorganized private consumers ('ultimate consumers' in the terminology of the period) in comparison with producers and governments as inter-mediate consumers, and (3) the advantages of making commodity test data available to private consumers in a readily utilizable form.

Chase and Schlink used the situation facing a car buyer as their point of departure. After rehearsing the irrational factors which might influence buying decisions of individual readers, they offered this generalization: 'You do not know, nobody in America knows, the real comparative value of your car, for the money you pay for it, and for the average use it will be put to' (Chase and Schlink, 1925: 153). In this passage, the expression 'real comparative value' constitutes an important move in redefining the problem of buying. 'Real comparative value' is determined not from the perspective of the individual buyer's experience, but rather in terms of an organization of knowledge based on scientific testing:

> For the expenditure of about a million dollars, it would be possible to take every current type of motor car made, over a standardized 10 000-mile road test under controlled conditions . . . At the close of the experiment, the figures for each make could be published in parallel columns, without comment. Just the cold figures – so many miles per gallon of gas and oil, so many failures of one kind or another per 1000

miles, so much braking ability from a given speed, so much accelerating capacity, so much tire wear, and so on. (Chase and Schlink, 1925: 153)

The publication of such data was to permit a reading practice whereby consumers would make choices strictly in terms of the demonstrated utility of products:

> Would this help you in choosing your next car? Not if you were an exponent of conspicuous consumption. But if you really wanted to get back of the advertising, the high-powered salesmen and the dandy little jiggers on the dashboard, and find out what was the best car for your needs and for your money – it would help tremendously. As the motor car becomes increasingly a utility and decreasingly an emblem of swank, the help to the main body of purchasers would be untold. In the end such a list would set up standards of performing excellence, and force persistently inferior types off the market altogether. (Chase and Schlink, 1925: 153)

The conception promoted here differs fundamentally from earlier consumer movements such as consumer cooperatives and consumers' leagues. The former sought to establish communally based alternatives to exploitive commercialized distribution and retailing; they did not assume the commercial mass market as a given. The latter sought to enlist the influence of middle-class women as consumers in the struggle to reform unfair labour conditions; they did not stress the consumers' *own* troubles. In contrast, what Chase and Schlink proposed is essentially an engineer's conception of consumer problems. The possibility of developing test data and presenting them in a usable form ('published in parallel columns, without comment') was clearly central to their conception. Inasmuch as the provision of test data was presented as an alternative to advertising and other organized marketing practices, their approach assumed a decision environment already rife with confusing claims and misleading appearances. Further, it was assumed that significant numbers of consumers would come to make choices on the basis of utility, rather than a quest for 'emblems of swank'.[3]

Having devised this account of what is and what might be, Chase and Schlink next sought to establish that their vision was not utopian. The 'working model of how to do it' which they considered was based on established government purchasing practice. They noted that the US government, in acting as a large buyer of consumer goods, used scientific information to guide its buying:

> in buying much of this material, the several purchasing agents pay no attention to pretty girls or magazine covers, nor yet to super-salesmen with pants like the Prince of Wales. They pay attention to instructions from the Bureau of Standards. Half-way between Washington City and Chevy Chase, these great laboratories and testing rooms rise –

magnificently on guard. Skilled chemists, physicists, engineers, research workers in a hundred fields are passing continually and relentlessly upon the relative quality of the goods which the purchasing agent proposes to buy. (Chase and Schlink, 1925: 153)

In the Chase/Schlink rhetoric, this account of the US Bureau of Standards furnished not just a working model but also a tableau of mythic proportions: the Bureau is 'magnificently on guard'; scientists in 'a hundred fields' work 'continually and relentlessly', etc. (Compare Chase's description of Consumers' Research, Inc., below.)

Chase and Schlink then showed quality testing to be part of a larger set of practices which culminates in the writing of a specification:

The methodology of scientific purchasing is roughly as follows: When a given product is under consideration, the Bureau of Standards' engineers first secure samples of all varieties in the field, and subject them to rigid tests. Thus they inform themselves as to current status of the technical art, and also determine comparative quality. Secondly, they go into the field of pure theory and ask, what is the highest quality obtainable; what is the perfect product? There is some higher mathematics and a formula or two. Then the engineers write a *specification*, based both on theory and on the available types. The specification represents the best type for the purpose at hand as governed by the practicable limits of manufacturing and reasonable cost. (Chase and Schlink, 1925: 154)

They offered the following example of a government specification for the purchase of foodstuffs:

Chocolate – best quality, unsweetened: to contain not more than 3 per cent of ash insoluble in water, 3.5 per cent of crude fibre, 9 per cent of cocoa starch, and not less than 45 per cent of cocoa fat per pound.

The ability to write and use a specification had its basis in the resources which the government, as a large consumer, could command. Private consumers lacked not only the means for conducting tests, but also the resources for even using existing specifications:

The invaluable data which save the government a hundred million [dollars], are not available, in a form that can be used, to that wider body of consumers who pay the government's bills. A consumer can secure a specification – the chocolate one for instance – by writing to the proper government service, but he cannot secure the results of tests made on products now in the market, and so guide his buying. With the naked specification only, he must hire a chemist or an engineer to find out what makes, if any, meet it. Practically, then, the specification can only help the large buyer. (Chase and Schlink, 1925: 154)

In this passage, Chase and Schlink revealed an organization of knowledge which left private consumers disadvantaged, even though it was they who – as taxpayers – had paid for the production of that knowledge. Specification use remained the privilege of large-scale buyers. What was needed, then, was a different organization of knowledge in which product test data would become available in a form useful to private consumers.

The discovery of 'the new illiteracy'

In the second instalment of their broadside, Chase and Schlink turned to the question of how to respond to the problems they had posed. Scientific testing was viewed as the key element of an organized response. Yet existing testing bodies were chiefly geared to the practices and resources of large consumers. Established facilities included those operating at various levels of government in different departments (including the US Bureau of Standards, the Food and Drugs control of the Department of Agriculture, etc.), private bodies attached to trade associations, and the testing laboratories and specification departments of individual large corporations such as the Bell Telephone System, the Westinghouse Company, and General Electric. None produced information in a form usable by ultimate consumers. Testing bureaus geared to the ultimate consumer included the Good Housekeeping Institute, the Popular Science Institute of Standards and the New York Herald-Tribune Institute. Chase and Schlink observed that these bureaus were compromised by an unwillingness to 'alienate advertisers by showing the relative rating or technical standing of different brands'. Possible bases from which consumers might organize a demand for product testing included 'the organized labour movement, the women's clubs, the teachers' unions, producers and consumers' cooperative associations' (1926: 182). Leaving the choice open, Chase and Schlink emphasized the need for action: 'The practical problems are how to organize the consumer, and under what auspices to maintain the testing bureaus' (Chase and Schlink, 1926: 182).

The programme set out in these passages marked the beginning of a new phase of the consumer movement in that it established a new kind of organizational basis for defining the consumer interest and mounting a programme of action. The question of adequate purchasing information was to be placed at the core of efforts to organize and educate the consumer. These ideas were given a more extensive treatment in a bestselling book by Chase and Schlink entitled *Your Money's Worth* (1927), which Lynd later called the

Uncle Tom's Cabin of the consumer movement. As a result of public response to the book, Chase and Schlink decided to set up Consumers' Research Inc., a private-consumer product-testing association. By 1935, *Business Week* was able to observe that, 'Consumers' Research is universally ranked as Advertising Enemy No. 1' (*Business Week* 1935: 8). A labour dispute at Consumers' Research that year led to the formation of Consumers' Union, an organization which quickly surpassed its rival's membership and went on to become the leading organization within the consumer movement during this period (on this, see Silber, 1983). Chase and Schlink's vision of the consumer gazing at 'figures . . . published in parallel columns, without comment' thus formed the originating kernel of the vast self-help literature epitomized by *Consumer Reports*. The 'Few Billions for Consumers' articles inaugurated a new set of practices for dealing with consumer problems, practices which were designed to centre the organization of consumers squarely on the demand for information to increase the utility gained from purchasing activities.

The specifics of the programme envisaged owed much to Schlink's background as an engineer (he had been associated with the US Bureau of Standards), and in subsequent writings Schlink's abiding concern was with the benefits of standardization and testing for private consumers. Chase's concerns were far more diverse. He produced an outpouring of diagnoses and commentaries which sought to show how science could be employed to address a broad array of public issues (Westbrook, 1980). Relying on a knack for popularizing the scientific ideas of the day, he adopted the role of self-appointed problem-constructor. Consider, for example, how he formulated the larger significance of the issues he had explored with Schlink. Those endeavours were reformulated, in *A New Deal* (1932), as a response to 'the new illiteracy'. This vivid phrase (actually, a paraphrase) was borrowed from the Lynds, who had characterized the difficulties facing women shoppers as a new kind of 'social illiteracy'. Chase wrote:

> If anyone has not yet heard of the new illiteracy, let him turn back to *Middletown*, in which Robert and Helen Lynd coin the phrase. It means the ignorance of the consumer, in the face of high pressure salesman-ship, and the difficulty of securing his money's worth in the modern market. Housewives no longer have cottage industries as bench marks; tin cans and delicatessen stores have all but abolished them. So housewives buy what national advertising forces them to buy, after it has laid down a smoke screen of psychological appeals to shame, fear, sex, mother love, success, and greed. (Chase, 1932: 232)

This passage not only sensationalized the Lynds' observations, but also redefined consumer problems as *the* new illiteracy. The result was a considerably truncated rendering of the broad changes in the social basis of practical knowledge studied by the Lynds. Chase's formulations also revealed a curious equivocality concerning the gendering of consumer problems. Note the abrupt shift from the consumer 'securing *his* money's worth' to housewives being forced to buy. This peculiar transition – in which it is the generic male consumer who has the problem, while the housewife engages in the actual practices of consumption – exemplifies a recurrent ambiguity in the literature of consumer problems during this period.

Having named and defined the problem, Chase invited readers to imagine a response from the standpoint of centralized planning:

> Here, obviously, is a large order for the planning authority. Such practices must be rigidly controlled. The consumer must be protected against himself. One visions boards, juries, laws, restrictions on wholesalers, retailers, advertising agencies, newspapers; armies of inspectors. The vision is not alluring . . .

For Chase, the problem of consumer illiteracy did not necessitate the expansion of a bureaucratic control apparatus. Dismissing this option, he raised the possibility of reforming purchasing directly, through consumer education:

> I propose that first we experiment with an entirely different and far simpler method. Suppose we employ the well known technique used in tax collecting of 'stoppage at source'; suppose we show the consumer directly the difference between honest goods and trash. Suppose we counter the high pressure fraternity with an intensive course in sales resistance. If this is feasible, many of the boards, laws, restrictions, inspectors disappear. (Chase, 1932: 232–3)

Evidence of the viability of this approach was to be seen in the work of Consumers' Research, Inc.,

> whose purpose was to furnish consumers plain, authoritative information about the goods they buy . . . Sponsored by scientists and public men of high standing, incorporated as a non-profit organization under the laws of the State of New York, the integrity of the advice was guaranteed . . . Subscribers to the service – who pay $2 a year – have a double motive. They are enabled to get more value for their money, and they take very human satisfaction in being permitted to peer behind industrial false fronts, and observe at first hand what actually goes into toothpastes, cosmetics and tin cans. The second appeal is important, countering as it does the emotional strings upon which advertisers so astutely play. (Chase, 1932: 233–4)

For Chase, Consumers' Research's bulletins were the prototype for textually transmitted expert advice which could 'show the consumer directly the difference between honest goods and trash' (232–3).

The provision of plain, authoritative information might prompt an awakening which would make consumers' choices 'really free' and bring the whole system of commercial exploitation crashing down:

> If all consumers should wake up literate tomorrow morning, the commercial fabric would be torn to pieces. It has been patiently reared on the assumption that we are natural-born damn fools. (Chase, 1932: 235)

Compared with Chase and Schlink, Lynd was not optimistic about the prospects for organizing consumers on the basis of educational or advisory programmes. He doubted that such efforts could play more than a minor role in changing the consumers' situation. He envisioned a different involvement for experts, with a different organizational basis.

New forms of social illiteracy

In his writings on consumption during the early 1930s, Robert Lynd outlined a set of unprecedented social conditions which confronted persons seeking to satisfy their everyday needs. They included (1) the decline of home production and corresponding shift to 'buying a living', (2) growth of the range of choices available, (3) manipulation by advertising, (4) connected with these, inability to judge new products and purchase rationally (illiteracy), (5) the lack of organization of consumers as compared with business, labour, and government, and (6) inadequate public recognition of all of the aforementioned as a problem, and thus the need for attention by social scientists, government, etc. In examining how Lynd sought to formulate the 'problem of the consumer' (Lynd, 1934b), I will focus particularly on Lynd's conception of consumer illiteracy as it relates to both everyday knowledge and science-based initiatives directed towards social change.

In *Middletown*, the Lynds had used the expression 'social illiteracy' to focus attention on individuals' lack of preparation for dealing with changes in the institutions which shape everyday life:

> even while Middletown prides itself on its 'up-to-date' schools with their vocational training, the local institutional life is creating fresh strains and maladjustments heretofore unknown; the city boasts of the fact that only 2.5 per cent of its population ten years of age or older cannot read and write, and meanwhile the massed weight of advertising and professional publicity are creating . . . new forms of social illiteracy, and the invention of the motion picture is introducing the city's population, young and old, week after week, into types of vivid experience which they come to take for granted as parts of their lives, yet have no training to handle. (Lynd and Lynd, 1929: 222)

They observed that in a situation marked by increasing reliance on the market for provisioning the household, women lacked access to knowledge appropriate for the task:

> It is characteristic of the customary lags and friction of institutional life in a period of change like the present that women, thus forced into the market to buy and urged on by a heavily increased advertising appeal, must as yet perform this task dependent almost entirely upon the counsel of the selling agent, whose primary concern is to capture the market. In the absence of the knowledge requisite for buying on the basis of quality, the Middletown housewife must in the main, as noted above, depend upon 'looks' and 'price'. (Lynd and Lynd, 1929: 166)

Although the concept of 'social illiteracy' did not receive extended explicit treatment in *Middletown*, the Lynds were clearly sensitive to (1) changes in what people needed to know to act effectively in everyday life, and (2) elements of what we might call the textual basis of this change, for example the new importance of magazines, motion pictures, and advertising, and the diminishing role of traditional lore. This sensitivity to changing demands on knowledge is also evident in Robert Lynd's formulation of 'consumer literacy' in 'The People as Consumers':

> *Consumer Literacy* – The increase in new kinds of goods and services, the decline in home handicraft knowledge, the increased complexity of mechanical devices and fabricated commodities, new pressures on the consumer to buy, and new tensions within the consumer, all make new demands for consumer literacy. This problem of literacy involves two things: knowledge of commodities and of what one can afford. (Lynd and Hanson, 1933: 881)

In a note they explained:

> 'Literacy' is used here to denote the ability to understand and use the complicated symbols and formulae of technologically processed commodities and to make needed discriminations among such processed, advertised, branded, and priced goods. (Lynd and Hanson, 1933: 881)

As a result of these changes, the nature of the task of consumption had changed; persons not equipped to handle those changes were said to be in a condition of illiteracy:

> A profound illiteracy is involved in the shift from finger-knowledge of textiles, foods and other commodities to the present great obfuscation of the values inherent in commercial articles. The housewife may finger a heavy silk knowingly after the manner of her mother and yet be totally ignorant of the fact that it is tin loading that makes the silk 'heavy' and therefore speciously 'good': according to her inherited equivalence of those two adjectives as applied to silk . . . And so the buying of so simple an article may become a technical problem and a source of indecision and personal tension. (Lynd, 1932: 89)

Further, as Lynd reiterated in a number of writings, the lag between coping ability and change was intensifying:

> It seems probable that under the pressures of modern business development, the consumer is becoming confused and illiterate as a buyer more rapidly than the combined positive factors of education, standardization, and so on are succeeding in making him literate as a buyer. (Lynd, 1934a: 4; cf. Lynd, 1934b: 46; Lynd, 1936: 514; and Lynd and Flynn, 1933: 7)

The tendency towards a deepening illiteracy was compounded by the fact that consumers were relatively isolated, compared with other groups:

> The consumer faces his problems alone, save for such counsel and support as other members of the family may happen to be able to give; while the productive and merchandising agencies operate in increasingly coordinated masses, aided by trade associated and acute specialized services, and backed by a general governmental policy concentrated on helping business rather than the consumer. (Lynd, 1932: 87)

The problem of illiteracy was thus not unconnected with the more general problem of organizing consumers into a collective force for change.

Making standards useful: the social basis of consumer knowledge

As an activist social scientist,[4] Lynd went beyond the provision of a diagnosis in his approach to consumer problems. He became involved in projects which responded more or less directly to the problem of illiteracy. As a result of the stature which he had achieved through the *Middletown* study, Lynd had been invited to contribute a chapter on consumers to the Hoover commission study, *Recent Social Trends* (Lynd and Hanson, 1933). The latter established Lynd as an authority in the field of consumer affairs; soon after, he was asked to join the Consumers' Advisory Board which had been set up as part of the New Deal's National Reconstruction Act.[5]

In particular, Lynd was appointed as head of the Board's Committee on Consumer Standards. One result of this association was the production of a document entitled 'Proposal to Develop Standards for Consumer Goods by Establishing a Consumer Standards Board and Funds for Basic Testing', which came to be called '*the* Lynd Report' (Consumers' Advisory Board, 1933). In this report, one can see an attempt to win recognition for a new kind of mandate for dealing with consumer problems. As with Chase and

Schlink, this mandate was grounded in a perception of changed conditions which made it urgent to put consumer buying onto a more scientific basis.

Several points from the Lynd Report (supplement entitled 'Reasons for Action') should be noted. First, the report argued that consumers faced new conditions which reduced their ability to judge the quality of retail goods. The familiar, simply fabricated goods of the past had been replaced by a large array of highly fabricated goods marketed through brand-names and advertising. The necessity of using standards and eliminating 'unscientific consumer buying' had become even more pressing as a result of the Depression. Through the use of specifications government agencies, industries, and other large buyers had gained access to a scientific basis for purchasing, yet 'Under present conditions, this group knowledge is suppressed and the tendency is all too frequently to give the buyer merely what he asks for' (Consumers' Advisory Board, 1933: 2). Moreover, existing standards for producers' and intermediate consumers' goods were not appropriate for consumer use:

> their specifications and grades are customarily drawn from the commercial point of view, and their nomenclatures are often misleading to the purchaser at retail. They are drafted primarily with an eye to the competitive conditions of producers and distributors. (Consumers' Advisory Board, 1933: 2)

In contrast, useful standards would have to be constructed in a way which took into account the perspective of the consumer:

> Satisfactory consumer standards must be built upon analysis of commodities in their final forms in which they are purchased over-the-counter at retail; this analysis must be in terms of actual consumer use-conditions; and the standards must be presented in terms of specifications and grades determined in the light of such use-conditions and useable by non-technical purchasers at retail. (Consumers' Advisory Board, 1933: 2)

Given their lack of organization, consumers urgently required an agency which could establish a programme of consumer standards:

> The fact that industry and commerce are organized, and have possessed extensive financial resources, has led to the preoccupation of technical personnel and laboratories with industry's problems, while the unorganized consumer has been very largely neglected. (Consumers' Advisory Board, 1933: 4)

The Lynd Report thus paralleled the Chase/Schlink definition of the consumer's problem in several respects: the conditions which call for scientific buying, the need for standards, the disadvantaged position of the consumers when compared with large buyers, the need to organize. They differed, however, over the question of auspices. The Lynd Report argued with some reservations in favour of government action as the means for extending the benefits of standardization to the alleviation of consumer problems. It was pointed out that this would involve a major shift in the allocation of government services, which had up until then heavily favoured producers over consumers. The central recommendation of the report was the setting up of a Consumer Standards Board operating under the federal government. Inasmuch as the proposal was eventually rejected, the document can be regarded as an interesting failure. However, it should also be viewed as the culmination of an effort to make social science responsive to the problem of the consumer. In this respect, it constituted the formulation of a mandate for action in the consumer interest which, in accord with Lynd's sociological vision, addressed the social conditions under which consumers acted, and exposed the organizational arrangements which ensured their inability to command the necessary resources for dealing with those conditions.

Grade labelling as cultural reform

During the late 1920s and early 1930s the ideal of standardization formed a crucial axis for conceptualizing consumer problems. In the Chase/Schlink version, standards would be used to generate unbiased information which could guide consumers' buying. Literacy would take the form of learning to plan purchases on the basis of brand-name ratings of products as determined by test results. Lynd also drew a connection between consumer illiteracy and the standardization movement, but he made different assumptions about consumer practice. The solution favoured by Lynd was the development of grade labels.

In the work of the Committee on Consumer Standards, the point was not to issue brand-name ratings, but rather to introduce standardized terms of reference at the retail level. The use of 'grade labels' would translate the technical language of specifications into a form meaningful to the ultimate consumer:

> The label is assurance that a product answers to certain technical descriptions – called specifications – such as are established by the staffs of many Government and industrial laboratories.
>
> The specifications are often so detailed and technical that to mark them on a product might confuse rather than inform the buyer. For that reason a label is used to designate the specifications, thus becoming a consumer-short-cut to information which the industry itself has about its product. (Consumers' Division, 1934: 6–7)

In 'Why the Consumer wants Quality Standards', Lynd made a similar appeal for grade labelling. He argued that

> The development of standards, grades, and precise labelling will in no sense mean either the stereotyping of American life by the elimination of variety, or bureaucratic paternalism telling people what they must buy. Variety and style will remain wherever economy or matters of taste give a real basis for variety. The person who wants a cheap towel can still buy a Grade C or D towel, or a cheap silk a Grade C or D silk with a plainly specified amount of weighting. (Lynd, 1934b: 15–16)

The assumption which Lynd made about the practice of consumer literacy is evident in a subsequent passage:

> The person who uses a commodity should be the judge of what he wants to buy, just as in the case of governmental and industrial purchasing. This means that a market exists to help people with use-needs to match those needs as quickly and precisely as possible with the particular commodities best able to meet them. It also means that since people are of varied education and intelligence and not the coldly rational calculators which the classical economics assumed them to be, everything possible should be done to make buying fool-proof. (Lynd, 1934b: 46)

But why should buying be fool-proof? Was it because consumers were, in Chase and Schlink's terms, 'poor boobs' who deserved to 'stew in their own juice' unless they undertook to educate themselves (Chase and Schlink, 1926: 182)? I think not. The approach to standardization adopted by Lynd was consistent with attention to the social basis of consumer illiteracy, and the personal and cultural resources available for changing these. His hope lay not so much in transforming individuals through education (or what in a later period would be called consciousness-raising), but rather in changing the institutional basis of consumer practices. It was not so much that 'the consumer must be protected against himself' (Chase, 1932: 232) as it was that consumers should be provided with institutional support for releasing their potential for literacy.

In Lynd's view, American cultural tradition made it unlikely that consumer illiteracy could be eliminated by direct educational means. He observed that Americans tend to be preoccupied with their role as producers, and to regard their consumer problems as private problems. Within this tradition, the favoured solution was to earn more money rather than to adopt a design for living which could maximize the purchasing power of one's present income (Lynd, 1936: 513–14). These observations on consumer habits should be set alongside the broad hypothesis concerning the relation of culture and rational action which Lynd ventured in *Knowledge for What?*:

The chance of securing more coherent, constructive behavior from persons depends upon recognizing the large degree of irrationality that is natural to them and upon structuring the culture actively to support and encourage intelligent types of behavior, including inevitably opportunity for creative, spontaneous expression of emotion. (Lynd, 1939: 234)

Lynd sought this possibility through cultural reform rather than transforming actual individuals into ideal rational actors:

the structuring of a dull, methodical culture is not the aim. The aim is rather to create a cultural situation which, by minimizing occasions for wasteful mistakes, would free energy and resources for the vital creativities of living. Our present culture's false reliance upon the rational omni-competence of the adult tends to cramp deep, vital spontaneities by institutionalizing superficial whims, and to institutionalize reckless irrationality in the name of rationality as 'the American way'. (Lynd, 1939: 235)

Lynd's advocacy of consumer standards, grading, and labelling was thus consistent with an overall approach to social change that would place emphasis on 'seeing that intelligence was encouraged and supported at every critical point in daily living' (Lynd, 1939: 235). In this way, Lynd's response to consumer illiteracy emphasized the social basis of the problem. It was not a question of reforming the individual, of turning actual consumers into 'dull methodologists'. It was rather a question of providing appropriate institutional support which would make literate conduct possible while taking into account the limits of cultural traditions and the value of creative and spontaneous conduct.

Organizing the consumer

The innovations proposed by consumer activists like Chase and Schlink, on the one hand, and Lynd, on the other, were not attempts to insert reading practices where none had existed before. They clearly took themselves to be dealing with consumption practices which were already textually mediated in various ways. Their point of departure was a situation in which consumers were already inundated with a welter of claims and images conveyed through advertisements, popular magazines, motion pictures, mail-order catalogues, and the like. As a rubric, 'literacy' captured the increasingly important connections between social competence and involvement with texts. These writers recognized that the illiteracy of consumers was not the result of a wilful ignorance of textually transmitted messages, but rather of the massive and partly intended confusion which characterized consumers' reading environment. In different ways, they sought to weave resistance to manipulative marketing into the fabric of consumer practices by changing existing reading practices and establishing new ones. They also knew that attempts to organize consumers would meet with hostile responses from a press dominated by business interests (for example, see Lynd, 1936: 513).

In turning to standardization, these writers sought to anchor consumer literacy in a way of organizing information which had the impartial, systematic character of science. In the most general sense, a commodity standard – as articulated by Chase, Schlink, and Lynd – was a description which was employed to coordinate diverse, temporally specific, and geographically dispersed sites of the production and use of a type of product.[6] The standardization discourse assumed that a multitude of particular products and the sites of their production and application could be linked by representing them in uniform and unambiguous terms, thus permitting exact comparisons relevant to concrete user experiences. Commodity standards would provide a master discourse which would make scientific buying possible, and against which other consumer discourse (advertising or business journalism, for example) could be measured.

Through standardization, everyday experience and scientific text would be linked, so that the latter became the ground of the former. Here, one might interject: so scientific purchasing emerged alongside similar undertakings in other fields. The application of scientific method to problems of private consumers was even a belated event, since scientific management (with respect to paid labour) and domestic science (with respect to unpaid domestic labour) had emerged by the turn of the century.[7] But this observation fails to grasp the specific character of what was being recommended. This becomes evident as soon as one focuses on the particular forms of textual mediation involved. The two versions of consumer literacy we have been considering involve not only different ideas about the relation of science and everyday life, but also different concrete practices of reading and buying.

For Chase and Schlink, standardization was to be the point of departure for arriving at brand-name ratings. Consumers who seriously hoped to maximize the utility of their purchases would engage in a reading practice in which they used the ratings to coordinate their needs with the locally available products. Surveying the larger regional and national markets, the test reports would show the exact ability of each brand and model of a type of product to perform in ways relevant to the satisfaction of the typical needs with which it was associated. Order would be introduced into the market, wherever and whenever possible, through the provision of trustworthy advice. As scientific buyers, consumers would exercise an unremitting advice-based vigilance, and they would seek to purge from themselves any impulse not related strictly to the utility of the objects for sale. In this way, standardization would become the basis for a kind of popular education which might neutralize the invidious effects of advertising.

In contrast, the beneficiaries of Lynd's mandatory system of commodity grades would concern themselves with matching a general set of graded levels of performance to their current needs and financial resources. They would be able to assume that any can of peas labelled Grade A would meet certain criteria of size, taste, purity, and appearance, so that – having decided they needed Grade A peas for a given purpose – they could confidently choose from among the Grade A products available in the store on the basis of price. The labelling code would introduce enduring order into the market by ensuring conformity with uniform descriptions. Whereas the ratings user must in each case use ratings – if available – to assemble the local market array into a rational order, the grade label user must become familiar with the grading system which is supposed to ensure in advance that each marketed product is already located within a stable and clearly demarcated order of quality. In this way, standardization would be the basis for a far-reaching innovation in the institutional basis of consumption which would not make unrealistic demands on consumers' competence for rational action or turn them into dull calculators of utility.[8]

To be sure, the results of these alternative strategies for dealing with consumer illiteracy were, in themselves, somewhat disappointing. During the period considered, their promise remained largely unrealized – although the threat of its realization was taken seriously in business periodicals such as *Business Week*. Yet it should be evident by now that the often ineffectual-seeming self-organization of consumers as a movement was surrounded and intersected by a much more pervasive social organization of 'the consumer' as an object and subject of knowledge. This broader process of organization involved the development of forms of discourse, subjectivity, and association which were registered selectively through the more focalized concerns of leagues, cooperatives, product-testing agencies, investigations, advisory boards, councils, and the like. The institutional bodies – with which 'organization' in its substantive sense might be equated – were the formally constituted zones of a much wider field of social organization which enabled both 'the consumer' (as a category) and consumer organization (as a movement) to appear, along with the administrative and market apparatuses into which they were set. This wider field of social organization was without relief textually mediated. The organization of the consumer can therefore be depicted (Figure 1) as a reflexive relationship in which efforts to elaborate the category also mark out a field of possible movement activism (or government regulation or marketing initiatives, etc.), while emergent forms of activism (or regulation, marketing, etc.), in turn prompt efforts to rework existing categorizations in a manner relevant to the practical or theoretical purposes at hand.[9] Lynd involved himself with this reflexive relationship at a crucial juncture. One might say that he both produced a conception of consumer literacy (as an analyst) and then became limited (as an activist) by its practical implications.

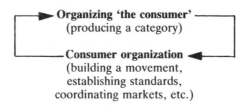

Figure 1

Conclusion

How, then, should Lynd's contribution to the consumer discourse be characterized? The basic terms of the discourse can be recalled, along with Lynd's emphases: First, 'the consumer' is an actor who makes choices on the commodity market in order to achieve use-values. Lynd stressed that present social conditions imposed 'buying a living' as a circumstance of everyday life. We are not 'free to choose' this basic condition of obtaining satisfactions. Secondly, the mastery of knowledge required to choose effectively was called 'consumer literacy' by Lynd. But this need for literacy was in a sense a false need, for it was structurally imposed by market arrangements which themselves were unreasonable. Thus in speaking of 'illiteracy', Lynd did not wish to engage in blaming the victim. Thirdly, the solution lay in changing the information environment. The development of consumer standards was to be a strategy for making the terms of choice uniform and unambiguous. For Lynd, the point was to neutralize as much as possible the knowledge disadvantage which hampered individual consumers. The fact that 'shopping about' had come to appear normal and necessary was viewed by Lynd – to use his own expression – as 'a consumer pathology' (1936: 492) which ought not to be perpetuated. Thus, unlike other consumer activists, Lynd did not stress a further development of 'buymanship', since the structurally produced pressure to know was itself the deep cause of consumer perplexity. Lynd recognized the need to balance a reasonable level of literacy and knowledge with freedom from excessive demands on consumers' attention. This contrasts with the pattern of standards use developed in the consumer advice literature, which continued to shift the burden of the work of consumption onto individuals. One can speculate that Lynd would not have been surprised to discover that today for many middle-class consumers, the quest for a 'best buy' has become an added dimension of the pursuit of conspicuous consumption.

After World War II the link between consumer problems and social research which Lynd both developed and relied upon began to be superseded by new relations. The practical consumer around which a movement had been developed was being uncoupled from the sociological consumer which Lynd had played a central role in constructing. The activist meaning of the category 'consumer' underwent a truncation in which technical troubles were emphasized at the expense of social ones, rather than being connected to them. The rhetoric associating the consumer movement with left politics receded. In the pluralist outlook which began to predominate, consumer activism was no longer regarded as an alarming outburst, but rather as the more or less legitimate expression of one interest group among others. The strategies for remedying consumer illiteracy developed during the 1930s continued to have organized support, but increasingly had the semblance of solutions integrated into the political mainstream. As David Riesman noted, the call for 'literacy' no longer had a critical edge, since the acquisition of competence in handling consumer problems was now treated as a requisite feature of the normal course of socialization (Riesman and Roseborough, 1955). In social research, emphasis on the passivity of the consumer reached new heights, while efforts to connect social analysis with the remedy of consumer problems virtually disappeared. The most general tendency was to treat the consumer as both victim of and accomplice to a process of cultural decay viewed as part of the fate of modern mass societies. By the 1960s, when consumer activism had begun to regain a critical edge, sociological attention was focused on poverty, race, youth, women (and slightly later, the environment) in ways which made the very notion of 'the consumer' problematic. Ironically, the politics of consumption made itself felt vividly on a variety of fronts, but not in a manner which upheld 'the consumer' as such as a key figure in the struggles of the day.

Nevertheless, the problem with which Lynd wrestled persists, namely the relation of individual competence and social organization. For example, in the contemporary field of life-skills education[10] one can find an echo of the kind of dilemma which Lynd faced when he became concerned with consumer problems. The term 'life skills' now functions as a generic label for the identification of a range of everyday coping problems (such as budgeting or handling personal relationships) which Lynd would have diagnosed as manifestations of 'social illiteracy'. But like the consumer advisory programme promoted by Chase, 'life-skills training' involves changing the individual while leaving the society as it is. The further rub is that acquisition of life skills is often imposed as part of a mandatory training programme, and there is no hint that waking up 'skilled for life' will bring an exploitive system crashing down. Lynd clearly saw that such a direction was unpromising, and so he struggled to shift the consumer discourse in a direction which would place the burden for change on the system itself, and not on those who suffered within it even as they were caught up in its reproduction.

Notes

An earlier version of this chapter was presented at the 1987 annual meetings of the Canadian Sociology and Anthropology Association in Hamilton, Ontario. Research activities involved in its production were supported by a grant from Trent University, Peterborough, Ontario. I am grateful to Dorothy E. Smith, Ann Duffy, William Buxton, Frank Nutch, Dieter Misgeld, Daniel Abondolo, and Kamini Maraj Grahame for their encouragement and support. Correspondence to: Department of Behavioral Sciences, Bentley College, Waltham, Massachusetts, 02154, USA.

1   In the context of a seminar conducted at the International Summer Institute for Semiotic and Structural Studies (Toronto, June 1982), Foucault used the term 'historical pragmatics' as a retrospective gloss for what he had been aiming at in his work.

2   For a contemporary discussion of the narrowness of economic interpretations, see Creighton (1976).

3   According to Leiss et al., the mid-1920s mark a transition from product-oriented, 'reason why' advertising copy to copy emphasizing 'qualities desired by consumers – status, glamour, reduction of anxiety, happy families – as the social motivations for consumption' (Leiss et al., 1986: 124). This suggests that advertising strategies were geared to a trend opposite to the Chase/Schlink emphasis on utility: from the marketing perspective, the 'emblem of swank' was in fact the ascendant type of meaning associated with product use.

4   For views on Lynd's consumer activism, see M.C. Smith (1979) and Fox (1983). It has been remarked, for example, by Lee (1978) and Birnbaum (1971), that a generation before Mills wrote *The Sociological Imagination*, Lynd had already sought to practise a critically committed form of sociological analysis. Fox asserts that Lynd was converted into a technocrat during his consumer activist period, and

Westbrook (1980) lumps Chase and Lynd together as 'technocratic progressives'. However, the differences between the Chase/Schlink form of activism and Lynd's own are merely glossed over by labelling them 'technocratic'. In contrast, I hold that close attention to Lynd's textual strategies shows his diagnoses and recommendations to be grounded in a distinctive sociological vision which stretches from *Middletown* to *Knowledge for What?*

5   On the detail of these developments, see Campbell (1940) and M.C. Smith (1979).

6   Commodity standards thus exemplify what D.E. Smith (1984) has described as the power of texts to provide for extra-local forms of organization.

7   On the emergence of scientific management, see Braverman (1974). On domestic science, see Rothman (1978) and Ehrenreich and English (1978).

8   Curiously, it was in Canada rather than the United States that the collective strategy of mandatory grade labels would prove viable as a key objective of the consumer movement. While it lacked the resources for setting up testing laboratories, the Canadian Association of Consumers enjoyed the good relations with government which US organizations clearly lacked during their formative period. The ideal of being an adviser to government, while conferring a largely illusory sense of power, sustained the Canadian organization in its emphasis on consumer-oriented policy rather than product information.

9   The reflexive relation between linguistic expressions and the circumstances of their production and use has been extensively discussed by ethnomethodologists. For a recent discussion, see Heritage (1984). Through a series of studies, D.E. Smith has addressed the particular forms of reflexive embedding through which documents organize an extended set of relationships and circumstances; for a summary, see D.E. Smith (1984).

Gusfield (1981) has recommended treating the development of categories as a feature of cultural organization, while viewing the 'who does what' element of social problems as part of social organization. My own preference is to see both categories, on the one hand, and movements, government regulation, marketing, etc., on the other hand, as involving the cultural production of organized spheres of social action. Both the ethnomethodological treatment of reflexivity and Foucault's reflections on knowledge and power (for example, Foucault, 1979) suggest that cognition and action are everywhere intertwined in the construction of social problems.

10   For discussions of life-skills education, see Grahame (1988) and Griffith (1988).

References

Abercrombie, Nicholas, Hill, Stephen and Turner, Bryan S. (1980) *The Dominant Ideology Thesis.* London: Allen & Unwin.

Birnbaum, Norman (1971) *Toward a Critical Sociology.* New York: Oxford University Press.

Braverman, Harry (1974) *Labor and Monopoly Capital.* New York: Monthly Review Press.

Business Week (1935) 'Kallet vs. Schlink'. 7 September, p. 8.

Campbell, Persia (1940) *Consumer Representation in the New Deal.* New York: Columbia University Press.

Chase, Stuart (1932) *A New Deal.* New York: Macmillan.

Chase, Stuart and Schlink, Frederick J. (1925) 'A Few Billions for Consumers', part 1. *The New Republic,* 30 December, pp. 153–5.

Chase, Stuart and Schlink, Frederick J. (1926) 'A Few Billions for Consumers', part 2. *The New Republic*, 6 January, pp. 180–2.

Chase, Stuart and Schlink, Frederick J. (1927) *Your Money's Worth.* New York: Macmillan.

Consumers' Advisory Board of the National Recovery Administration, Committee on Consumer Standards (1933) Proposal to Develop Standards for Consumer Goods by Establishing a Consumer Standards Board and Funds for Basic Testing, Reasons for Action. (The Lynd Report)

Consumers' Division, National Emergency Council (1934) *Standards of Quality.* Bulletin no. 3.

Creighton, Lucy Black (1976) *Pretenders to the Throne: The Consumer Movement in the United States.* Lexington, MA: Lexington Books.

Dyer, Gillian (1982) *Advertising as Communication.* London: Methuen.

Ehrenreich, Barbara and English, Deirdre (1978) *For Her Own Good: 150 Years of the Experts' Advice to Women.* New York: Anchor/Doubleday.

Ewen, Stuart (1976) *Captains of Consciousness: Advertising and the Social Roots of the Consumer Culture.* New York: McGraw-Hill.

Foucault, Michel (1979) *Discipline and Punish,* tr. Alan Sheridan. New York: Vintage.

Foucault, Michel (1980) *The History of Sexuality*, Volume I: *An Introduction,* tr. Robert Hurley. New York: Vintage.

Fox, Richard Wightman (1983) 'Epitaph for Middletown: Robert S. Lynd and the Analysis of Consumer Culture', in Richard Wightman Fox and T.J. Jackson Lears (eds), *The Culture of Consumption, Critical Essays in American History 1880–1980.* New York: Pantheon Books. pp. 101–41.

Garfinkel, Harold (1967) *Studies in Ethnomethodology.* Englewood Cliffs, NJ: Prentice-Hall.

Giddens, Anthony (1987) *Social Theory and Modern Sociology.* Stanford, CA: Stanford University Press.

Grahame, Peter R. (1985) 'Criticalness, Pragmatics, and Everyday Life: Consumer Literacy as Critical Practice', in John Forester (ed.), *Critical Theory and Public Life.* Cambridge, MA: MIT Press. pp. 147–74.

Grahame, Peter R. (1988) 'Curriculum or Common Sense? A Study in the Production of Useful Knowledge', *Journal of Educational Thought*, 22: 237–46.

Griffith, Alison I. (1988) 'Skilling for Life/Living for Skill', *Journal of Educational Thought*, 22: 198–208.

Gusfield, Joseph R. (1981) *Drinking–Driving and the Symbolic Order.* Chicago: University of Chicago Press.

Habermas, Jürgen (1979) 'What is Universal Pragmatics?' in *Communication and the Evolution of Society,* tr. Thomas McCarthy. Boston: Beacon Press.

Heritage, John (1984) *Garfinkel and Ethnomethodology.* Cambridge: Polity Press.

Horkheimer, Max and Adorno, Theodor W. (1972) 'The Culture Industry: Enlightenment as Mass Deception', in *Dialectic of Enlightenment,* tr. John Cumming. New York: Seabury. pp. 120–67.

Jamieson, Frederick (1983) 'Postmodernism and Consumer Society', in Hal Foster (ed.), *The Anti-Aesthetic, Essays on Postmodern Culture.* Port Townsend, WA: Bay Press. pp. 111–25.

Lasch, Christopher (1979) *The Culture of Narcissism: American Life in an Age of Diminishing Expectations.* New York: Norton.

Lee, Alfred McClung (1978) *Sociology for Whom?* New York: Oxford University Press.

Leiss, William, Kline, Stephen and Jhally, Sut (1986) *Social Communication in Advertising, Persons, Products, and Images of Well-being.* Toronto: Methuen.

Lynd, Robert S. (1932) 'Family Members as Consumers', *Annals of the American Academy of Political and Social Science,* 170: 86–93.

Lynd, Robert S. (1934a) 'The Consumer becomes a "Problem"', *Annals of the American Academy of Political and Social Science,* 173:1–6.

Lynd, Robert S. (1934b) 'Why the Consumer wants Quality Standards', *Advertising and Selling,* 4 January, pp. 15–16, 46, 48–9.

Lynd, Robert S. (1936) 'Democracy's Third Estate: The Consumer', *Political Science Quarterly,* 51: 481–515.

Lynd, Robert S. (1939) *Knowledge for What? The Place of Social Science in American Culture.* Princeton: Princeton University Press.

Lynd, Robert S. and Flynn, John T. (1933) 'The New Deal and the Consumer', radio debate between John T. Flynn and Robert S. Lynd, 23 December on NBC. Transcript reprinted in *Economics for Consumers under the NIRA and After.* Washington, NJ: Consumers' Research, Inc., 1934.

Lynd, Robert S., with the assistance of Hanson, Alice C. (1933) 'The People as Consumers', in *Recent Social Trends in the United States: Report of the President's Research Committee on Social Trends.* New York: McGraw-Hill. pp. 857–911.

Lynd, Robert S. and Lynd, Helen Merrell (1929) *Middletown: A Study in Modern American Culture.* New York: Harcourt, Brace & World.

Riesman, David and Roseborough, Howard (1955) 'Careers and Consumer Behavior', in Lincoln H. Clarke (ed.), *Consumer Behavior,* Volume II: *The Life Cycle and Consumer Behavior.* New York: New York University Press. pp. 1–18.

Rothman, Sheila M. (1978) *Woman's Proper Place: A History of Changing Ideals and Practices, 1870 to the Present.* New York: Basic Books.

Schudson, Michael (1984) *Advertising, the Uneasy Persuasion: its Dubious Impact on American Society.* New York: Basic Books.

Silber, Norman Isaac (1983) *Test and Protest: The Influence of Consumers' Union.* New York: Holmes & Meier.

Smith, Dorothy E. (1984) 'Textually Mediated Social Organization', *International Social Science Journal,* 34: 59–75.

Smith, Dorothy E. (1987) *The Everyday World as Problematic: A Feminist Sociology.* Toronto: University of Toronto Press.

Smith, Marc C. (1979) 'Robert Lynd and Consumerism in the 1930s', *Journal of the History of Sociology,* 2: 99–119.

Westbrook, Robert B. (1980) 'Tribune of the Technostructure: The Popular Economics of Stuart Chase,', *American Quarterly,* 32: 387–408.

Williamson, Judith (1978) *Decoding Advertisements.* London: Marion Boyars.

PART TWO

POLITICS IN THE FIELD

5

Local Cultures and Service Policy

Jaber F. Gubrium

A few years ago, Geertz (1983) collected together and published a series of his essays in interpretive anthropology entitled *Local Knowledge*. The title, drawn from one of the essays, meant to convey the 'always ineluctably local' shape of ethnographic knowledge (1983: 4). Geertz's view was that the distant ideas of interest to anthropologists were, in some sense, accomplishments – meaningful assignments – of those concerned, both natives and social scientists. This chapter takes its point of departure from the idea of local knowledge, contending that local knowledge forms into local cultures and that the accomplishments of local cultures present a considerable conceptual challenge to policy.

Local cultures are more or less regularized and localized ways of assigning meaning and responding to things. The *regularities* are organized features of the activities of those concerned, among them, the formal settings, jobs, audiences, informal groupings, professions, work schedules and shifts, and their respective systems of classification. The regularities occur according to place, time, or both. The cultures under consideration are *localized* in that those concerned engage differential ways of assigning meaning and responding to things, in and about their immediate everyday lives. It is not so much that a general culture specifies life's realities, as that such local circumstances as individual formal or informal organizations offer particular sets of codes of specification. The idea of a general culture, as anthropologists have traditionally conceived of it, is too broad to represent the diverse realities of everyday life. Localizing culture is a means of drawing generalities of common meaning into the disjointed particulars of everyday living. Policy typically glosses over localized interpretations, treating them as hindrances to successful general application. The *things* referenced, while including any variety of object or event, in this chapter will be limited to what Emerson and Messinger (1977) have called 'troubles'. Put simply, troubles pertain to bothersome personal matters, from juvenile delinquency and white collar crime to emotional disturbance, senility, and caregiving.

Based on data gathered in a variety of human service settings, the purpose of the chapter is to show how local culture 'always ineluctably' shapes the reality of troubles. The chapter falls into three parts. First, the approach and method are described, featuring the analysis of local cultures as cultural criticism. Second, three aspects of local culture pertinent to the possibility of generalized service policy are empirically illustrated. Third, in the light of the evidence, the rhetorical nature of troubles is addressed in relation to policy, linking policy with cultural criticism.

Approach and method

Cultural criticism is taken to be a form of commentary on public life that searches for and discerns its practical, rhetorical basis. Focal are the communicative designs that simultaneously construct and communicate the troubles of everyday life. The critical function is to 'deconstruct' these things in order to make visible their moral, yet practical connections (Derrida, 1977).

In linking troubles, local cultures, policy, and cultural criticism, we are treading at the margins of what are often distinguished as the 'is' and the 'could'. As far as policy is concerned, the business of doing something about people's troubles, until recently, has been considered a matter of systematically contending with them, using the by-products of research to somehow alter the lives concerned. Whatever the kinds of trouble, as 'is's', they were conceived as discernible upon close inspection. Whatever the mode of inter-vention or the bone of contention, the respective 'coulds' were taken, in principle, to be separate from, yet applicable to, the troubles under consideration. Is and could dwelt in different worlds – one more or less prevalent, the other more or less urgent – even while each was a commentary on the other.

The relationship between policy and research, of course, has varied. Bulmer (1982) presented three models: (1) empiricism, where research is taken to be a neutral and systematic means of gathering facts of use to policy-makers; (2) social engineering, where researchers acquire the data needed to scientifically plan the changes believed to be appropriate to particular problems; and (3) Enlightenment, in which alternate possibilities for dealing with troubles or problems are presented to policy-makers. Silverman (1985) treats the three models as versions of what is described as the research role and politics of the 'state counsellor'. He further distinguishes the independent scholar and the partisan, who, respectively, operates separately from policy considerations and takes up political action. While the models or roles differentially emphasize the connection between is and could, each nonetheless assumes the existence of concrete worlds of troubles, separate from, yet potentially subject to, policy consideration.

Foucault (1981: 12–13) criticizes the conventional separation of is and could. His analyses have been historical, offering detailed evidence of the totalizing 'gazes' that virtually conspire behind our backs in taken-for-granted discourses of is to reveal the apparent facts of human troubles, which, with a different gaze, *could* cast facts otherwise. The approach taken in this chapter is ethnographic and aims to make visible the moral, yet practical, sources of everyday troubles. As a moral vision of social facts, and against the general formulations of policy, it is a way of going beyond Enlightenment.

A local culture is simultaneously an is and a could. As far as is is concerned, a local culture provides means of interpreting troubles, which we might call its codes, or, following Goffman's (1974) cognitive emphasis, its frames. For example, the fact that we have both a disease code and a code of mirth to describe body weight means that we can classify and denote girth in terms of sickness or as (hilariously) normal. Extended to the activity of eating, we could identify the eating disorders that lead to pathological bodily states. The contrasting and contending framework of human sins and pleasures catalogues an entirely different set of bodily conditions – of is's – such as gluttony or vain disfigurement (compare Lyman, 1978). As more or less regularized and organizationally circumscribed ways of assigning meaning and responding to the body, a local culture might offer one code or the other, or both, for conveying the experiential reality of weight, girth, and indulgence.

A local culture is also a could. In contrasting local cultures, we find that, as Casteneda (1971) might have put it, is's are 'separate realities', and thus possibilities, alternate embodiments of experience. Where bodies are conceived and denoted in terms of pathology, there appear the symptoms of eating disorders; where bodies are conceived and denoted otherwise, the facts display different experiential choices. As such, in and about everyday life, what we actually behold in front of us, in one body or another, are not merely things knowable and known, but integrally both known and locally chosen. To merely refer to what is, is not only indicative but a practical selection from among manifold possibilities – a virtual negation of other choices – cognitive by-products of the link between local knowledge and power (Foucault, 1980). What is local about this is that those concerned – from the troubled to the interested – engage diverse, everyday resources and preferences for discerning the realities of things in different places at varied times.

While it has been said that there are 'organizational cultures', meaning designs for seeing the world and doing business specific to particular organizations (Frost et al., 1985), the concept of organizational culture has suggested internal uniformity. Local culture, in contrast, specifies immediate and regularized codes for assigning meaning to things which, in principle, could appear to be at considerable odds with each other, but are taken nonetheless to be 'the ways things are thought out' in one place in contrast to another. For example, with respect to the conduct of troubled children, any one formal organization might be a culture of diverse experiential options, locally combined in particular ways. A private service agency like Cedarview, which is a residential treatment centre for emotionally disturbed children (Buckholdt and Gubrium, 1979), had codes of both disturbance and spiritedness as optional designations for children's conduct. The children were really one thing or another – disturbed or excited – depending on local cultural application. The code formally applied in Cedarview's psychiatric conferences was a discourse of disturbance. Yet, with cognitive segmentation, a contrasting framework in the same conferences could turn children's conduct into classes of more or less spirited boys and girls, glossing their psychiatric tenor.

As a local culture of codes for troubled children, Cedarview differed from the children's households. While Cedarview staff members called upon both codes of disturbance and spiritedness to represent children's conduct, it was evident in Cedarview's so-called 'parent effectiveness training classes' that family members at home mostly communicated what they saw in their children in other terms – of right and wrong, self-control, and misbehaviour – things not spun from psychiatric cloth. Of course, the households differed in this regard, too, some of whose interpretive cultures designated understandings of conduct closer to disturbance than others. At the same time, it was evident that as family members participated in the training classes, they learned Cedarview's local culture and categorical options. In due course, various family members began to 'see' the things staff members saw in the children's conduct. We might refer to this learning process as a kind of local cultural diffusion. As participating parents and staff members accordingly taught each other and alternately convinced and unconvinced themselves of the meaning of children's troubles, it was evident that the is's under consideration could not be separated from the 'coulds' the varied local cultures tacitly urged them to discover in the children's troubled lives (compare Gubrium and Lynott, 1985). The connections were not so much rational as rhetorical and linked with the categorical press of their separate contexts.

The term 'local' is intended to experientially place diverse, everyday configurations of meaning, not permanently secure their geography. While a local culture of disturbance abounded on Cedarview's physical premises, it also was clear that the facility, at times, was a complicated domestic premise, as it tended to be in parent effectiveness training classes. As a social worker once noted in one of the classes, 'Sometimes when I listen to these parents, you wouldn't even know you're here [at Cedarview]. Sounds like they're right at home, doesn't it?' Together with other references to place, time, and meaning, the comment suggested that local cultures are not so much units of cultural geography as important points of reference for discerning how those concerned presently think about things. While local cultures are anchored in both time and place, their application is subject to the continuing question of which local culture circumscribes a particular premise. Local cultures not only preconfigure the possible meanings of troubles, but, in practice, also engage those concerned in affirming or redesignating the local culture informing the concern.

This way of thinking about culture – as locally diverse and practical – not only confounds the is's and coulds of everyday troubles, but ineluctably subjects troubles to local construction and transformation. Silverman's (1986) third of his seven rules for qualitative method – 'the phenomenon escapes' – is relevant here. Adapted to the concept of local culture, Silverman would warn us that policy not only must confront the diversity, but also the *practical construction*, of troubles. In a manner of speaking, those concerned with troubles at Cedarview do not always 'do' emotional disturbance in their cognitive encounters with children. As I shall discuss at greater length below, 'after hours' (meaning after 5 p.m. and on weekends) they are likely to 'do' something else. In this way the local experiential reality of disturbance shows its temporal borders, the margin of is and could. Putting it in terms of local culture, we find that the very stuff for which policy is formulated alters its everyday reality according to the localization of culture, something as simple as the time of day or the discernment of what now it is time to do, and what place suggests is 'going on here' at the moment.

While those concerned do not use the term 'local culture' as we do, they do take into account experiential codes and boundaries. They are attuned to, or tune into, the diverse things which the sights and sounds of their concrete concerns are and could be. To the extent the concerned engage is/could – which I contend they do in the practice of everyday life – local culture is essentially policy-relevant. As Laing (1967) once put it, those concerned continually engage a 'politics of experience' as they figure the troubles of their lives.

Displaying engagements with local culture calls for something well beyond what Hammersley and Atkinson (1983) label 'naturalistic ethnography'. It requires a deconstructive field method, one which makes visible the practical articulation of the policy-relevant realities of everday life (Gubrium, 1988). Accordingly, field data are interpreted to show both the variety of understandings for troubles and the margins of usage.

Three policy-relevant features of local culture

I now turn to three interrelated, policy-relevant features of local culture and illustrate them as a way of making visible the everyday linkages of is/could in the matter of troubles: (1) the diverse codes of local cultures, (2) organizational rhythms and cultural variation, and (3) the descriptive activity of local culture.

The diverse codes of local cultures

As part of a field study of the social organization of care in the Alzheimer's disease (senile dementia) experience, support groups for caregivers were observed in two North American cities over a period of three years (Gubrium, 1986). Some groups were comprised of caregiving spouses, mainly the elderly wives of dementia patients cared for at home. A few groups were limited to the adult children of demented parents, often caregiving daughters. Most were attended by a mixture of familial caregivers, including the rarer sibling or friend who provided home care.

From the support group literature we learn that some groups have a didactic mission while others are more socio-emotional. The didactic group aims to teach and guide participants to think and feel in particular ways about the troubles ailing them. The socio-emotional group functions as a forum for the expression of feelings, with little or no mandate for offering a guide to living. Support groups also are said to vary in leadership, some facilitated by the experienced membership at large, others led by professional service providers.

The support groups observed in the Alzheimer's disease study combined the aims and leadership styles. At times, some groups were mainly didactic and, at other times, chiefly socio-emotional.

Leadership style, while formally prescribed in some groups, depended on the particular issues under consideration. Any group could become decidedly anti-professional and member-guided when the professional ignorance of caregiving complications was at issue; the same group could be singularly attentive to expert leadership when so-called 'medical breakthroughs' were discussed.

Each group had a local culture that, regardless of aim and leadership, served to frame the experiences which participants brought to each other's attention. While the groups could be compared for, say, their leadership styles and, thereby, be subject to evaluation according to some overall policy tenet such as the effectiveness of member-facilitation for drawing out member expressiveness, it was evident that local cultures provided their own, separate and particular, designs for interpreting the value of experiences shared.

Each group's interpersonal history could be thought of as a configuration of codes for comparing and assessing individual caregiving experiences. For example, in one of the support groups studied, it was evident that the notion of the 'really' ideal caregiver was an especially persistent background concern of participants, presenting them with a local code for evaluating their caregiving responsibilities. One caregiver in particular, who no longer attended the group but who was influential in local Alzheimer's disease service activities, was taken to be a virtual exemplar of 'total devotion' to the home care of a demented family member. In this support group, the exemplary caregiver – call her Jessica – presented participants with a basis of comparison for the evaluation of caregiving activity, felt strain, and sentiments about continued home care and possible institutionalization. Participants used Jessica's legendary experience to assess how they 'were doing' personally, whether, say, their individual contributions were 'all that great' in comparison to 'what Jessica does for her husband'. According to received wisdom, the husband was 'a living vegetable', who, as it was commonly put, presented Jessica with a real '36-hour day' burden of care.

Still, in this support group, Jessica's legendary status as an ideal caregiver was not continually positive. When the condition known as 'denial' was entertained, which was believed to be a tacit refusal to acknowledge the reality of an event or experience, Jessica became an exemplary instance of overdevotion, bringing to bear a different code for interpreting filial responsibility. She was still an ideal caregiver, though not to be emulated. In the framework of denial, Jessica was used to evaluate whether, in comparison, one was being realistic about continued home care. In this context,

Jessica served as a basis for assessing whether one had 'gone too far', that is, to the point at which a totally devoted caregiver becomes the disease's so-called 'second victim', caught in a spiral of overconcern and the denial of personal and familial strain.

In this support group's local culture, the issue-linked quality of Jessica's exemplary status offered support for diametrically opposed decisions in the matter of institutional placement. When Jessica presented the positive ideal, participants hesitated to speak of the possibility of placing their demented loved ones in a nursing home. It was not uncommon for those considered to be too (coldly) rational in assessing their home situation to be thought of as rushing to judgement in deciding 'it's time', a common expression referring to the moment it was appropriate to consider an alternative to home care. When Jessica portrayed the negative ideal, participants discussed at length the indirect and insidious impact of the dementia on the caregiver and other members of the household. It was on the latter occasions that one was likely to hear participants entertain denial as underpinning overdevotion in general against their possible overconcern in particular.

From this support group, we learn that such ostensibly measurable qualities as the degree of impairment, felt stress, and the inclination to institutionalize the patient – components of what I have elsewhere called the 'care equation' (Gubrium and Lynott, 1987) – do what Silverman referred to as the phenomena 'escaping'. Depending on the issue under consideration, either devotion or denial, Jessica's exemplary status shifted from being a positive to a negative standard of comparison. Paralleling this, participants who used Jessica as a standard of comparison for their own caregiving experience and decisions, stood to experience rather dramatic alterations in understanding their own circumstances and testimony. As such, it seemed altogether sensible for caregivers to report that how they felt about the burden of care and possible institutionalization 'depends', as some put it to those who interviewed them about their related thoughts and feelings.

Not all of the support groups studied had such singularly prominent exemplars. While singularly prominent exemplars provided some support groups with solid sources of individual comparison, they tended to homogenize the meaning of the burden of care over time, as diametrically opposite as their concrete details might be. Support groups lacking such a folklore provided a winter spectrum of evaluative options for the interpretation of individual experiences, and, at the same time, engaged participants in more intensive efforts to designate standards of comparison.

The local culture of each group was not simply given, once and for all. In communicating his or her caregiving experiences to the group, each participant contributed to its growing and/or changing local culture. The process of interpersonal comparison was not just a chain of inter-individual contrasts, but, at the same time, entered into its own exemplary background for further comparison. Each comparison and resultant judgement became, in its recollection, a local standard for subsequent contrast and judgement. As such, the local culture of each support group was, to some extent, always both old and new, ramifying the availability of codes for designating the meaning of caregiving troubles.

A comparison of the local cultures of support groups indicates a strong linkage between the is's and coulds of everyday life, such as presenting concrete exemplary is's as possible personal identities. When participants prefaced descriptions of their loved one's impairment, their own felt stress, and their thoughts about whether 'it's time' with the provision that what they conveyed 'depends', I took them to imply that one ought to consider seriously the local cultural values of such matters in the interpretation of experience. In taking stock of the diversity, we link is and could. Any caregiver who learns what he or she is as a caring spouse in the contexts of one group, experiences what is at the expense of what could be in other contexts. The conclusive is's of everyday experience are decisively factual only *against* diverse factual possibilities.

An important point to raise here is the relation between the local is's and coulds of everyday life and the is's and oughts of service policy. Taking both into account would require us to move beyond Enlightenment into that complicated realm we might call folk Enlightenment. Not only do researchers and policymakers offer enlightened suggestions for public consumption, but we also recognize that those for whose lives we offer solutions are also, perhaps, inadvertently, in the Enlightenment business. As the diverse codes of local cultures show, the business is not a simple inventory of concrete troubles more or less subject to possible intervention. Local cultures have a separate market of is's and coulds, with a brand of experiential politics that is at once both about the troubles and the diverse things troubles can be.

Organizational rhythms and cultures of troubles
I have argued the need to geographically locate the interpretation of troubles, not to literally place particular cultures on distinct premises but as a way of appreciating an important means by which those concerned anchor the interpretive contexts of what ails them. Geography does not so much fix local cultures as it provides

concrete clues to the understandings those concerned are likely to take into account in interpreting experience.

Time is an important regulator of the meaning of one's premises. While a particular place might formally be known, say, as a residential treatment centre for emotionally disturbed children, the local culture of treatment, progress, and recovery is bound to that premise's organizational rhythms, such as its hours of operation. At Cedarview, one such centre, the hours of 8 a.m. to 5 p.m. roughly circumscribed the application of psychiatric categories for children's conduct (Buckholdt and Gubrium, 1979). Before and after those hours, Cedarview was the location of a different means of framing conduct and dealing with its distinct behavioural programming. One might say, roughly, that, after 5 p.m. Cedarview's local culture of troubles was rather distinct from what it was during regular business hours. Indeed, during evening hours and on weekends, it was not unusual to hear the skeleton staff comment on 'how different' it all seemed at those times, how things that mattered so much during the week gave way to other priorities.

In the varied field sites where the social organization of troubles were studied – from the residential treatment centre for emotionally disturbed children (Buckholdt and Gubrium, 1979) to nursing homes (Gubrium, 1975, 1980a, 1980b), a physical rehabilitation hospital (Gubrium and Buckholdt, 1982), and caregiver support groups (Gubrium, 1986) – it was evident that, over the course of the day and week, a formal organization was not a single cultural entity. For one thing, workshifts altered local culture. At Murray Manor, a nursing home studied some 15 years ago, staff's talk and approach to patient troubles on the day shift contrasted with their counter-parts on the night shift (Gubrium, 1975). For example, on the day shift, dementia was more likely to be framed as a therapeutic problem than it was during evening hours. Staff spoke of the various kinds of 'therapies' they used in dealing with confused patients during the day; they tended to be more concerned with, and talked of, patient management later in the day, especially in the night shift, which spanned the hours from about 11 p.m. to 7 a.m. when most patients were asleep but some were awake and 'wandering'. Again, putting it in terms of Silverman's apt phrase, workshifts showed that the phenomenon of confusion escaped: what confusion was in practice shifted in meaning with changing daily cultures of troubles.

It is important to note that I am not arguing that troubles disappear in some objective sense. Rather, it is the interpretation of whatever is considered to be troublesome that varies with organiz-ational rhythms. Murray Manor's confused patients did not simply stop being 'confused' after regular business hours; what was made of the conduct changed. Cedarview's emotionally disturbed children did not abruptly cease doing what was commonly called 'acting out' after 5 p.m.; what was made of the conduct changed.

Consider the weekend as part of the organizational rhythms that regulate the local culture of troubles. At Cedarview, most of the children, aged 6 to 14 years, were sent home for the weekend. Those remaining attended what was called the 'weekend programme'. On the weekend, few, if any, therapeutic and treatment staff were to be found on the premises; the special education teachers, psychologists, social workers, consultants, and administrative staff were absent. The weekend staff was composed of the few child-care workers chosen to supervise the small number of children who were gathered together in one cottage (dormitory) for their stay.

It is regularly noted that night shifts in work organizations are virtually different work settings from day shifts, even though the formal design of work and its location remains the same. Likewise, in the matter of interpreting troubles, weekends at Cedarview presented a setting for different kinds of encounters between staff members and children. No one, of course, suggested that the children stopped being emotionally disturbed on the weekend. The difference came in what was made of conduct otherwise perceived in the framework of emotional disturbance.

Take the written materials of Cedarview's official treatment programme, a regimen of behaviour modification tailored for each child and organized into assessment, goal specification, and therapeutic intervention. For each child, staff members targeted the particular manifestations of disturbance to be treated, developed behaviour-modification programmes to alter the manifestations, and periodically evaluated progress. A central component of the programmes were so-called 'point charts', in effect for each child at various locations in the institution. Point charts were posted prominently and contained the points awarded by the staff to the children for 'being appropriate' in targeted areas. For example, there were point charts in the various cottages that targeted behaviours like swearing, the failure to complete assigned tasks following breakfast, or fighting. Other point charts were located in the children's classrooms and in the offices of the children's social workers.

During regular business hours, with a full complement of treatment staff present, communication concerning the point charts highlighted treatment and modification. The progress that children were making on their programmes was shown by the accumulation of points for appropriate behaviours. The success of staff's intervention also could be read from the figures. While there was evidence that child-care workers, like others, haphazardly used the point charts to manage children's conduct, such as might be evident in threats not to award earned points if a child ignored a staff warning, it was clear, too, that the categories of communication still, by and large, reflected the institution's treatment machinery.

As the cultural relevances of the institution changed with its organizational rhythms, staff altered its orientation to the charts. On the weekends, the child care staff, of course, continued to be responsible for monitoring the children's behaviour and awarding points for appropriate conduct. While the weekend behaviour of the children changed somewhat because, among other conditions, there were fewer children present, the children nonetheless manifested many of the behaviours that would, during the week, be considered grossly inappropriate.

The weekend brought a rather different configuration of usages for the point charts. Social control was secured differently. During regular business hours, while emotional disturbance was a problem of social control as much as it was a pathological condition, it was secured by a general institutional understanding that there was programming and modification going on 24 hours a day. On weekends, in contrast, social control was further circumscribed by the fact that all concerned knew it was, 'after all', the weekend, in which emotional troubles were not as urgent a matter as they otherwise might be. For example, it was not uncommon on weekends for treats by staff members regarding points charts – such as, 'If you don't do your morning job, I'll be really watching you for your afternoon points' – to be followed by pleas that, 'after all', it's the weekend, or Saturday, or Sunday, and that, 'after all' things aren't the same as during the week. The different comments audibly reflected the organizational rhythms that regularly shifted the meaning of the concrete troubles ostensibly evident in emotionally disturbed children.

The term 'regular business hours' represented a local cultural boundary as much as it specified organizational access. It is in this sense that we can say that the phenomenon of emotional disturbance, even as materially represented in points and charts, escaped as an experiential category with the timely movement of institutional relevancies. While the use of point charts for the purpose of interpersonal control occurred throughout the week, it took its relevance from the different urgencies or contrasting experiential oppositions of regular business hours and weekends. During regular business hours, the use of charts for social control was engaged against the background of serious behavioural conditioning. During the weekend, the use of charts was engaged against everyone's knowledge that it was, 'after all', the weekend. The set of opposites represented by social control and serious behavioural conditioning, on the one hand, and the set represented by social control and the comparative irrelevances of the weekend, on the other, organized differential local cultures and, of course, different practical realities as well. Like nightwork in general, the weekend was an alternate experiential frontier for all concerned (compare Melbin, 1978).

Each local culture as descriptive activity
The codes or framings of troubles were not only geographically organized into local cultures and regulated by institutional rhythms, but the comparative relevance of individual framings were sorted by means of descriptive work (compare Gubrium et al. 1982). Features of communication such as who speaks, under what auspices, and to whom, were taken into account in deciding how to interpret the possible senses of trouble contained in each local culture. As such, besides the various coulds for troubles tacitly apparent in diverse local cultural codes and transformed with organizational rhythms, those concerned worked at establishing what a trouble ought to be for local purposes.

During regular business hours at Cedarview, for example, the local culture of emotional disturbance was a mélange of framings, from the deep affective troubles perceived by a consulting psychiatrist to the inappropriate activities tallied by behaviourists and the characteristic spiritedness and savvy of the children observed by all when the latter's 'spunk' or resilience was under consideration. Auspices came into play when the facts of diverse framings had to be combined into, say, the behavioural data of the formal reports of an agency officially operating with a behavioural mission. Whom the facts of disturbance were conveyed to – the audience – was also an important consideration in sorting the framing options of the local culture. The staff members who participated in psychiatric conferences with a consulting psychiatrist in attendance literally heard the deep affective facts of children's troubles; the 'same' facts (is's) were transformed in writing by social workers into targeted activities (other is's), not feelings, for the semi-annual reports submitted to the county welfare departments who paid Cedarview for behavioural treatment.

Choosing a local cultural option for the meaning of trouble was not automatic. Among other questions, it entailed deciding which local cultural frame was relevant for the purpose at hand. Consider a situated complication regarding audience as it occurred on the occasion of a family conference at Wilshire, a physical rehabilitation hospital whose everyday treatment languages were a focus of study (Gubrium and Buckholdt, 1982).

Wilshire treated the physical dysfunctions associated with conditions such as stroke, brain trauma, spinal cord injury, hip fractures, and amputation. Physical and occupational therapists provided regimens of bodily exercise and guidance to rehabilitate patients to optimal functioning. Since most patients were discharged from the hospital with the prospect of chronically compromised physical functioning, familial support figured significantly in progress reports and discharge planning.

The local culture of treatment and progress at Wilshire was organized around two contrasting codes – educational and medical. In working with patients, staff members spoke of their clinical activity in educational terms. Patients were regularly reminded that staff could not 'cure' physical dysfunctions, only 'teach' those affected how to gain the most function from their handicaps. Staff also told patients that successful rehabilitation was as much a result of motivation and learning as it was a matter of bodily resuscitation. However, in communicating with third-party payers, like insurance companies, considerable effort was expended to convey treatment and progress in medical terms. The advances due to patient motivation in the context of an educational framing became successes derived from clinical intervention. In further contrast, when the family served as the audience for staff's communication, the family was presented information about treatment and progress in either educational or medical terms, depending on the relative success of rehabilitation. When the patient was making what was believed to be adequate to good progress, staff spoke to family members in terms of effective clinical intervention. When the patient's progress fell short of what was expected, staff talked of the educational deficits of the case, in particular the relative lack of motivation or unsatisfactory learning. The varied framings linked with audience showed that rehabilitation took its meaning as much from communicative activity as bodily dysfunctions in their own right.

Circumstance had a way of complicating audience designations and the framings believed to be appropriate to them, such as on the occasion of one of the several family conferences that staff members held during each patient's average four- to six-week hospital stay. The family was represented by the patient's sister and adult daughter. A recently widowed, elderly stroke patient was being discussed who, according to the physical therapist, had been making some progress in regaining function in her right arm. The patient's speech also had been compromised and the speech therapist reported to the family that, even though things were a bit slow, the patient had shown some progress in articulation. It was evident in what the various staff members shared with the patient's sister and daughter that, while clinical intervention was highlighted as the source of progress in treatment, progress was not evident enough to warrant full clinical plaudits. Between descriptions of successful intervention, one staff member or another would speak of the need, sometimes, to 'get her to push herself along'. Yet, until midway into the family conference, talk of pushing the patient along was auxiliary to the clinical messages.

Following the presentation of each treatment team member's report of progress and midway into the conference, the patient's adult daughter and sister were asked if they had any questions. This was the typical format of a family conference, where individual staff reports were followed by family questions and discussion of the domestic side of continuing care. Notable for its impact on the framing of this patient's treatment and progress was a comment made by the adult daughter as she responded to the staff's request for questions. The adult daughter prefaced a question with the statement, 'Having once been a physical therapist myself . . .'. It was evident that the statement presented the staff with a communicative challenge, for, following the statement, staff's treatment-and-progress language became decidedly educational, especially as staff members proper and the adult daughter mutually elaborated on what it was like working with rehab patients. At one point, the rehabilitation team's physical therapist remarked to the adult daughter:

> Of course, you know the kinds of problems we have with getting them [patients] interested in their progress. You know how many of them come in here thinking that this is a hospital and it's going to cure them. You run up against that kind of thing all the time, and it's a real job just to get them to think in terms of pushing ahead on their own.

The adult daughter responded that she knew perfectly well what the physical therapist meant and that, putting herself in the physical therapist's shoes, she felt that progress in rehabilitation was more a problem of motivation than it was a matter of medical intervention. Communication and a shift in audience thus displaced the medical framing of matters as the educational problems of progress in working with rehabilitation patients took the forefront. For the time being, in sharing the daily trials of the working patient, both staff members and the adult daughter were speaking the language of motivation as the key to progress.

This was eventually to be reversed. The adult daughter changed roles – and audience – when she soon prefaced another question to staff with the comment that, 'as her [the patient's] family, we need to know what we can expect when we bring her home'. Following this, the figure and ground of educational and medical framings once again shifted to highlight clinical intervention and prognosis. The patient had made some progress, as reported earlier, and, according to the staff, there was reason to believe that continued physical, occupational, and speech therapy would result in greater mobility. Audience, language, and the respective framings showed that rehabilitation seemed to be as much a matter of doing troubles with words as it was a matter of treating them, once again linking is with could in the work of defining the troubles at hand.

Local cultures and service policy

The particular codes, transformations, and descriptive activity of local culture present a considerable challenge to the idea of policy as an ought essentially separate from the troubles or problems for which solutions are prescribed. At this level, the challenge to policy is in the organizationally tentative nature of experiential realities, on the one side, engaged by policy which, understandably, is formulated to address concrete troubles or problems, on the other.

There is another level at which the challenge to policy is more subtle, extending to communicative grammar (compare Sandywell et al., 1975). Against the experiential horizons and diversities of local cultures, policy's apparently neutral designations for data (its is's) are grammatically invalid, something which challenges even this chapter's own grammatical constructions. To write or speak of 'troubles' as the entities which are transformed between the separate realities of local cultures is a kind of grammatical tyranny of free-standing nouns. To properly align writing with a local cultural argument would have required us to inscribe each local cultural designation of 'a' trouble (such as emotional disturbance) as the-trouble-in-accordance-with-its-weekend-framings or the-trouble-in-accordance-with-its-regular-daytime-framings, and so on. Even this improved grammar would not have done justice to the diverse natural attitudes which, in practice, circumscribe the experiential horizons of one sense of trouble or another. Beyond codes, transformations, and descriptive activity, we can't seem to grammatically convey a neutral – a free-standing – form of the thing under consideration. Indeed, we might as well go ahead and write the-trouble-for-policy as another candidate for the entity being written about. Policy needs its particular brand of concrete designation as much as each world of experience denotes the sense of its own.

Regardless of the level at which we consider the sense of concrete trouble – whether as practice or grammar – we find that its free-standing, positive forms and formulations, *rhetorically* support the realities they reference as much as their concrete traces (what we observe and hear) inform us that such matters of everyday life bother those concerned (compare Derrida, 1977). Even if we agree to recognize 'trouble' and like entities as useful shorthands for the separate realities that each can be, in time we stand to lose sight of an initial convenience. Things have a way of urging us to attend to their actual points of reference. What is more, a convenient recognition of the essential ties of is/ought is easily eclipsed by pressing 'needs' like the ostensible need to do something about one trouble or another.

I have argued and attempted to show how there are two moral worlds at stake in policy matters – the is's and coulds of everyday life and the is's and oughts of policy proper. They are parallel domains of knowledge/politics. Their juxtaposition stands in considerable tension with the is versus ought designations respectively assigned to troubles and policy in Bulmer's models. The parallel domains suggest that we link their modes of analysis, tying service policy with cultural criticism. So bound, policy would not so much be an engagement with irony as it would publicly force us to address the experientially productive character of troubles. Just as the codes and circumstantial character of local cultures enter into definitions of experiential reality, the separation of fact and possibility derived only from the categorical differentiation of research and policy rhetorically secures the troubles that intervention services.

A culturally critical methodology exists only in field research that systematically provides detailed documentation of the constitution and experiential organization of everyday troubles. It is not a naturalistic methodology but one that attends to the everyday construction of things like troubles (see Hammersley and Atkinson, 1983). As I have noted elsewhere (Gubrium, 1988), whether the everyday structures or the articulation of trouble is emphasized, there is ample evidence from field research to show that politics does not begin and end with the desires and influence of those concerned with troubles, but is part of our very senses of the latter's reality.

To link policy with cultural criticism is to redefine the moral relationship between research and policy. No longer would they merely serve each other. Rather, the documented is's and coulds of local cultures would provide a basis for making visible the political character of the very facts produced by conventional social research, no matter how objective the latter's immediate methodological aims. Adapting Derrida's (1977) terminology, the systematic 'deconstruction' of trouble, as a research mandate, would establish trouble as a cultural category, and policy as a fundamentally moral enterprise. Short of that, in separating the language of policy from local cultural criticism, we stand to reaffirm the essential troubles we otherwise desire to alleviate.

Linking policy with cultural criticism is a beginning. It only suggests that they should not be categorically separated and dealt with as entirely different endeavours. It does not tell us how to form the linkage in practice, which would ineluctably draw us into local interests as well as local cultures.

At the same time, local interests aside, given the urgency of 'doing something' about a trouble that will not seem to go away, no matter how sophisticated its healing apparatus, it might be useful to entertain a shift in local culture as a 'healing' option. Silverman (1987) seems to have had this in mind when he recommended an alteration in the site of the medical encounter as a way of providing for other interpretations of a problem to emerge. We have seen, for example, that weekends at Cedarview – as a kind of re-siting – spawned an understanding of problem children quite different from that in effect during regular business hours. Applying this to local cultures, we might suggest that one way to transform troubles – literally make them go away – is to alter their defining context. Thus, we might suggest that in the case of emotional disturbance, the trouble could very well become something other than emotional disturbance if the boys and girls concerned were not placed in residential treatment but in a different setting, say, a 'willing' family residence. The groundwork for such an alternative would require more than the legal and financial arrangements for substitute family custody; it would require an openness to a new site's innovation in dealing with a problem child. The strategy would be to allow those concerned to work out their own cultural connections for troubles, which, incidentally, could very well mean that the behaviours formerly signalling trouble might be transformed into something categorically different.

While alternate sites and their respective emergent cultures would provide for other possibilities in interpreting troubles, that would not, of course, make for an end to interpretation. The child will be something or other. Yet the strategy of alternate sites would permit the new possibilities that a stable context does not. Cultural criticism cannot offer an end to culture, only an openness to the possibility of diverse understandings of experience.

References

Buckholdt, David R. and Gubrium, Jaber F. (1979) *Caretakers: Treating Emotionally Disturbed Children*. Beverly Hills, CA: Sage.
Bulmer, Martin (1982) *The Uses of Social Research*. London: Allen & Unwin.
Casteneda, Carlos (1971) *A Separate Reality*. New York: Simon & Schuster.
Derrida, Jacques (1977) *Of Grammatology*. Baltimore, MD: Johns Hopkins University Press.
Emerson, Robert and Messinger, Sheldon L. (1977) 'The Micro-politics of Troubles', *Social Problems*, 25: 121–35.
Foucault, Michel (1980) *Power/Knowledge*, ed. C. Gordon. New York: Pantheon
Foucault, Michel (1981) 'Questions of Method: An Interview with Michel Foucault', *Ideology and Consciousness*, 8: 3–14.
Frost, P.J. et al. (1985) *Organizational Culture*. Beverly Hills, CA: Sage.
Geertz, Clifford (1983) *Local Knowledge*. New York: Basic.
Goffman, Erving (1974) *Frame Analysis*. New York: Harper & Row.
Gubrium, Jaber F. (1975) *Living and Dying at Murray Manor*. New York: St Martin's Press.
Gubrium, Jaber F. (1980a) 'Doing Care Plans in Patient Conferences', *Social Science and Medicine*, 14A: 659–67.
Gubrium, Jaber F. (1980b) 'Patient Exclusion in Geriatric Staffings', *Sociological Quarterly*, 21: 335–48.
Gubrium, Jaber F. (1986) *Oldtimers and Alzheimer's: The Descriptive Organization of Senility*. Greenwich, CT: JAI Press.
Gubrium, Jaber F. (1988) *Analyzing Field Reality*. Newbury Park, CA: Sage.
Gubrium, Jaber F. and Buckholdt, David R. (1982) *Describing Care: Image and Practice in Rehabilitation*. Boston, MA: Oelgeschlager, Gunn & Hain.
Gubrium, Jaber F., Buckholdt, David R. and Lynott, Robert J. (1982) 'Considerations on a Theory of Descriptive Activity', *Mid-American Review of Sociology*, 7: 17–35.
Gubrium, Jaber F. and Lynott, Robert J. (1985) 'Family Rhetoric as Social Order', *Journal of Family Issues*, 6: 129–52.
Gubrium, Jaber F. and Lynott, Robert J. (1987) 'Measurement and the Interpretation of Burden in the Alzheimer's Disease Experience', *Journal of Aging Studies*, 1: 265–85.
Hammersley, Martyn and Atkinson, Paul (1983) *Ethnography: Principles in Practice*. London: Tavistock.
Laing, R.D. (1967) *The Politics of Experience*. New York: Penguin.
Lyman, Stanford M. (1978) *The Seven Deadly Sins: Society and Evil*. New York: St Martin's Press.
Melbin, Murray (1978) 'Night as Frontier', *American Sociological Review*, 43: 3–22.
Sandywell, Barry, Silverman, David, Roche, Maurice, Filmer, Paul and Phillipson, Michael (1975) *Problems of Reflexivity and Dialectics in Sociological Inquiry*. London: Routledge & Kegan Paul.
Silverman, David (1985) *Qualitative Methodology and Sociology*. Aldershot: Gower.
Silverman, David (1986) 'Seven Rules of Qualitative Method', unpublished paper, University of London, Goldsmiths' College, Department of Sociology.
Silverman, David (1987) *Communication and Medical Practice*. London: Sage.

6
Corridors of Power

Don Slater

To talk about a politics of field research is to talk about formulating practical intent within relations of power. Few researchers today doubt that, by such a definition, all research has a politics. The current source of angst is rather the implausibility of formulating a practical intent which is not, with more or less subtlety, complicit with relations of power: the problem is imagining how a properly *critical* intent can be pursued. Foucault, above all, has provided the organizing image of the contemporary 'dilemma of complicity': an image of power as all-pervasive, unavoidable, inscribed in the very heart of any project of knowledge, provoking yet simultaneously structuring all resistance to itself.

David Silverman (in this volume) has usefully described two strategies in the politics of research, providing labels which link them to Foucault's diagnosis of the complicity of knowledge and power in the modern era. The Enlightenment model, which links objective research science to rational progress by serving the pursuit of policy, is complicit with the production of modern institutional power, not only in serving and legitimizing power, but by virtue of the fact that the very object of knowledge – the patient, the criminal, the student – is produced by knowledge and power together. Research cannot but be part of a process of control and normalization. The only alternative to complicity with the technocratic, policy-based administration of social subjects appears to be a matter of taking the side of the (potentially) autonomous social subject: that attention to 'authentic' speech which Silverman has dubbed Romantic. Yet the language in which we and they formulate such speech is the same objectifying discourse which subjects them to new forms of power. Indeed, the very 'incitement' to speak has come to be recognized as a distinguishing strategy of modern power, exemplified in human sciences which not only discipline the body but claim the soul. The very logic of resistance appears to be self-contradictory insofar as the dilemma of complicity identifies knowledge itself with domination.

How can a politics of research be formulated with a critical intent when, whether we aim our knowledge at enlightened policy or 'real needs', we are simply following the lines of power and extending them a bit further? Silverman's terms evoke an authentically poignant sense of the dilemma of complicity, but they, like the dilemma generally, seem to emerge from a very particular area of social research and from the social position of particular human sciences: the knowledges and powers in terms of which this complicity is defined (and to which the diagnosis is almost exclusively applied) are those which involve the public sphere, and particularly the State, those in which claims to truth correspond to institutions which claim to act in the general interest.

In this chapter, I want to examine this problematic of complicity in the light of a different category of social concern in order to explore how the terms might change, how different the dilemma might appear, what other options might open up. Advertising belongs to the domain of civil society and private interests. In advertising, the relation between knowledge and power is not shrouded in claims to universal reason or authentic being: power has been the conscious and ambivalent focus of public discussion on advertising since its inception. After exploring how this power is defined, I will argue that it has set the research agenda for the study of advertising throughout the century. Finally, I will take issue with this research agenda and propose an alternative which points to a different way of conceptualizing the dilemma of complicity from which we started.

The public and the private

Advertising stands apart from those classic topics of social research around which the problem of complicity has been formulated, and which are well represented in the rest of this book. In the sociology of medicine, social services, law, the human subjects constituted by the human sciences have generally been those for whom a public responsibility has been claimed. Foucault for example, like most social scientists, has studied the mad, the bad and the ill: the constitution of the subordinated, the victimized, the marginal, the non-normal – the classic underdog. These social subjects come to be objects of knowledge and objects of intervention in the process of becoming wards of the public sphere. Ultimately they are wards of the State, the institutionalization and symbol of the public interest and of public responsibility. But in and around the State is the broader Enlightenment project which proposes a universal interest in rationally grounded progress, an interest with which all specific social interests can or should identify. In the name of this universalized public sphere, the marginal can be the legitimate object of public concern and intervention, with all the apparatus of power that accompanies such a status.

The cost of this project – which Foucault counted so well – is the power of normalization. But the human sciences which arose within the modern institutionalizations of power all claimed a legitimate and humane public interest not just in social order but in greater freedom. The subjects upon whom they operated could be called 'redemptive subjects': with the mad, the bad and the ill, scientific progress could be linked to the liberation of the subject; the human sciences and the caring State could bring these poor souls back into the human fold, into the democratic community, into full citizenship. This is the Romanticism at the heart of the Enlightenment: the production of real humanity, a social harmony based on the real and fully human person: as the tradition of critical theory constantly underlines, we understand the normalizing, rationalizing, subjectifying power of such sciences precisely against the backdrop of their claims to reason, the public good and the redemption of unfree subjectivity. The relation between reason and power is one which has constantly to be *discovered*. It is as covert as it is profound. The particular interests of power have to be uncovered beneath the public, general interest and the scientific–universal language in which their knowledges are expressed.

If the Foucauldian human sciences are tied to the public sphere, advertising belongs to civil society and the realm of private interests. It is, in a sense, shameless: like other forms of private, corporate activity – which Foucault scarcely addresses – it openly declares its interest in power (the management of consumers, needs and market forces); and it does not justify this power in terms of universal, public interests (its power is on sale to specific interested parties, whose own legitimacy, in capitalist societies, is based precisely on the pursuit of self-interest). Moreover, advertising does not exercise its power over the 'underdog', the ward of the State, does not normalize the pathological and call them to a higher humanity. On the contrary, it seeks control over the most 'normal' (and normative) citizen of the modern West, the consumer who is seeking rationally to satisfy his or her needs in the free market, to pursue his or her own interests. Finally, and crucially, the very normality of this citizen is defined precisely by its private character: consumption, in the modern West, is considered the most private of domains, one which cannot be regarded as the legitimate object of public and 'universal' interests, or of privately wielded power.

From the point of view of the 'enlightened' human sciences

(including, above all, economics) advertising has always been a *problem*, even an embarrassment, an irrational force in the march to a rational society. Not invariably so: at certain periods – the early twentieth century, the 1950s, the 1980s – during which private greed has been normatively and unashamedly identified with a national mission of economic growth, advertising has claimed public responsibilities and a general good. The early century is particularly well documented (for example, Marchand, 1986; Pope, 1983; Ewen, 1976): advertising's proclaimed role was to create the modern consumer, to train it in the consumption habits necessary for an affluent, mass-production society. It even – in America at least – claimed to be creating a unified nation in the process of creating a homogeneous mass market: it was part of a massive exercise in normalization known as 'Americanization'. Even more in the Enlightenment vein, advertising very early on declared itself to be 'scientific', to be based on psychological principles, to use social and psychological research, or to possess such an intimate humanistic or salesman's sense of the consumer's mind that it could be said to operate on the basis of certain knowledge, with equal certainty of success. Advertising was part of that rational management and organization of the forces of production on the basis of organized knowledge which constitutes modernization.

In contrast, however, to the explicitly public projects of Enlightenment knowledge and power, such claims instantly and continuously generated public concern. The very claim to the public good is worrying when raised by demonstrably self-serving interests: such an identity of private interests and public good is implausible to the most doctrinaire utilitarian. Moreover, this relation between knowledge and advertising, science and commerce, produces the most ubiquitous characterization of advertising throughout the century: advertising as 'persuasion' or 'manipulation' refers specifically to a sense that advertising possesses a special expertise in communication, a technology of domination based on knowledge of what makes the consumer 'tick'. We could certainly consider advertising in terms of intimate surveillance: market intelligence, psychographics, detailed electronically collected data on the movements of goods and consumers throughout the commercial system. The point is that from the turn of the century, conservatives, radicals and muck-raking journalists have frequently agreed to regard advertising as a science which will dominate the free and sovereign consumer, a theme which reached its height in Vance Packard's *The Hidden Persuaders,* but which is continuously revived (for example, Clarke, 1988).

Thus at precisely the point where advertising purports to be an

Enlightenment project, on the basis of both 'science' and a public interest, it is widely understood as a technocratic rationality and a serious danger. The complicity of knowledge with power has been a central theme. What underlies this theme, I would want to argue, is the division between the public and the private, state and civil society, and the forms of knowledge and power appropriate to each. The problem of advertising is not simply that it is wielded by private interests, but that it operates upon a sphere – consumption – which has been staunchly defended as private, as out of bounds to public scrutiny.

What I referred to as the 'redemptive subjects' of the Enlightenment are pathological and locked into a private, eccentric condition from which they are to be released by scientific understanding and humane social agencies. The object of advertising's efforts, on the other hand, is considered normal precisely by virtue of its privacy and eccentricity. This is, in the first instance, a question of individual autonomy: needs and wants lie at the core of identity and motivation to the extent that individual freedom is often identified with both the self-determination of desires and the range of choice available to satisfy them. We need only consider statements about freedom of choice in socialist countries, or contemporary Thatcherism. Moreover, this perspective is written into neoclassical economics: with its utilitarian foundations, the public good can only emerge from the pursuit of self-interest; but those interests must be self-determined if public good is to retain any meaning. Individuals pursue their needs within the economic arena – the free market – by formally calculating the intensity of their given desires in relation to price. But the desires themselves are utterly private and formed outside the market-place. If desires were determined by firms, prices would have no meaning in terms of optimally allocating goods. Needs may be treated as natural, rational, irrational or bizarre, but most fundamentally they must be treated as 'given'. As such they are both unquestionable and inexplicable. Indeed, the figure of the normal consumer is profoundly amoral: one cannot judge it by its substantive needs, values and goals, only by the formally rational way in which it goes about satisfying them in the market.

On the contrary, the consumer's sovereign needs are the court of judgement of the market as an efficient allocator of goods, the independent yardstick for measuring economic performance. At a higher level of abstraction, needs measure the relation between economy and society as a whole: does the economy meet human needs? The fear which haunts not only neoclassicism, but also critical theorists (such as Marcuse) and monopoly theorists (like

Galbraith), is the spectre of an economy which (through technologies like advertising) can determine needs and thus become self-
legitimating. It would call into existence only those needs which it
can profitably satisfy. Needs would no longer constitute either a
regulating mechanism or a critical category by which to judge the
system.

It is in this context that advertising is seen as a problem: it is
an attack on this autonomous, economic subject whose sovereign,
undetermined needs constitute the normative basis of the social
order (for conservatives) or the basis of critique (for critical
theorists). The apogee of capitalist competition, advertising simultaneously sounds its death-knell by undermining the autonomous
subject which grounds it. It is in this context, too, that the central
thrust of research into advertising emerges: the key question is
whether or not advertising does wield such power over economic
subjects, the capacity to alter needs and wants, and with what
effects. Much social science and public discourse has been preoccupied with proving whether or not advertising does influence an
otherwise autonomous subject, in order to protect that subject
through the regulation or restriction of advertising if it does; to
declare advertising silly but safe if it doesn't.

In a sense, we could almost say that neoclassical economics plays
the role of Romanticism in theorizing the private sphere. In the free
market, consumers always already know what they need and want,
and rationally express their desires (and their relative intensities)
through the free allocation of their incomes to the purchase of
goods. Advertising creates or distorts needs and wants, making
them false, which in turn destroys the rationality of free markets.
From this perspective, advertising, as an Enlightenment project of
knowledge, power and progress, appears much as critical theory
characterized mass culture in general – as psychoanalysis in reverse.
Far from raising the bemused citizen through layers of obfuscating
fog to the redemption of unconstrained reason and communication,
advertising creates a pathological consumer.

More broadly, however, we can say that an Enlightenment model
of research – in which social knowledge serves administrations
technocratically in order to produce enlightened policy – has never
pertained because advertising understood in these terms could
never be the serious object of policy – of regulation, yes, for
example, the restriction on the advertising of cigarettes or toys or
medicine partly on the basis of social scientific claims about the
effects of advertising – but not policy. For what would policy mean
in this context? Advertising, part of a broader structure of
marketing and commerce, is part of the way in which capitalist

economies mediate the relation between production and consumption, the way they organize the meeting of needs. Policy in this context means public intervention in that domain of consumption which has always been considered utterly private. Policy means public political agreement on consumption on the basis of over-arching social values and goals.

On the other hand, while the idea of consumption as the object of either public policy or private power may be anathema to major ideological currents, it constitutes the fulcrum of critical social theory. Here the entire issue is precisely the transfer of needs and wants from the private to the public sphere. Much critical thought also starts from an autonomous social subject, a subject possessing real and sovereign needs. However, a society based on commodity production, hence private interest, distorts these needs or replaces them with false needs functional to economic production and political docility, not least through advertising. A democractic society would satisfy and develop real human need. In such critical thought, the autonomous subject of need thus again becomes a critical category (it is a critique of existing arrangements in their failure to meet real need) and a redemptive one (this is the subject who would be truly autonomous under different arrangements). Raymond Williams (1980), for example, introduces a distinction between users and consumers, the former representing authentic needs embodied in a social subject to be redeemed by a political decision to choose socialism and thus to regard needs and consumption not as private and individual but as social and open to rational, public, democratic discussion. The figure of the user stands as a critique of the capitalist production of false needs.

There are two interlinked problems with this formulation of practical intent. The first is a problem of essentialism: the positing of needs outside social constructions of need. This links with the second problem of universalism: the positing of real needs simultaneously posits a discourse which knows the truth of all needs, which therefore constitutes subjects of need at the deepest level, and which – once institutionalized – is potentially totalitarian: we will be told what we need by a socially empowered knowledge of needs. What we have seen most vividly over the past century, and most clearly described in Foucault's accounts, is precisely the removal of need-provision and need-definition from the private to the public sphere in the name of universal and therefore normalizing knowledges of need: health, education, correction, moral regulation and so on. Certain needs have been declared social rather than private – such as care of the mad, bad and ill – and thus have become objects of policy. The movement from private to public – carried out as a critique of domination by private interests – promises the liberation of a truly autonomous subject as opposed to the false and only formally autonomous subject of neoclassical economics. But it does so at the cost of essentializing and universalizing particular versions of need; and institutionally it seems to entail precisely those technologies of power, State power, which produce a new normalization. Thus, neither the defence of the private subject of need nor its democratization seem viable as critical practice.

On the other hand, post-structuralist critiques of universalized subjects seem to demolish the grounds of any deeper critique or practical intent: deprived of either an autonomous subject to defend or a critical subject of need to promote to the public sphere, we seem to have little basis on which to descry current arrangements even as a problem. Indeed, many of the wilder ironies of post-modernist thought seem to return to the empty amorality of neoliberalism: desire, or in other thinkers, the code, emerges as the inexplicable but unquestionable generator of critically unassessable needs. We are simply left to wallow in consumer culture or post-modernity, which ecstatically reveals the fatuity of critical discourse.

Thus the problem of advertising has to do with the ostensibly private and autonomous nature of consumption and the problems of reformulating consumption as part of a political discourse: the inability to formulate policy on consumption which submits it to public, democratic, collective will-formation without installing a new, universalized and technocratic power.

Advertising, ethnography and power

Advertising, then, straddles a complex ideological force-field at the centre of which is a problem of power: do advertisements wield a power over those formerly sovereign and autonomous consumers who are central to both the legitimation and critique of modern societies and economies? Can they alter needs, create false ones, provoke or compel behaviour? Do they persuade and manipulate and on the basis of what knowledges of the human mind?

These questions have, consequently, set the agenda for research and commentary on advertising: a focus on the 'effects of advertising' which forms part of the general 'effects of the media' research concern. We can summarize this research focus as a 'paradigm of communicative power': does advertising produce texts – words and images – which have the power to sell, or to construct consumers, or to train them to a consumerist way of life, or to reproduce ideological systems? On the one hand, this paradigm has fed effects studies, cognitive psychology and theories of consumer behaviour, which may or may not seek to contribute to the industry. What is important is the extent to which they are circumscribed by the question of individual autonomy: the approach is to assume that consumers would normally be self-determining, to then isolate advertising as an independent variable, and to seek to determine whether it has a unique and specific effect on consumers, a communicative power arising from exposure to advertisements. On the other hand, semiotic approaches to advertising also fit within a paradigm of communicative power: the focus on the construction of meaning and reproduction of ideology within the advertisement is the basis for theorizing its social impact as part of general ideological, subject-constituting processes.

It is crucial to recognize that the focus on communicative power, the result of a particular set of ideological themes, has been so exclusive that there has only been one serious ethnography of the advertising agency to date (Tunstall, 1964). With the gaze firmly on the effects of advertisements, little attention has been paid to understanding how advertisements emerge from commercial practices and a commercial system. Yet understanding this process might well lead us to reconsider assumptions about the way needs and consumers are formed which underlie the paradigm of communicative power. Field research certainly generates quite different problems and concerns. The central question for ethnography would be, how do advertising agents produce advertisements and carry out the other functions they take on; how do they constitute their activities as rational, regular, orderly, etc? In raising such questions, the communicative-power paradigm is itself made problematic, for the research has to leave open to question any assumption that advertising agencies themselves organize their practice in terms of concepts of communicative power.

In carrying out field research, one cannot impose the communicative framework on advertising practice, but must regard it as one possible organizing rationality within the construction of advertising practice. Indeed one major problem in the study of advertising has been the tendency to produce theories of communicative power which are then assumed to provide an adequate account of the actual process of producing advertisements. For example, psychological accounts of advertising effects are often treated as if advertising agencies either do, or could, operate on the basis of a knowledge of the psychological processes put forward by the theory. Similarly, semiotic accounts, such as that of Judith Williamson (1978), account for advertising power in terms of the ideological structure of advertisements and the processes of reading such texts. Such theories are then used to ignore the actual social practice of advertising, implying instead that the ideological structure of language itself can account for the specific character of advertisements.

The ethnographer courts serious difficulties in keeping such distinctions clear, not least because advertising is saturated with discourses about power. After all, the industry *sells* power to its clients, and must substantiate and justify its claim to power to many different audiences. However, this diversity of audiences also makes for conflicting claims, as does the fact that advertising is conscious of the ideologically problematic character of its power, as described in the previous section. Thus it is a cliché in the industry that agencies promise their clients total and infallible power over the consumer's behaviour while telling the public that it has no power at all and merely reflects current trends or provides information. The problem, in the midst of these different formulations of power, is to ascertain not which theory of advertising power is empirically correct, but which discourse on power is actually active within the agency: what formulation of advertising's power is operative in the actual production of advertisements.

A further problem is that the paradigm of communicative power has at times proved very useful to the advertising industry itself. Consider the obvious: the advertising agency, as an institution, depends for its existence on selling to institutional clients images and media time and space on the rather weak assumption that they further corporate commercial aims: that is, that in some direct or indirect, mediated manner, advertisements will alter public attitudes or behaviour. The agency exists by claiming to sell a form of power – a most nebulous product, as well as an ideologically fraught and somewhat disreputable one. But in terms of the agency's survival and profit – indeed that of the industry as a whole – the primary question is one of rationality: can plausible reasons be put forward that advertising 'works', that agencies do more than construct images arbitrarily or impulsively, that the agency's work is based on knowledge, principles, verifiable and efficacious technology, that the client's money is being rationally spent?

More than this, however, the advertising industry needs to claim to possess a knowledge or power which the client does not possess, or cannot cost-effectively duplicate, that its expertise is somehow apart from ordinary marketing knowledge. Moreover, each agency would like to claim that *it* has a power no other advertising agency could provide its client. That is, discourses of advertising power are weapons of competition as well as legitimation and 'proof'.

Claims to communicative power solve all these problems. For

example, the claims to a scientific psychology of advertising, discussed above, provide grounds for arguing that advertising is rational and powerful because it possesses scientific principles concerning persuasive communications. By arguing that this scientific key to successful advertising has to do with a specific knowledge of communications – rather than of markets, retailing, commerce – the industry can claim that it is entirely different from the normal business practice of its clients. Finally, each agency can claim a different set of underlying psychological concepts or associated research techniques.

Advertising's claims to power and rationality have not always been stated in terms of science: its history, and agencies, abound with 'keys to successful advertising'. For example, agency 'philosophies' have been crucial: agencies simultaneously differentiate themselves competitively from each other, and claim effectiveness for their practice, by arguing that either 'hard sell' or 'soft sell' approaches are the key, or 'brand identity' or 'product image'. Alternatively, there is a constant claim to what might be termed 'humanistic' knowledge: creative personnel in particular claim a special intuitive knowledge of the consumer's mind and how to communicate with it. Again, the presumption is that the client – usually caricatured as over-rationalistic and remote from the consumer – cannot possess this knowledge.

These are all publicly voiced discourses of advertising power, some made to clients, some more widely. The question for field research is whether it is in these terms that advertising agencies constitute their own practices as rational for themselves, whether any of these discourses bear any relation to the logic by which advertisements are actually produced. In this regard I have stressed the extent to which versions of 'communicative power' could serve the industry's aims, while at the same time involving them in an ambivalent attitude to such power. However, the claim to communicative power, operating on an autonomous consumer, fits in well with the preoccupations of liberal social science. Social science saw its own problematic – the power of the media – reflected back to it in advertising's instrumental claims. It treated claims to scientificity as truth-claims to be empirically tested rather than as instrumental speech-acts tied to institutional interests. It therefore did not investigate, ethnographically, the extent to which a scientific rationality was actually constitutive of advertising practice. Nor did it attempt to discover what actually did constitute advertising and its power. Unless advertising could be shown to possess a special communicative power which threatened the autonomy of the economic subject, there was in fact no problem with it. Insofar as advertising did possess this power, it could be regulated or damned. What was ruled out of court was the possibility that advertising was part of a normal social process of defining consumption.

The most important ethnography to date, that by Tunstall, was carried out shortly after the height of the *Hidden Persuaders* furore, and the question of manipulation and scientific power over the consumer set the context for his research. Tunstall argued that far from being infallible scientific salesmen, advertising's claims to power were a symptom of its powerlessness and irrationality: it had no scientific basis, was at the mercy of omnipotent and capricious clients, led a life marked more by insecurity and angst than by scientific certainty, and consequently inflated its claims. Tunstall was quite correct in treating advertising's claims as strategic moves rather that truth-claims. However, in concluding that advertising was irrational he concurred, at a more fundamental level, with the paradigm of communicative power: a verifiable claim to communicative power was the only possible basis on which advertising *could* be rational. There is a complicity here with the underlying problematic of power – if advertising possesses a communicative power over the autonomous individual it is dangerous; if not, it is rather pathetic and requires no further investigation. For Tunstall, concerned with communicative power, the agency's dependency on its client indicated its lack of a rationality; he missed the possibility that this close integration of agency and client could be the basis of a more durable rationality.

The central question for field research, then, is precisely a relation between rationality, power and practice, and the fact that researchers meet in advertising a model of power – communicative power over the autonomous individual – which precisely matches their own concerns, and with which social science has been intimately involved. It was in order to get around this problematic that I undertook an ethnography of the advertising agency (Slater, forthcoming). The research took in a total of seven large agencies, focusing on advertising as a commercial, rather than a communicative operation, and thus on its relation to everyday business practice. Specifically, this involved looking most closely at marketing and advertising strategy – and thus at the work of account handlers rather than creative personnel – as that area which was likely to show the continuity of advertising with 'normal business practice', rather than its discontinuity as a specialist technology. At one level, this work produced an alternative paradigm – which I will call the 'marketing paradigm' – which I believe to be closer to the way advertising agencies actually carry out their work, and the way in which they come to see it as a rational practice on a day-to-day basis. At another level, this paradigm linked up with a model of consumption which treats needs not as properties of individuals which advertisements alter, but as outcomes of social processes in which advertising intervenes.

I would like to introduce this work at a fairly abstract level which relates consumption, needs and advertising in terms of the economic conditions in which advertising is carried out, namely a competitive market. Marxists and neoclassical economists can agree that a commodity must be recognized as a use-value or utility before it will be exchanged in the market. Reverting to Marxist terminology, use-value is a necessary condition for the firm's aim of realizing exchange-value. This necessity grounds the formal operation of the capitalist economy in the task of providing goods which fill substantive, culturally specific needs. Firms may thirst only after the abstract form of value, but they can only acquire this by matching specific goods to specific needs. Whereas theorists tend to reify or naturalize use-value, or to take it for granted in one way or another, practising advertisers see it as a highly complex and changing social construction. We can formulate their perspective through a definition of use-value which conforms to that of an anthropological sense of material culture: use-value is a relation between perceived attributes of a product and the social relations and practices within which that product is defined as needed or wanted. That is to say, goods can be defined as in some way integral to culturally specific modes of life, as sustaining them, defining them, allowing them to achieve specified ends, and so on. The construction of this use-value relationship between modes of life and material provision has many variables: those which go to construct the product, those which go into defining a mode of life and its versions of needs and wants, and those which relate product to modes of life. The construction of this relationship is a central social operation; and control over this process is a core operation of power: in defining and producing a way of life we are also constructing needs; in defining use-values, cultures are reinterpreted and related to the economic arrangements by which use-values are produced and distributed. The power to define use-values is therefore a political matter: it is part of producing, changing and reproducing culturally specific ways of life.

During the development of the modern corporate enterprise, there has arisen a discourse/practice known as marketing which can be defined by its objective of developing practices which intervene in *all* the variables, in the entire field over which use-value is constructed, as a means of producing definitions of use-value which will produce optimal sales. Marketing has developed a veritable arsenal of technologies which range from product development, design and packaging through retail distribution and sales forces to promotions and – most visibly – advertising. This covers the gamut of the use-value relation, allowing the firm to conceptualize and carry out interventions in all those areas which make up the central precondition of exchange. Marketing develops specific knowledges and analyses of both social relations and competitive relations in terms of which it can conceptualize and assess definitions of its product as a use-value. It can then deploy its technologies in the attempt to actualize, to make socially current that product definition which it believes will produce optimal sales. As part of this operation, marketing strategies are constructed which are designed to coordinate, integrate and discipline all the technologies – including advertising – towards the achievement of that product definition which stands at the core of the strategy.

To take an example, the advertising agency Young and Rubicam were involved in long-term planning for Johnson's Baby Oil. The product had a near monopoly in the infant care market and the client could see no further growth there. It sought new markets, and considered a range of possible use-values for the product. Twenty-seven possibilities were given consideration, including cosmetic remover, bath oil, sun-tan lotion, skin care product, and so on. Each of these possible product definitions defined use-values: they indicated different target consumers (women of different ages, classes, consumption habits), different relations to different cultures of health, hygiene, the body, each with different potential sales patterns. At the same time, each possible use-value definition indicated different market relations to contend with: different competitors, markets with different levels of competition and activity. The agency could provide advice on the advertising implications of each possibility, but had to do so in relation to the broader marketing operation of the client and the long-term implications of any choice for the client. At all levels of the firm and agency, calculations were made as to both the cultural and the competitive possibilities, and their relation. The final choice of a use-value would then form the framework for any advertising work.

Put crudely, the client does not walk into the agency and deposit a product on the copywriter's desk with the injunction to 'Sell it' with the agency's special communicative magic. The agency does not autonomously devise appeals and allures according to some special logic of semiotic power. Every step it takes is constituted and disciplined by advertising's place in a broader institutional context whose operating logic is a logic of market calculation and cultural intervention: an analysis of consumption relations in terms of competitive market positions. The agency does not autonomously decide to sell Johnson's Baby Oil with images of women luxuriating in baths: it may have some involvement in a decision to enter the bath-oil market which will then structure creative options. If the advertising then depicts a particularly alluring form of life, its foundations and structure are the result of quite mundane marketing.

Mundane but powerful: by virtue of the implicit definition of use-value, such mundane marketing involves intervening in diverse aspects of defining a mode of life, including the actual physical provision of goods. By virtue of the form of calculation, this intervention is a highly instrumental one: marketing is about regarding material culture through categories designed to relate ways of life to the consumption of commodities, designed to redefine cultural relations in terms of market relations and private interests of the firm.

Ethnographically, we can observe the marketing paradigm operating within the advertising agency as a constitutive rationality. Whereas the advertising agent *par excellence* is generally thought to be the 'creative person', the real centres of power in most agencies are the account handlers. Their role is to liaise between client and agency, to brief the creative and media people, and to be the main administrators of the account. They also tend to be the majority of board members and thus play the guiding role in the agency's own long-term planning. The feature of their job which promotes such a crucial position is their role as 'bearers of the brief' – this phrase denotes that it is the account director who, in liaising with the client, is briefed in the client's marketing situation and policy, participates in formulating the client's market problem and strategy (at least in relation to advertising) and translates this marketing brief into an advertising strategy, that is, into a task which advertising can carry out and which will fit into and carry out the client's overall marketing aims. The account handler oversees the work of the creative team, ensuring that it conforms to the advertising strategy, and eventually presents the advertisement to the client, again justifying it in terms of marketing strategy.

Strategy, especially in the form of a written brief, plays a disciplinary role: one hears it quoted verbatim in countless situations, as the answer to any question concerning directions that might be taken. For the question is always, does the advertisement 'fit the brief'? A common practice is to hold an internal meeting prior to presentation to the client, in which senior account handlers play the role of client and require the creative team to justify their work in terms of client marketing strategy.

Strategy, however, is not just a discipline on creative work: it is constitutive of the creative personnel's sense of what they are doing. Regardless of what might be said in public about creative flair and maverick art directors, within the agency the sole notion of professionalism in terms of which people make sense of their jobs and judge performance is the ability to fill a strategy brief: creative skill is defined within the framework of strategy. More fundamentally, advertising personnel generally regard their advertising work and final products as rationally grounded and potentially effective when, as they say, 'We've got the strategy right'. That is to say, in terms of giving reasons as to why work might or might not be successful, the discourse (of power and reason) does not revolve around the images *per se*, but around the correct implementation of a correct strategy, a correct definition of market and consumption relations.

An ethnography of the agency, then, shows a marketing rationality at work, and this rationality is rooted in economic and cultural conditions which run counter to the paradigm of communicative power and the problematic of autonomous individuals and needs from which we started: marketing, and advertising as manifestly integral to marketing, needs to be theorized not in terms of a relationship (of persuasion or information) between texts and subjects, but in terms of a broad intervention in a social process. Needs are not properties of subjects which can be (illicitly) altered by powerful communications. Needs are the outcome of definitions of forms of life and their relation to modes of material provision. In producing such definitions, marketing does not aim to discern either essential needs or generalizable ones, but focuses first on the particularity, the singularity of specific cultural modes of life; and secondly on the logic by which social relations and material goods are defined in relation to each other.

Finally, marketing represents a specific logic for producing and intervening in definitions of cultural modes of life, a logic which emerges directly from market conditions, from the firm's need to define a cultural use-value for their goods as a condition of their sale on the market. This logic means that culture is defined and developed in terms of profit and private interest rather than alternative logics which could be tied to public interests. Alternative logics do exist – for example, the logic of public provision of services under the aegis of social need; or the 'local logics' by which specific consumer groups actually make sense of the goods on offer – and marketing has historically been engaged in a contest for the power to define consumption.

Conclusion

In the case of advertising, where power is overt and thematized, the politics of field research revolves less around the exposure of power than a disentangling of the types of power and claims to power by which the practice is carried out, legitimated and criticized – each of which may involve different concepts of power, all confusingly interrelated. The question of complicity concerns less the choosing of sides than the sharing of assumptions: the concern with individual autonomy seems to lead both critics and apologists up the same path, away from a sense of what is going on, as opposed to what is being claimed.

Both Enlightenment and Romanticism as models of research relationships between knowledge and forms of power seem problematic. This is not so much because of their claims to universality and reason on the one hand, and authenticity on the other, but because both these claims are tied to the figure of the autonomous individual, one to be redeemed (through public intervention), the other to be articulated (through authentic speech). On this basis, consumption and material provision continue to be seen as essentially private affairs, and their essentially social, collective nature is missed: we lose sight of what is going on, the production and reproduction of forms of life and the different logics by which this process might be carried out.

What both, on the other hand, offer, and which cannot be so lightly dismissed in the private sphere of economic as opposed to State power, is the claim to a right to public, democratic discussion of consumption and material provision. We might, on this basis, argue for *more* Enlightenment (where the public good is understood as democratic consensus on needs rather than public definitions of need which can then be bureaucratically administered); and *more* Romanticism (where authentic speech is understood not as the articulated essence of the individual but as the process of unconstrained, public discussion of how a way of life is to be defined and carried on).

In this context, the problem of field research is to avoid that problematic of individuals and power which incites it to put forward an agenda of 'real needs' or simply to accept or reject advertising on the basis of proven powers and 'effects'. Its proper concern is to comprehend the competing social logics by which material cultures might be defined, and assess these in terms of democratic potential, in relation to the social, culture-forming nature of consumption.

To conclude with a paradox: I think the marketing paradigm, the understanding of advertising as a social intervention in markets and cultures, points in two directions, towards Foucault and towards Habermas: on the one hand, need is relativized and made specific to particularistic modes of life which are constituted within relations of power, not least marketing as a technology of power which invades consumption. Needs are cultural agendas set in the present: they are properties of collectivities, formed in their myriad contingent ways, whose needs are defined in terms of an ongoing way of life and change. Research with a practical intent must start from this contingency and specificity: it cannot be concerned with a singular, consensual and therefore bureaucratically convenient notion of need. The focus has to be on needs in the plural, on the relations of present power in which they arise and on their ungeneralizable quality. Much like the marketer, we might describe our method as case study, or as genealogy.

At the same time, needs constitute political agendas: they are claims to support for a form of life, claims for material provision for a culturally specific community. In this they carry a presupposition that political and economic arrangements must be subordinated to collectively decided values, that ends must dominate over means, that the formation of collective identity is rooted in communicative rationality rather than strategic action. Consumption at a social scale requires the politicization of needs: a policy not in the sense of fixing needs as a basis for rationalized public provision; but rather in the sense that the political sphere must ultimately be about installing as commanding social purpose the reproduction of specific and diverse modes of life. In defining use-values we define a way of life: the process is intrinsically political, is intrinsically a matter of social policy even when, as at present, policy is formulated by private economic interests. The logic of this argument points to a critique of institutional arrangements which define needs and cultures in terms of instrumental rationality oriented towards profit; a critique which is not grounded in a universalized or essentialist notion of need but in the norms of collective discourse and collective will-formation.

References

Clarke, Eric (1988) *The Want Makers*. London: Hodder & Stoughton.
Ewen, Stuart (1976) *Captains of Consciousness*. New York: Basic Books.
Marchand, Roland (1986) *Advertising the American Dream: Making Way for Modernity 1920–1940*. Berkeley: University of California Press.
Packard, Vance (1977) *The Hidden Persuaders*. Harmondsworth: Penguin.
Pope, Daniel (1983) *The Making of Modern Advertising*. New York: Basic Books.

Slater, D.R. (forthcoming) *The Political Economy of Advertising*. Cambridge: Polity Press.

Tunstall, Jeremy (1964) *The Advertising Man in London Advertising Agencies*. London: Chapman and Hall.

Williams, Raymond (1980) 'Advertising: The Magic System', in *Problems in Materialism and Culture*. London: Verso.

Williamson, Judith (1978), *Decoding Advertisements*. London: Marion Boyars.

7

Evaluation Research and Quality Assurance

Lindsay Prior

Commodification

'A commodity', said Marx (1970: 72), 'is a mysterious thing simply because in it the social character of men's labour appears to them as an objective character stamped upon the product of that labour . . .' It was an insight which Lukács took up and developed in his analysis of the reification process which he considered to be 'the central, structural problem of capitalist society in all its aspects' (Lukács 1971: 83). Lukács, of course, read Marx 'through spectacles tinged by Simmel and Max Weber' (1971: ix), and so it is not surprising that we can find numerous links between his particular exposition of commodity structure and some similar ideas which were advanced by other Weber scholars, the most notable of which were the members of the 'Frankfurt School'. On the Marxist side of the balance sheet, however, Lukács' debt was clear and like Marx, he envisioned the essence of commodity structure in the objectification of labour. Thus, for him, the basis of commodity structure is clear.

> Its basis is that a relation between people takes on the character of a thing and thus acquires a 'phantom objectivity', an autonomy that seems so strictly rational and all-embracing as to conceal every trace of its fundamental nature: the relation between people. (Lukács, 1971: 83)

In fact, it was by marrying this Marxist concept of commodity fetishism to the Weberian one of rationalization, that Lukács felt able to discuss the reification of consciousness which seemed to pervade every aspect of the modern world. Indeed, for Lukács, it was a process which 'progressively sinks more deeply, more fatefully and more definitively into the consciousness of man' (1971: 93), and thereby stamps its imprint upon the entire fabric of social life. Reification is manifest everywhere. We may see it in the labour process where alienated labour power and the worker are progressively decomposed into productive and unproductive parts, we can see it in forms of factory organization where manufacturing processes are arranged according to rational principles of production, and we can see it in forms of social science such as industrial psychology which extend the process of rational assessment 'right into the worker's "soul"' (1971: 88). Yet, it is not only physical artefacts which are reified as objective commodities, but all human processes including services. For, according to Lukács, with the rationalization of the world, human activities in general become standardized and subjected to an increasingly formal treatment, and consequently human services as well as physical artefacts are metamorphosed into 'thingness'.

As I have said, this particular analysis of reification has direct parallels in the writings of many of Lukács' contemporaries. Indeed, the critique of the reification process constituted a fundamental policy aim of the Frankfurt School. It is evident, for example, in Horkheimer and Adorno's (1973) analysis of the self-destruction of the Enlightenment and the commodification of human culture. So too in Adorno's (1973) analysis of German existentialism and, of course, Marcuse's (1964) analysis of advanced industrial society. More to the point, however, and on the basis of Lukács' 1922 essay, I would like to emphasize how commodification is evident in our contemporary orientation to both material things and the provision of services. For it is through the process of commodification that humanly produced phenomena become reified as things which stand apart from their producers. And it is through the critique of such processes that we may come to see the social basis on which the appearance of such 'things' rests. As Lukács and his German contemporaries suggested, the tendency to reify human activity pervades all forms of social action and may even be reinforced through the construction and adoption of particular types of epistemological framework, research strategies and 'methodologies'. It is to the analysis of one such form of knowledge that I wish to turn in this chapter. In fact, in what follows I hope to illustrate how certain schemes of thought and ways of thinking can entice us to regard both organized forms of human interaction and human bodies as objective commodities. I also hope to show how the dominance of such ways of thinking poses practical problems for the sociological researcher, and I hope to be able to illustrate some of the resultant dilemmas by drawing on examples from my own research on facilities for the rehabilitation of psychiatric patients in an Irish town.

Evaluation research, quality assurance and social interests

One group of research strategies which fit in particularly well with the tendencies toward commodification are those which exist under the rubric of 'evaluation research' (ER). Evaluation research, of course, is supposedly designed for use with what are sometimes called human service programmes. In that sense ER can be, and is, applied to educational programmes, health care programmes, poverty programmes and the like (see Attkison et al., 1978). Since the actual strategies of research take many different forms it is not particularly easy or accurate to discuss ER as an undifferentiated entity, but there can be little doubt that ER expresses an ethos or mode of thought about the nature of the world which can be effectively described. It is, in fact, an ethos which dovetails very neatly with the demands of instrumental reason and, as I shall seek to show, encourages both the commodification of organized forms of human interaction and, very often, of the human and bodily properties of those who are subject to assessment.

Evaluation research is usually presented as an atheoretical and objective method for examining the world. Wortman (1983), for example, states just that, 'Evaluation research is an applied, largely atheoretic, multidisciplinary activity spanning the social sciences' (1983: 224). And most texts on the subject of evaluation present ER as a set of practical, objective and systematic (scientific) procedures which are entirely decontextualized from the mesh of social interests which ordinarily serve to structure human social organizations. Evaluation research is thus regarded as a value-free way of measuring efficiency, effectiveness, organizational outcomes and processes. In this respect it has, for example, similarities with certain research trends in health economics in which quantifiable economic measures and techniques are presented as nothing but a 'useful adjunct' to decision making processes (Gudex, 1986: 1). Indeed, many texts open their accounts of what ER is by listing a set of 'neutral' questions which any rational person may reasonably ask and which ER is presumably designed to answer. Thus, Rossi et al. (1979) claim that ER asks such questions as: 'Is the [social] intervention reaching the appropriate target population? Is it being implemented in the ways specified? Is it effective? How much does it cost? What are its costs relative to its effectiveness?' (1979: 20) Whilst Shipman (1979) in his discussion of in-school evaluation tells us that, 'The purpose of evaluation is to increase the effectiveness of schooling'. Other writers (Rutman, 1977; Patton, 1980) emphasize the objective and practical nature of ER in all its settings. Whilst Attkison et al. (1978) eulogize about the value of ER in ameliorating human and social problems in general. This emphasis on performance and the measurement of outcomes is redolent of the origins of 'evaluation' in industrial settings, and especially of the systems of statistically based quality control which were developed in the war time industries of the UK and USA (see Duncan, 1952). Thus the emphasis given to the study of means/ends relationships (or means/objectives relationships to be precise), the use of measurement, and the desire to develop and/or draw upon nomological knowledge is as apparent in ER as it was (and is) in industrial systems of quality control. In fact, ER in the human sciences more often than not adopts what Simons (1981) aptly terms 'product efficiency models' of evaluation.

In some ways, there is little that one could object to in all of this in so far as the aim of improving the effectiveness and efficiency of human activity seems self-evidently desirable. What, for example, could possibly be misplaced in the desire to pinpoint deficiencies in the sequence of production and to subsequently correct them? Nothing could, it would seem, until we recall that in the Marxist scheme of things which I referred to at the opening of this chapter, 'deficiencies' can be located either in the instruments of production or in the social relations of production, and once we take into account the latter we are forced to realize that any discussion which treats of 'outcomes' and 'performance' as decontextualized and neutral objectives is, to say the least, sociologically naïve.

The naïveté of the approach rests in the fact that it holds to an (implicit) assumption that human organizations are structured in common purpose and that they are consensually organized for mutual benefit. But, (and this takes us back to many of the older sociological discussions of social order), human organizations are not necessarily like that. Indeed, if we return to Marx's commodity we can readily see the critical point, for a commodity (that is, objectified labour power) embodies not simply social relationships *per se*, but antagonistic and conflicting social relationships. The antagonism and conflict emanate, of course, from the opposing social interests inherent in the organized production of commodities. In other words when we examine performance, efficiency and the like we must do so in some context, and that context will invariably encompass diverse social interests, many of which may be conflicting. In this sense there is not and can never be an objective analysis of human performance.[1]

Oddly enough, this point does not go entirely unrecognized in ER literature, though it is not perhaps recognized in quite the way I have stated it. Thus, Rossi et al., for example, make the claim: 'Now, however, it is clear that evaluation research is more than the application of methods. It is a political and managerial activity' (Rossi et al., 1979: 25). And the recognition of the managerial potential is evident in Shipman's remark that, 'Evaluation is a basic management tool in all organizations' (1979: 1), though it is quite clear that 'management' in this context is viewed in the same detached and decontextualized manner as is evaluation in general, that is, as a supposedly neutral process geared towards the enhancement of the common good. But even if those who practise evaluation recognize that ER occurs in a context of social interests, they still seem to be incapable of taking on board the notion that such interests are more often than not conflicting and, possibly, inherently and necessarily antagonistic.

Strangely, the recognition that research is inextricably bound up with social interests is, I suspect, as plain to those being researched as it is obscure to the proponents of ER. It is certainly an issue which crops up in my own work with some frequency, and my informants are always keen to know under whose 'umbrella' (to use one euphemism) I am working, who it is that will eventually have access to the research data, and how the data will eventually be used. Indeed, it is something which is readily evident in the following exchange which occurred between myself and one of my informants who was considering how she should introduce me to a third party.

> *I*: Who shall I say you are?
> *LP*: . . . and say that I'm doing some research into the facilities available for rehabilitation.
> *I*: No. Don't say that. People are wary of researchers. For [the Board] 'research' always means cutbacks and people get worried about their jobs.

It is not unreasonable to argue, then, that ER is a management-inspired activity, or, at least, an activity which, whatever its motivational origins, appeals to the practical stance which health and social service programme managers are required to adopt in an age of monetarist economics. (Though things are much more complex than a glib reference to the requirements of monetarist economics would suggest.) Indeed, much more than the transient interests of a managerial group are involved in the adoption of ER, and a far wider set of forces are at work here. They are, I would suggest, linked to the broader themes of technical control and rational calculation which Weber first referred to through the concept of rationalization and with which Lukács was concerned in his seminal essay.

Evaluation research, of course, is essentially about the assessment of entire programmes. Within such programmes, however, are people; sometimes patients, sometimes clients, sometimes pupils, and sometimes offenders. Forms of evaluation which centre on clients rather than programmes are often referred to as schemes of

Quality Assurance (QA). Naturally enough there are significant differences between QA and ER (see Woy et al., 1978), but the guiding principles of enquiry tend to be similar. Thus, Woy et al., for example, state that,

> Quality assurance of clinical care is a process designed to identify and correct deficiencies in services provided to patients . . . Analogous to quality assurance is the concept of quality control in manufacturing where acceptable tolerances are set and items exceeding those tolerance limits are rejected. (Woy et al., 1978: 416–17)

This same concern to present QA as a technically neutral and objective managerial activity is equally evident in the King's Fund (1986) report, and the WHO (1985) document on *The Principles of Quality Assurance*. In the latter, QA is said to be concerned with such things as technical quality, efficiency, risk management, and patient satisfaction – 'To assure that each patient receives such a mix of diagnostic and therapeutic health services as is most likely to produce the optimal achievable health care outcome for that patient' (1985: 5). And this language of managerial economics resurfaces in Shaw's (1986) King's Fund document in which direct parallels are drawn between the production of health and the production of things. Thus, states Shaw, 'One way to consider health services is to consider them as a production line generating "health" from a defined set of resources (or inputs)' (1986: 12). Indeed in these schemes 'quality' becomes something of a misnomer for a process whereby amorphous human processes are reduced to observable and measurable outcomes through which conclusions about effectiveness and efficiency are consequently arrived at. Indeed, in this sense we can begin to see affinities with the measurement schemes used in the QALYS proposals of the health economists (see Mulkay et al., 1987).

From the standpoint of this chapter it is of some significance to note that, for 'client-centred' evaluation, the touchstone of measurement is even narrower than many of the items selected in ER programmes. For, in QA, one of the most favoured dimensions of measurement is 'behaviour'. In other words, when we ask questions about the effectiveness and efficiency of a mental health (or any other form of) programme, we will most likely be encouraged to give answers in terms of the 'terminal behaviour' of the client. It is a behaviour whose success or failure will be measured against that other phenomenon much loved of behaviourists – the 'objective' and it is a position well summed up in the following claim which I have taken from a relatively early text on evaluation. 'Evaluation is a process best approached through objectives stated in behavioural terms' (Armstrong et al., 1970: 21).

In summary, then, ER is presented as an objective, neutral and rational means of assessing human performance, which places particular emphasis on instrumental concerns and the analysis of means/ends relationships (Attkison et al., 1978; Rossi et al., 1979; Patton, 1980; Rutman, 1977; and Wortman, 1983). It is especially fond of causal analysis and the discovery of lawlike regularities (Attkison et al., 1978; Fitz-Gibbon and Morris, 1978; Wortman, 1983), and to that end it employs quantitative measures and indices in abundance (see, however, Cook and Reichardt, 1979). Consequently, I would argue that the adoption of ER techniques not only implies a commodification of both human services and of the interactive processes which are expended within them, but also restricts our (sociological) vision to matters of technical success or failure. It thereby deflects our attention away from many basic social and moral issues. When applied to active human subjects instead of mere programmes, ER entices us to adopt a particular view of personhood, namely, one which reduces persons to little more than the behaviours which they exhibit and which structures the subject as a behaviourist machine (see Armstrong et al., 1970; Attkison et al., 1978). It is through the discourse of behaviourism that the commodification of the body occurs.

Ultimately, then, ER commodifies social and health services by treating those services as mere things to be measured and compared. This usually implies a valorization of human activities. The viability of human relationships is, in other words, assessed in relation to such factors as 'output', 'turnover' and 'cost', and the qualitative basis of human interactive processes tends to be lost among the numerous indices which serve to mark out the success or failure of service programmes. Quality assurance in turn tends to measure such success and failure on the behavioural condition of the human body, and so partial skills and specific human attributes are selected and emphasized at the expense of all other actual and potential skills and set against the total personality of the 'client'. But rather than talk further in terms of such abstractions, I would prefer to describe how such ideologies work themselves out in concrete human practice. To that end I intend to discuss the nature of ER in a study on the rehabilitation facilities for psychiatric patients in an Irish town.

Evaluation and sociological research:
an outline of some difficulties

Some preliminary concerns
My own encounter with ER was via an involvement in a small

research project on the provision of facilities for the rehabilitation of psychiatric patients. In what follows, and on the basis of that encounter, I shall attempt to highlight some of the ways in which ER may be considered restrictive of both sociological, social and moral interests, and I shall also attempt to indicate how the adoption of measurement schemes in the human sciences so easily encourages some wider tendencies towards the commodification of human characteristics in general.

The evaluation of mental health care programmes has a considerable pedigree in the US (partly, perhaps, on account of the 1972 Congress legislation which established the necessity for Professional Standards Review Organizations). Consequently, numerous ER schemes have been used (see Beigel and Levenson, 1978; and Woy et al., 1978). These, as I have already suggested, lay great stress on the analysis of means/ends relationships. Indeed, and according to most ER texts, one should always establish the policy goals of the organization under study and then determine the extent to which the available resources have been effectively and rationally brought to bear on the stated objectives. In fact, even those forms of ER which claim to be 'goal free' (Scriven, 1972) lay primary stress on the emergent means/ends relationships of organizations, and according to Rossi et al.: 'Unless goals can be clarified and objectives operationalized, it is unlikely that an adequate evaluation can be attempted' (1979: 63).

What is more, many ER texts argue that the question of effectiveness is ultimately dependent upon analysing relationships of causality. Thus: 'In the largest context, the problem of discerning the effectiveness of a program is identical with the problem of establishing causality' (Rossi et al., 1979: 162).

This concentration on the issue of causality and the consequent emphasis on the use of the research strategies beloved of positivist social science was brought home to me more than once in the course of my own research – mainly by managers (usually nurses) who wished to know what 'hypothesis' I was testing. And it was this apparent equation of a social service with a thing to be tested that struck the first discordant note in my own consciousness. It subsequently became clear that those who were keen on hypothesis testing saw all true research in the image cast by the randomized clinical trial. In other words social experimentation was regarded as a 'superior means' (Riecken and Boruch, 1974) of gaining dependable knowledge about social interventions, and consequently all other forms of research were seen to constitute greater or lesser deviations from this revered ideal, (see also Kinston, 1983).

The study of organizational goals and causal relationships is, of course, both important and revealing and, as Dingwall and Strong have indicated elsewhere in this volume, the issue of effectiveness is not to be ignored. In fact, and as I shall indicate shortly, the organizations referred to here were often confused, unclear and ambiguous about what they were trying to achieve. But, as instructive as the development of such findings may be, a concentration on goals and means can encourage one to by-pass something which is (sociologically speaking) even more revealing, namely the study of the conceptual and theoretical premises on which an organizational apparatus is built. In the framework of this chapter, I am referring to the study of the discourse through which the social world of the psychiatric patient is structured, and by 'discourse' I mean to refer not merely to linguistic activities, but to the entire field of social practices and organizational arrangements through which any given mode of thought is expressed (see Woolgar, 1986). And I shall argue that it is important to explore the programme goals and the technology of rehabilitation in terms of the broader cultural and historical setting in which they are located. This demands moving beyond the study of instrumental (means/ends) relationships so as to ground the programme in its wider sociocultural context. In a sense, it is only through the prism of discourse that the examination of specific means/ends relationships can make sense.

Naturally, in a short chapter such as this, I cannot hope to provide a detailed and thorough account of the discourse on rehabilitation. Instead I intend to concentrate on some selected features of rehabilitation as they appear in a hostel for discharged mental hospital 'patients'. The hostel, of course, is part of a much wider mesh encompassing both the hospital itself and the day centres and workshops which surround it, and with appropriate references to these other sites I hope to be able to say something about the ways in which nurses, psychologists and psychiatrists, as well as social workers, structure their understandings of the psychiatric 'client' and the rehabilitation process in which that client is managed.

The hostel

The hostel system (to which I have alluded above) is complex and multifarious. Here I intend to concentrate my attention solely on the 'assessment hostel' which often acts as the first point of entry for the discharged mental patient (many of whom have been hospitalized for over 20 years). The assessment hostel was designed to accommodate up to 10 'clients' and is managed by Ballybreen Social Services Department. It is situated in a large three-storey house located in a busy part of Ballybreen.[2] Its informal title (that is, assessment hostel) gives a clue to one of its purposes.

The stated aims of the hostel are numerous, but rarely clear. For example, one is never certain whether it is designed as a training unit in which clients can learn elementary skills such as cooking, cleaning, shopping and the like, or whether it is strictly an assessment unit. In fact, both things occur continuously and any given staff observation on a client can be used to either stimulate further training or as the basis of an 'assessment'. In addition, the hostel is sometimes used as a 'retreat' for a patient who is living at home, and sometimes as a temporary base for a discharged patient whose immediate need is for housing. On top of this, one is able to discover all manner of written aims, some of which overlap, some of which contradict, and some of which dovetail with the aims I have already mentioned. Take the following as examples, all of which I extracted from documents drawn up in the hostel at various points during the previous two years: 'to provide a supportive learning environment', 'to encourage independence', 'to provide a homely environment for [those] who cannot live independently', 'to provide a system of assessment', 'to encourage, stimulate and instruct continuously'. Such multiple goals naturally give rise to multiple activities, but it is clear that the hostel makes no claims to offer a treatment for illness – though illnesses have, of course, to be managed within the context of the hostel (usually by means of chemical control). Indeed, the lack of what hospital psychiatrists called a 'medical input' was regarded by them as a weakness of the hostel system.

In the everyday routine of the hostel a division between staff and clients is always maintained. The division is not rigid but it is always hierarchical even at its most informal. Usually, however, members of the staff ordinarily relate to the clients as whole persons. That is they relate to an Agnes, or a Tom as full and complete individuals who require help or advice or encouragement or whatever in some specific task or other. In that sense staff seek to understand, comprehend, and communicate with clients on the basis of everyday language and gesture. Thus Tom may be applauded on his strike in the bowling alley, Agnes complimented on her sewing skills and Stan on his cooking ability. On a day-to-day basis, therefore, the staff can be seen to be dealing with other 'persons' who have histories, minds, experiences and behaviours. Once out of the client's hearing, however, the results of these interactions are often re-analysed in terms of a specific (and professionalized) linguistic framework. Thus, a game of ten-pin bowling is re-analysed in terms of 'motor-skills'. A discussion about food is re-analysed in terms of coping skills. A lapse of memory is discussed in terms of a syndrome and a leisure-time activity is analysed in terms of affective disorder. Above all, however, clients are ultimately assessed in terms of behavioural measures. In fact, client 'problems' are in many respects newly created through the application of behaviourist discourse to what are called 'activities of daily living'. Thus, the admission of new inmates is normally accompanied by a thorough assessment of context-specific behaviours in which clients' problems are 'identified', and modes of intervention devised for correcting those problems.

The use of behavioural measures for the assessment of client progress dominates the world of the mentally ill. Long before the hostel clients emerged into Ballybreen, they were rigorously assessed according to a number of behaviour rating scales. They were scales specific to the hospital in which they were treated, though based upon and designed along the same lines as some of the better-known scales of this kind (see, for example, Baker and Hall, 1983). In fact, following the results of a hospital-wide survey on behaviour patterns, patients were 'graded' according to their suitability for rehabilitation and discharge, and one of the major problems for the hospital-based psychologists was understood to involve the fine-tuning of the rating instruments so as to ensure better predictions about the outcome of a rehabilitation programme on any given patient. This question of behaviour is closely associated with the problems of assessment in general, and not only are behavioural measures used for selection to rehabilitation status, but for the assessment of almost every in-patient activity. Naturally, none of the (behavioural) scales used require any conscious input or response on behalf of the active 'patient'. In fact, patients often complain that 'no one really speaks to us in here' – which is untrue. What is true, however, is that all staff/patient interaction is mediated through a series of structured processes in such a way that what might be termed casual, informal or spontaneous discussion between staff and patients is rare. For nursing staff, in particular, each episode of interaction is seen as being 'part of the programme' and consequently there is an ever-present interest in formally structuring routine, day-to-day activities and conversations.

Ballybreen Hospital is not, of course, alone in relying upon behaviour as a central object of assessment, grading and measurement. Wing and Morris's *Handbook of Psychiatric Rehabilitation Practice*, for example, also lays a steady emphasis on such things. And Jaffe's (1975) account of the organization of treatment in a North American psychiatric ward made plain that the prime object of care, treatment and rehabilitation was behaviour. In fact, he described the nature of the ward in those very terms, thus. 'A remedial people-processing institution has people as its input and output. Its task is to change or alter their status or behaviour' (Jaffe,

1975: 27). And, of course, the influence of behaviourism on rehabilitation programmes in general is well established. Albrecht (1976), for example, extols the virtues of behaviourism in programmes for the rehabilitation of the physically disabled. He describes the aim of such programmes in the following terms:

> Within the behavioural framework, socialization after the onset of disability can be conceptualized in terms of identifying the problems that need to be solved and learning the adaptive behaviours necessary to solve these problems. (Albrecht, 1976: 24)

Shepherd (1984: 162) argues that, 'The process of rehabilitation can be thought to consist of three basic stages: Assessment, Treatment and Management. For assessment purposes the most accurate methods are those based on direct observation of criterion behaviour'. A behaviourist stance is also evident in the Royal College of Psychiatrists' 1980 report on the nature of psychiatric rehabilitation, and the design of nurses' observation scales and social-behaviour assessment schedules in psychiatric rehabilitation programmes has generally become something of an established subfield (see Affleck and McGuire, 1984). Behaviourist terminology, however, doesn't necessarily exhaust the ways in which one might describe either rehabilitation or care in general (see Gubrium and Buckholdt, 1982 and Buckholdt and Gubrium 1985).

The adoption of behaviourist discourse in effect means that the client as person and as personality becomes fragmented into different types of conduct. Mind and consciousness become invisible. Reference to the social conditions and social networks in which individuals have to live and work is secondary and taken to constitute one of the many background factors which may or may not influence the outcome of an illness – though even 'illness', always present, fades into the background as diagnosis and assessment are reduced to the recording and study of isolated behavioural indices. The assessment sheets used by the hostel staff in Ballybreen, for example, are composed in terms of such categories as the following: use of toilet, personal hygiene, grooming and appearance, making the bed, social graces and so on. Indeed, the inmate world is almost entirely constructed in a behaviourist mesh. 'Objectives' are established for each client. 'Programmes' are drawn up for each individual as well as for the residents as a group. Time is carefully parcelled out, and activities are structured in timetables and charts which are placed prominently along the walls of the residency. All cognitive and affective as well as psychomotor properties are reduced to levels of behaviour. Indeed, it is often assumed that unless we reduce human qualities to observables, evaluation is impossible. Thus, according to Armstrong et al. (1970) even such inner states as understanding, comprehension, and appreciation do not refer to anything that is directly observable and thus 'do not permit evaluation to be carried out in a systematic manner' (1970: 16). In psychiatric settings, of course, 'cognitive deficits', as they are called, are also assessed, but the assessment and study of cognition lies low in most rehabilitation settings.

In the hostel, then, there is little discussion of thoughts, feeling or awareness, still less of wider socioeconomic forces or even such things as family and friendship structures. When any such discussion does take place it tends to be couched (though not invariably so) in behaviourist terms. Persons are confronted as isolated individuals and their decontextualized behaviour is problematized and assessed according to behaviour rating scales. They become nothing but the behaviour which they exhibit. Furthermore, despite the fact that clients are regarded as having illnesses and diseases, there is little discussion about such things. Schizophrenia, depression and mania are, of course, mentioned but the treatment of such disorders is regarded as a matter for psychiatrists and hospitals. When an 'illness' does get out of hand, further medication is sought and once again the primary aim is to control the client's behaviour – normally by chemical means.

The emphasis on behaviour, and client assessment by means of behaviour, is also plainly evident in some of the workshops which the rehabilitation clients attend. Once again the goals of the workshops are sometimes mixed and fused together. One such description of workshop aims emerged as follows.

> *LP*: What would you say the main purpose of the Unit was?
> *I*: [*Silence*]
> *LP*: I mean. What, from your point of view, are you trying to do here?
> *I*: [*Pause*] Discipline. [*Pause*] To get people used to discipline and the discipline of work. Er . . . To motivate people for work.

This discipline, however, was achieved through the use of routine, repetitive and boring mechanical tasks (such as packing cotton wool). Indeed, the rehabilitation status of the client was in part judged according to his/her acceptance of the tedium involved in assembly-line packing processes. More important from our viewpoint, however, is the fact that discipline as an aim was intertwined with both therapeutic tasks and the means of client assessment. In addition to this, workshops also claimed to offer training in daily 'life skills'. And, once more, the problem of assessment loomed large as is evident from the following statement of a workshop manager.

We're expanding beyond industrial training. An assessment centre and a social skills unit is being built on the top floor. Clients will be taught the skills of daily living. Coping skills. They will be assessed to determine whether they are suitable for working in the community, for sheltered living, or for independent living. A series of training and assessment programmes [are] being developed . . .

Indeed, it is clear that in the vocabulary of psychiatric rehabilitation, a small number of key terms dominate the entire discourse. 'Assessment', 'behaviour', 'management', 'monitor', 'objectives', 'programmes' and 'selection' form a semantic field through which everyday practice is structured. And it is evident from what I have said that the evaluation of the organizational system associated with this vocabulary could take many forms. Evaluation research, however, would encourage one to devise observable measures by which one could judge either the progress of the client or the success of the hostel. The extent to which clients re-present themselves to hospital psychiatrists, for example, might be one such measure. Yet, as appealing as such a methodology might be, I would argue that this form of investigation tends to place in abeyance some fundamental social and practical issues. One such issue involves the utility of judging psychiatric qualities or human well-being according to behavioural manifestations. For, in many respects, behaviourism is only another form of reification in which human 'problems' are projected onto the isolated, decontextualized human frame and detached from the meaningful contexts in which they occur. Thus, people become bodies who behave, and their problems are seen to rest in their behaviour rather than in their social condition. Their behaviour is consequently sorted into constructive and unconstructive, useful and useless, dependent and productive categories. And it is only by reifying social properties on human anatomy and commodifying the body that QA and ER find it possible to exist.

The perplexities of social research

I have talked of forms of knowledge and of the discourse of rehabilitation. I have suggested that the latter takes as its object of focus 'human behaviour' and consequently I have tried to indicate how a number of social practices inexorably follow in the train of that focus – for example, the development of behavioural measures and scales, the construction of specific forms of description, as well as the manufacture of forms of therapy and forms of medical organization. Thus, and in this sense, 'behaviour' isn't just a feature of individual action, but the product of an entire discourse. Indeed, behaviourism is not just a method of constituting human subjects but also a resource through which such things as health and social services are organized.

The sociological researcher, of course, is able to interpose him or herself into such a discourse in only one of two ways. The first involves a critique of the practices implied by the discourse, whilst the second involves a more direct engagement with it in such a way that one becomes part of the discourse. It is in the second context that evaluation is possible. In fact, in the latter stance the position of the sociologist is analogous to that which was underlined for me by a clinical psychologist, namely, 'The task is not to philosophize — only social workers do that — but to get on with the operational decisions'. And the pressures to follow this line of reasoning are many. For funding, for the image of an academic department, and even for gaining entry to a setting, ER can prove immensely beneficial. Yet, and as I have attempted to illustrate, the evaluation of organizational means/ends relationships can only make sense in a wider context. Indeed the weaknesses of product-efficiency models of ER in ignoring wider contexts have, in fact, been recognized for some time in the field of educational research (see, for example, Lacey and Lawton, 1981). For my part, however, I would argue that the study of contexts necessarily involves the study of a discursive order (in the sense in which I have already specified that term). Failure to examine the latter means that the sociologist will be encouraged to ignore most of the wider social and moral issues which impinge on the problem at hand and to concentrate solely upon technical problems of causation. As a result, sociology will prove unable either to map out the limit of existing practice or to indicate alternative directions of social action.

In pursuing this last point, I shall offer only one brief example and it involves reference to social networks. The relationship between structured social networks and mental health (and illness) is well documented. Biegel et al. (1985) list, for example, some 1430 items in their bibliography on the subject. Yet, and as I have hinted, many psychiatric rehabilitation programmes make no reference to such an object. Social networks are, of course, no more nor less real than behaviour, but by focusing on the one rather than the other we engage ourselves in different forms of description, investigation, action, therapy and organization. In particular, a focus on networks involves examination of a far wider range of active subjects than just the psychiatric client, and it is, perhaps, apposite at this stage to refer to the Barclay Report (1982) on the role and tasks of social workers in Britain in which it was argued that the focus of social work should be tilted away from its traditional concern with casework and towards care in the community. Leaving aside the fact that many of the key concepts in the report were left rather vague, the implications were clear – a new object of professional practice brings in its train implications for the organization of care.

It may be argued, of course, that in encouraging the substitution of social networks for behaviour as an object of professional practice, we merely implicate sociology in the operation of a different (and perhaps more pernicious) form of social policing. It is an argument which, in many respects, serves to highlight the claim that there is no objective, scientific, rational means of selecting between a service which focuses upon the one rather than the other. In fact the choice hinges on a set of moral and ethical questions. Consequently, and to paraphrase Weber (1949), no 'science' can tell us what we ought to do, only what we can do and what the practical consquences of our choices are likely to be. The role of sociology, perhaps, is to outline the choices.

According to Lukács (1971) the main task of Marxist theory is to lay bare the basis of objectification, and to explain how the proletariat is the true subject of history. I would suggest that the task of sociology is in some respects a related one, namely to explain how the 'subject' is constituted in and through the practices of social life. Thus, in so far as human beings and their interactive relationships come to be viewed as objective commodities one of the central sociological problems is to explain the foundations and context of that objectification. And having done so it is also incumbent on sociology to detail the consequences of such forms of belief for the subjects involved. Thus, those methodologies and forms of social investigation which enter into the flow of commodification and treat the subject as an objective facticity whose behaviour can be objectively evaluated miss the essential target of social inquiry.

Notes

I wish to acknowledge the assistance of the Policy Research Institute, Belfast in enabling me to carry out the fieldwork on which part of this chapter is based.

  1   Exactly the same claim made on the basis of a distinctively non-Marxist analysis is contained in the paper by Mulkay et al. (1987).

  2   A pseudonym for a Northern Irish town.

References

Adorno, T.W. (1973) *The Jargon of Authenticity*. London: Routledge & Kegan Paul.
Affleck, J.W. and McGuire, R.J. (1984) 'The Measurement of Psychiatric Rehabili-

148   *Lindsay Prior*

tation Status: A Review of the Needs and a New Scale', *British Journal of Psychiatry*, 145: 517–25.

Albrecht, G.L. (1976) *The Sociology of Physical Disability and Rehabilitation.* London: University of Pittsburgh Press.

Armstrong, R.J., Cornell, T.D., Kraner, R.E. and Roberson, E.W. (1970) *The Development and Evaluation of Behavioural Objectives.* Worthington: Charles A. Jones.

Attkison, C.C., Hargreaves, W.A. and Horowitz, M.J. (eds) (1978) *Evaluation of Human Service Programs.* New York: Academic Press.

Baker, R. and Hall, J.N. (1983) *User's Manual for Rehabilitation Evaluation.* Aberdeen: Vine Publishing.

Barclay Report (1982) *Social Workers· Their Role and Tasks.* London: Bedford Square Press.

Beigel, A. and Levenson, A. (1978) 'Program Evaluation on a Shoestring Budget' in Attkison et al. (1978).

Biegel, D.E., McCardle, E. and Mendelson, S. (1985) *Social Networks and Mental Health: An Annotated Bibliography.* Beverly Hills, CA: Sage.

Buckholdt, D.R. and Gubrium, J.F. (1985) *Caretakers: Treating Emotionally Disturbed Children.* Lanham, MD: University Press of America.

Cook, T.D. and Reichardt, C.S. (eds) (1979) *Qualitative and Quantitative Methods in Evaluation Research.* Beverly Hills, CA: Sage.

Duncan, A.J. (1952) *Quality Control and Industrial Statistics.* Homewood: Richard D. Irwin.

Fitz-Gibbon, C.T. and Morris, L.L. (1978) *How to Design a Program Evaluation.* Beverly Hills, CA: Sage.

Gubrium, J.F. and Buckholdt, D.R. (1982) *Describing Care. Image and Practice in Rehabilitation.* Cambridge, MA: Oelgeschlager, Gunn & Hain.

Gudex, C. (1986) 'QALYS and their Use by the Health Service'. Discussion Paper 20. Centre for Health Economics: University of York.

Horkheimer, M. and Adorno, T.W. (1973) *Dialectic of Enlightenment.* London: Allen Lane.

Jaffe, D.T. (1975) 'The Organization of Treatment on a Short-term Psychiatric Ward', *Psychiatry*, 38: 23–38.

Kinston, W. (1983) 'Pluralism in the Organisation of Health Service Research', *Social Science and Medicine.* 17: 5: 299–313.

Lacey, C. and Lawton, D. (1981) *Issues in Evaluation and Accountability.* London: Methuen.

Lukács, G. (1971) *History and Class Consciousness. Studies in Marxist Dialectics.* London: Merlin Press.

Marcuse, H. (1964) *One Dimensional Man.* London: Routledge & Kegan Paul.

Marx, K. (1970) *Capital*, Vol. 1. London: Lawrence and Wishart.

Mulkay, M., Ashmore, M. and Pinch, T. (1987) 'Measuring the Quality of Life: A Sociological Invention Concerning the Application of Economics to Health Care', *Sociology*, 21(4): 541–64.

Patton, M.Q. (1980) *Qualitative Evaluation Methods.* Beverly Hills, CA: Sage.

Riecken, H.W. and Boruch, R.F. (eds) (1974) *Social Experimentation: A Method for Planning and Evaluating Social Intervention.* New York: Academic Press.

Rossi, P.H., Freeman, H.E. and Wright, S.R. (1979) *Evaluation: a Systematic Approach.* Beverly Hills, CA: Sage.

Rutman, L. (1977) *Evaluation Research Methods: A Basic Guide.* Beverly Hills, CA: Sage.

Scriven, M. (1972) 'Pros and Cons about Goal-free Evaluation', *Evaluation Comment*, 3: 1–7.

Shaw, C.D. (1986) *Introducing Quality Assurance.* London: King's Fund Publishing Office.

Shepherd, G. (1984) *Institutional Care And Rehabilitation.* London: Longman.

Shipman, M. (1979) *In-school Evaluation.* London: Heinemann.

Simons, H. (1981) 'Process Evaluation in Schools', in Lacey and Lawton (1981).

Weber, M. (1949) '"Objectivity" in Social Science and Social Policy', in E.A. Shils and H.A. Finch (eds), *The Methodology of the Social Sciences.* New York: The Free Press.

Wing, J.K. and Morris, B. (1981) *Handbook of Psychiatric Rehabilitation Practice.* London: Oxford University Press.

Woolgar, S. (1986) 'On the Alleged Distinction between Discourse and Praxis', *Social Studies of Science* 16: 309–17.

World Health Organization (1985) *The Principles of Quality Assurance.* Copenhagen: WHO.

Wortman, P.M. (1983) 'Evaluation Research: A Methodological Perspective', *Annual Review of Psychology*, 34: 223–60.

Woy, J.R., Lund, D.A. and Attkison, C.C. (1978) 'Quality Assurance in Human Service Program Evaluation', in Attkison et al. (1978).

8

Reconstituting the Sociology of Law

Susan Silbey and Austin Sarat

The sociology of law begins with a broad but simple claim that legal institutions cannot be understood without seeing the entire social environment. Nonetheless, scholars exhaust most of their attention studying the implementation of law, especially the ways in which non-legal, social factors intrude upon and undo legality. By looking at hard cases – at places where the law seeks to change behaviour and circumstances – scholars have been drawn to instances where legality fails and have described, much to their chagrin, the ineffectiveness of the law in the gap between law on the books and the law in action.

Law in its daily life is most often not studied. Sociologists look at the ways in which consumer protection laws are enforced, but rarely look at the ways in which the buying and selling of goods takes account of and accounts for its legal regulation. Researchers study the ways in which organizational constraints and professional interests influence the practice of law, but less often look to the ways in which lawyer–client interactions are constructed by, as they themselves constitute, the law. In general, sociologists of law have looked at violations of law but not at instances of law-abidingness.

Thus, the modern sociology of law is, for the most part, a sociology of state law. It studies the ways in which law disciplines state power or, more often, the ways in which legality fails to effectively control that power. It is, moreover, a sociology that speaks to and for the state apparatus as often as it speaks about the state apparatus. In this way the sociology of law has developed close ties and affinities to policy studies and the institutions of policy making and implementation. A typical research project in the sociology of law will begin with a policy problem, locate it in a general theoretical context, present an empirical study derived from the theory to speak to that problem, and conclude with recommendations, suggestions or cautions.

In Foucauldian terms the sociology of law has yet to join in cutting off the head of the king (Foucault, 1980); it legitimates state power even as it ignores the ways in which power has escaped the state. Paradoxically, the excessive emphasis on the juridical form of state law means that, again from a Foucauldian point of view, it is more archaic than dangerous. In important ways, this fixation on the juridical form seems to remove the sociology of law from the modern disciplinary apparatus and, at the same time, distances it from efforts to resist the controlling gaze of the institutions and practices of the human sciences. Yet it is precisely in this ironically archaic concern with state law that the sociology of law contributes to the empowerment of the disciplinary apparatus of modern society. It is precisely in its focus on and legitimation of state law that sociolegal research helps to blunt resistance. In its focus on the state, the sociology of law diverts attention, channels energies and focuses scholarship on the most visible and least penetrating aspect of the disciplinary apparatus.

In its attention to state law, the sociology of law is not unlike other subdisciplines of the social sciences which also, too often, focus research on a subject institution's own definitions and models of accepted practice. For example, Robert Strauss (1957) describes the role of sociology in medicine as a research practice which takes the events and processes medical practitioners define as problems as subjects to inquire about, to understand, and possibly to remedy. In contrast, Strauss defines a sociology of medicine as the study of how medical practitioners identify and construct those events and processes as problems. Thus sociological research in medicine might and often does study patient compliance with therapeutic regimes, while a sociology of medicine might study why doctors consider patient compliance a problem.

This chapter describes the preoccupation of sociolegal scholars with state law and roots that preoccupation in an Enlightenment conception of science, policy and progress. It argues that the sociology of law has been part of the modernization of state law and of the effort to turn law to the task of steering society. It calls for a revision of the epistemological and political assumptions of the sociology of law, for new understandings of what counts as knowledge and a broader view of what counts as law. In so doing, the effort is to make the sociology of law less archaic. But, a less archaic sociology of law might very well be a more dangerous sociology of law, one more closely tied with the modern constitution of the human subject. For us, however, resistance requires a clarity of vision which is incompatible with the more archaic and less threatening sociology of law (Fitzpatrick, 1986). We want to contribute to the demystification of state law, to a clearer vision of its power and its limits so that the sociology of law itself no longer stands as a barrier to a sociology of discipline and resistance.

The sociology of law and State law

The origins of the sociology of law can be traced to the eighteenth century when a distinction between law and society was postulated as part of a series of political struggles the object of which was to limit the power of the state (see Locke, 1690). The congruence of law and society had long been associated with forms of hierarchical oppression; thus, the effort to distinguish law and society was part of an effort to end, or at least to discipline, political control by the few.

Two themes from these early conceptions of the relationships among state, law, and society, can be detected in the modern sociology of law: a distinction between policy and politics and a vision of an unproblematic relationship between knowledge, science and power. The distinction between politics and policy is claimed on the grounds that policy analysis is value free and apolitical, a technical inquiry concerning the relationship of possible means to predetermined ends. This perspective reflects, while it propagates, a vision of knowledge and science independent of and removed from the sources of social power which it helps generate and support. This allows sociolegal scholarship to disclaim an advocacy role in the collective struggle over community values while it simultaneously rationalizes the outputs of that collective struggle.

By maintaining a distinction between policy and politics, sociolegal scholars align themselves with and reproduce the premises of liberal legalism which also rests upon a divorce of Politics, with a capital 'P', from policy, or politics with a small 'p'. In the classic formulations of liberal social theory, the larger questions of Politics, that is, how we shall live together and what is the good and just society – are resolved in favour of the free play of self-interested ambition; the messy, open-ended questions concerning the meaning of justice, the distribution of property and the definition of the public welfare are settled through the adoption of the institutional arrangements of liberalism – that is separation of powers, checks and balances, republican forms of government. These institutional arrangements define the tasks of government and of law as limited and instrumental: to monitor, and possibly to mediate, the largely self-regulating processes of competitive private ambition. Governance becomes a more circumscribed, and mechanical problem concerning the useful and effective adjustments within a fundamentally just, if flawed, arrangement. In this system, the tasks of government are not simply narrow but are removed from Politics. In the terms in which the American progressive reformers reinterpreted this ethos in the early part of the twentieth century, good government is a matter of technically proficient administration.

Thus, by attending primarily to the technical means of achieving legitimately established goals or policies, by studying the consequences and effectiveness of state law, sociolegal scholars reproduce the problematic distinction between the ends and means of political life characteristic of liberal social thought. Mainstream scholarship participates in the common political vision of an imperfect but just legal order in which approximate solutions to the larger questions of justice, equity, security and liberty are built into the framework of political institutions and need not be subject to the sort of probing examination which would reduce discourse to unresolvable debate and incommensurate arguments. By thus aligning themselves with the dominant conception of state and law, sociolegal scholars can do their work and imagine that they are speaking to benign, well-intended, and rational decision makers who also share fundamental assumptions about justice and legality, the primacy of rights, and the necessity of due process for balancing the interests of individuals and communities. By addressing this audience, scholars can do research and believe that they are doing good.

Sociological inquiry about law is, however, not only fuelled by the liberal distinction between politics and policy but also by Enlightenment views of the relation of reason and knowledge and the further location of both reason and knowledge in the scientific study of nature. The project of such Englightenment thinkers as Locke and Descartes was to expose the fallacious idealism of Aristotelian metaphysics and epistemology, to substitute a view of knowledge based upon empirical observation and neutral reason. The reasoning person, stripped of sentimentality and prejudice, approached a world accessible to disciplined inquiry. Such inquiry produces valid observations, that is, observations which, when subject to the discipline of method, could be repeated and would produce essentially similar results. Those observations provide the raw material for the mental operations of judgement. Given that such observations and operations could be performed by anyone trained in proper methods of investigation, Enlightenment epistemology promised that men could be freed from the authority of tradition and traditional religion. Thus as Engels (1959: 68) would later write, in the Enlightenment, everything had to 'justify its existence before the judgement seat of reason . . . Reason became the sole measure of everything'.

The Enlightenment's equation of knowledge and reason, and the assimilation of both to the methods of science, was, of course, part of, and associated with, a political revolution.[1] Reason was a political force. As Hobbes put it (1839: Vol. I, 7), 'The end of knowledge is power'. The emergence of and alliance between liberalism and science was itself a challenge to traditional political élites and modes of knowledge; empirical science provided the means for contesting both aristocratic and ecclesiastical power in the name of democracy and publicly demonstrable truths.

Reason, knowledge and science had to be useful to men in coming to terms with and managing the threats of nature,[2] and in developing a new political order. For Enlightenment thinkers the errors of political life were largely a result of distortions in man's understanding of himself and his world. Reason, knowledge and science applied to the task of producing a realistic picture of the social world would, it was hoped, produce a political life which would be rational and, as a result, more clearly subject to human adjustment and control.

Thus, from the Enlightenment onwards, political authority systematically shifted its claim to legitimacy from tradition, emotion and religion to increasingly rational and professional sources. By chasing away the Gods, as Weber claimed, the Enlightenment equation of reason and science seemed to make calculable and predictable what in earlier ages had seemed governed by chance. In a rather direct way, contemporary sociolegal scholars share the inheritance of the Enlightenment faith in the ability of science to further progress and human perfectability. Their authority rests upon specialized knowledge and skill which is not depleted or impaired when it is applied in the service of policy goals, but is rather enhanced by the deference reflected when expert advice is followed.

The address to power and the claim of authority, joining with the denial of politics, encourages the use of science as a source of legitimation (Lasch, 1977; Chomsky, 1967), and helps silence both political and moral challenges as well as voices which do not share its assumptions or speak its language. The prestige and organization of professional knowledge carries the risk that 'expertise is more and more in danger of being used as a mask for privilege and power rather than, as it claims, as a mode of enhancing the public interest' (Freidson, 1972: 337). The desire to be useful and speak authoritatively on public policies not only limits the kinds of arguments and perspectives that researchers offer, and the kinds of knowledge that are sanctioned, but it also fosters naïve and uncritical conceptions of progress and effectiveness.

Noting the emergence of scientific authority generally in political life does not mean, however, that state officials have been, or are, especially eager for, or attentive to, the results of social scientific studies of law. Those officials are, in one view, more interested in results than method, and are impatient with the tentative or cautious conclusions of much social science. In this view, policy makers eager for clarity, or at least certainty, about the consequences of particular courses of action care less about science than about the capacity of social scientists to recommend solutions for immediate problems. This understanding has much to commend it, and it certainly helps to illuminate the dilemmas faced by those who seek legal reform and address a policy audience.

Focusing on the impatience of policy makers with scientific method and nuance offers, however, too narrow an understanding of the relation of knowledge and politics. While policy makers may articulate their demands and discomforts in utilitarian and instrumental terms, state officials seek to use social science to legitimate, not merely to direct, policy choices. Reason is turned into a justification for, rather than a guide to, action. This turns the Enlightenment project on its head. The mere association of policy choice and scientific inquiry is politically useful in suggesting that those choices are deliberate, rational and guided by reasonable predictions of consequences as well as concerns for the public interest.

The ties of the sociology of law to state law, its complicity in advancing a distinction between politics and policy, and its legitimation of legal policy through the language of science, can be seen clearly in the work of the American legal realists and in the rhetoric and aspirations of much of the contemporary Law and Society movement in the United States. Both have tried to use social science scholarship on law to help produce more effective legal policy. Both have embraced, endorsed and advanced the reform aspirations of state law, and have portrayed state law as a valuable tool of social change and human liberation.

American legal realism, by no means a unified or singular intellectual movement, emerged as part of the progressive response to the collapse of the nineteenth-century *laissez-faire* political economy. By attacking the classical conception of law with its assumptions about the independent and objective movement from pre-existing rights to decisions in specific cases (Cohen, 1935; Llewellyn, 1931 and 1960), realists opened the way for a vision of law as policy, a vision in which law could and should be guided by pragmatic and/or utilitarian considerations (Llewellyn, 1940). By exposing the difference between law on the books and law in action realists established the need to approach law making and adjudication strategically with an eye towards difficulties in implementation.

Realists saw the start of the twentieth century as a period of knowledge explosion and knowledge transformation (Reisman, 1941). Some saw in both the natural and the emerging social sciences the triumph of rationality over tradition, inquiry over faith, and the human mind over its environment (McDougal, 1941). Some realists argued that the law's rationality and efficacy were ultimately dependent upon an alliance with science (see Schlegel, 1980). By using the questions and methods of science to assess the consequences of legal decisions, realists claimed that an understanding of what law *could* do would help in establishing what law *should* do (Llewellyn, 1931).

Social science could aid decision making by distinguishing empirical inquiry from normative debate and by thus providing the technical mastery necessary for effective legal regulation. By identifying the factors that limited the choices available to officials and, more importantly, by identifying the determinants of responses to those decisions, social scientists could help informed decision makers to adopt decisions on the basis of what was or was not possible in a given situation (Lasswell and McDougal, 1943). Rather than challenge basic norms or attempt to revise the legal structure, this brand of realism ultimately worked to increase confidence in state law and to foster the belief that legal thinking informed by social knowledge could be enlisted to aid the pressing project of state intervention. For social science, the unmasking of legal formalism and the opening of legal institutions to empirical inquiry offered, at one and the same time, fertile ground for research and the opportunity to be part of a fundamental remaking of legal thought. The possibility of influencing legal decisions and policies may have also suggested grounds for establishing social science's relevance and legitimacy.

The emergence of the modern Law and Society movement began with this legacy: it developed in partial reaction to the political retrenchment of the 1950s and in partial support of the political reformism of the sixties. Its emergence coincides with one of those recurrent episodes in American legal history in which law is regarded as a beneficial tool for social improvement, in which social problems appear susceptible to legal solutions, and in which there is, or appears to be, a rather unproblematic relationship between legal justice and social justice (Trubek and Galanter, 1974). By the mid-1960s liberal reformers seemed once again to be winning the battle to rebuild a troubled democracy; the political forces working, albeit modestly, to expand rights and redistribute wealth and power were in ascendancy. The national government was devoting itself to the use of State power and legal reform for the purpose of building a 'Great Society'. The courts, especially the Supreme Court, were out front in expanding the definition and reach of legal rights. Because law was seen as an important vehicle for social change, those legal scholars who were critical of existing social practices believed they had an ally in the legal order. Pragmatic social change was an explicit agenda of the state and an equally explicit part of the agenda of law and society research. Legality seemed a cure rather than a disease (Scheingold, 1974); the aspirations and purposes of law seemed unquestionably correct.

Thus, the modern law and society movement, like the realist movement before it, grew up in, and allied itself with, a period of optimism about state law. The period was one in which, 'the welfare regulatory state program of liberal capitalism was once again in the ascendancy' and in which,

> liberal legal scholars and their social science allies could identify with national administrations which seemed to be carrying out progressive welfare-regulatory programs, expanding protection for basic constitutional rights and employing law for a wide range of goals that were widely shared in the liberal community and could even be read as inscribed in the legal tradition itself. (Trubek and Esser, 1987: 23)

This period was, of course, also a period of extraordinary optimism in the social sciences, a period of triumph for the behavioural revolution, a period of growing sophistication in the application of quantitative methods in social inquiry.

In American legal realism and the Law and Society movement research on law is empirical, that is, it is based on the assumptions of normal science, and focused on the state. Both of these movements use knowledge to serve power,[3] to legitimate and rationalize state law. Both imply, although they don't argue, that the production of knowledge can be objective and value free and that law can and should be responsive to objective knowledge. State law is portrayed as struggling for effectiveness; state law is, nonetheless, portrayed as a central apparatus of control. By linking a scientific methodology with a preoccupation with state law the modern sociology of law legitimates law even as it misdescribes or neglects to locate law in the network of power which constitutes social life.

Beyond normal science

To the extent that sociologists of law continue to seek influence over state policy they are likely to be encouraged to adhere to a posture of 'deliberate detachment' (Friedman, 1986: 780). This is not to say that state officials are the only force encouraging sociologists of law to adhere to, or to adopt, the posture and canons of normal science; there are certainly others. Nonetheless, the policy audience offers a powerful invitation to sociologists of law to characterize their empirical work in the language of science (see Dror, 1975). That audience encourages sociologists of law to operate as if social behaviour could be understood in terms of a tangible and determinate world of facts (see White and Reim, 1977; see also Rich, 1977), to treat data as if they were an undistorted window on the social world, to treat the ambiguity of what we observe in an unambiguous way. Sociologists of law are invited to act as if there is a clear congruence between our representations of things and things themselves, and to accept the model of value-free, detached, objective inquiry in which empirical research seeks generally valid propositional knowledge about 'reality'. This attitude towards scholarship and presentation of research is one of the prices of attempting to speak convincingly to the powerful.

There are, we think, at least two related ways in which policy makers encourage or support those attitudes and tendencies. First, state officials seek and/or demand authoritativeness in the inquiries they commission, support or attend to (Lindblom and Cohen, 1979). As the reach of the regulatory state expands, and more public regulation is made at farther remove from democratic processes, policy makers seek and require new forms of authority and legitimation. Neither electoral mandates, nor public stature is sufficient to underwrite the expanding universe of contemporary public policy. The claim of scientific expertise seems, however, to offer a particularly useful form of legitimacy for the modern state.

It is rarely satisfactory for the purposes of the policy audience, however, to be told that research is partial, expresses the values of the researchers or that it is itself a relatively self-contained representational system. If sociolegal research is to be influential it must claim to have something that policy makers do not themselves have, that is, it must claim to have something which is different, and presumably better, than the ordinary understandings that policy makers themselves routinely acquire (Lindblom and Cohen, 1979: 22). Opinions are ubiquitous but knowledge is rare; state officials want knowledge, that is, advice that has a greater probability of predicting accurately the outcomes of alternative courses of action. Some of the realists understood, however, that social science could be a valuable tool for policy makers by providing its own kind of quality control and its own set of assurances about the truth value of its research products. Science then and now purports to be able to guarantee the reliability and validity of research results, to assure that research results can be replicated, and are therefore not the idiosyncratic product of a particular investigation. It provides both an assurance of quality and a hope that an objective realm of knowable conditions can be managed, or coped with, if not altered and changed.

Secondly, state officials require not only legitimation but also demand what Herbert Gans described as 'programmatic rationality'. Policy makers attempt 'to achieve substantive goals through instrumental action . . . that can be proven, logically or empirically, to achieve those goals' (1975: 4; compare Bok, 1983). State officials look to social research, not simply to supply justification through better or more reliable information but, in particular, to supply technical advice in the form of precise, conditional propositions about the relationships between specific social and legal variables. Only when scholars produce seemingly reliable estimates of the probable relations between means to ends – the elements of technical rationality – can scientific authority satisfy the demand for an allegedly apolitical justification for political choice.

While there is much sociolegal work that works hard to distance itself from the assumptions of normal science either in the choice of so-called soft methods or in its focus on particular cases (see, for example, Engel, 1980 and Yngvesson, 1985), the influence of science is not simply a choice of hard over soft or extensiveness over intensiveness. It is seen as much in attitudes towards data as it is in the choice of data itself. It is seen as much in the removal of the observer and the process of observation from the analysis of the things observed as in the choice of quantitative over qualitative methods, as much in a refusal to be as explicit about political commitments as in the choice of research methods.

The normal-science strategy of exempting the observer from the process of observation, writing as if the social scientist was exempt from, or outside, the social processes he describes and denying the politics of academic activity is, however, challenged by recent work in philosophy, epistemology and social theory which offers alternative accounts of what constitutes knowledge of the social world and its relationship to social power (Foucault, 1972; Unger, 1975; Derrida, 1978; Rorty, 1979, 1982; see Rajchman and West, 1985). This work challenges the premises of the Enlightenment, and the liberal alliance between scholarship and political power which appropriates and uses science in the name of an unquestioned pursuit of progress (Spragens, 1981). It builds upon traditions of philosophical scepticism in denying that any known mental activity is able to have unmediated access to a world of facts. What we call fact, it is argued, does not exist outside, or prior to, the categories of thought we construct to guide and make possible our inquiries. This argument puts the observer, and the process of observation, directly within the thing observed and collapses the distinction between subject and object.

Much contemporary philosophy has abandoned the traditional quest for congruence between appearance and reality. Instead some philosophers are now concerned with 'the quotidian, with the *Lebenswelt*', what Husserl called the life-world, or lived world, and with a 'philosophy free of the search for a "true world"' (Putnam, 1985: 29). Because, as Rorty writes, 'the notion of "logical analysis" turned upon itself and committed slow suicide' (1982: 227), contemporary philosophy is characteristically pluralistic, conventionalist, and historicist, as well as antireductionist. While there are differences of view within the philosophical community about how far to depart from the search for a 'sub-basement of conceptualization, or language' (Quine, 1960: 3), nonetheless, there seems to be a general consensus challenging the paradigm of normal science and the claims of positivism in sociolegal studies to be able to identify, through rigorous scientific methods, determinate responses to legal interventions. Moreover, this challenge suggests that the search for the kind of objectivity and clarity demanded by state officials may be ultimately self-deceptive. This challenge requires, or invites, sociologists of law to implicate themselves in their analyses and their scholarship. It requires, or invites, an effort to overcome the subject/object distinction and to consider the way sociolegal research constitutes its subject of study. Paying attention to these challenges threatens the alliance between the sociology of law and policy élites in the liberal state. It means returning to, and exploring the implications for empirical practices of, those deconstructivist strands in legal realism which have, to this point, played a small role in sociolegal studies (see Silbey and Sarat, 1987; Trubek, 1984).

Beyond state legality

The concentration of sociolegal research on state legality works to both overestimate and underestimate the importance and efficacy of state law. It overestimates by suggesting that state law is a, if not the, central mechanism of social control and social order. It does so by conceiving of the modern subject as a juridical subject, a possessor of legal rights and interests. Yet, at the same time that the sociology of law suggests that state law is central it implies that state law is not dangerous. The sociology of law concentrates on areas of state law where implementation and impact are most problematic (see Feeley, 1983; Robertson and Teitelbaum, 1973; Loftin et al., 1983; Lefstein et al., 1969; Casper and Brereton, 1984; Ross, 1973; Skolnick, 1966; Zeisel, 1982), on decisions or situations, where law is least likely to be effective. It produces pictures of a legal system struggling to retain what seems like a tenuous grasp on the social order (Abel, 1980; Sarat, 1985), and portray legal officials as vainly struggling against great odds to do law's bidding.

State law is by no means as weak as this picture would present it. Law in the realms in which it operates plays an important part in the reproduction and maintenance of social relations, yet as Foucault has shown, juridical power is only one among many sources of power in contemporary society. Power is decentralized; power has escaped the state. Thus the sociology of law, if it is not to mystify the nature of power in modern society, must itself cut free from its almost exclusive focus on state power. Attention needs to be paid to social processes themselves to identify the ways in which law in its daily life constitutes social relations, and conversely, the ways in which ordinary social processes, and the various forms of power there, help constitute law. We need to study the vast interstices of state law in which ordinary social processes and law are mutually constitutive.

Instead of studying the problematic enforcement of law, we might study the practices which make law unproblematic in social life, the normalcy of law which helps constitute ordinary daily life. For example, one might study the conventional and non-professional aspects of law that exist in many untroubled, non-conflicting social transactions. We might study the behaviours which lay behind the screen of legislation and decision but actually govern social relations, although only periodically become enacted in formal rules (compare Ehrlich, 1936). These norms define the taken-for-granted world of legal practices and legitimacy, and illustrate the power of law, rather than its inefficacy. Because legal forms are constitutive of the very forms which social relations and practices take, they are so embedded in the ways in which individuals act that they are virtually invisible to those involved. It is this invisibility, this taken-for-grantedness that makes legality and legal forms powerful.

From this perspective, one might study the ways in which law is routinely mobilized in constructing images of 'acceptable' human behaviour and 'normal' social relations. For example, Sarat and Felstiner (1986, 1988) have studied negotiations between lawyers and clients during the process of divorce. Through these discussions, lawyers and clients work out the means of dissolving a marriage. In the process, clients are instructed about how the legal system works and why it does not work in ways the client desires and expects. The discussions about how the legal system works, what strategies can be more or less successfully pursued, how to negotiate or whether to settle, are also a negotiation about who the client is, what kind of self is legally relevant, and what kind of person succeeds or fails in particular kinds of social transactions. What is at stake in these discussions is more than the dissolution of a marriage, the division of property, and the custody of children. The conversations involve a legitimation of some parts of human experience and personality and a denial of the relevance of others; they privilege financial considerations and denigrate emotional, normative and symbolic aspects of relationships. Rather than being ineffectual, here the law is powerful. It becomes a means by which those undergoing divorce are instructed about what it means to be a successful and effectual person.

In another study, Silbey (1987) observed the ways in which young adolescents begin to articulate their understandings of themselves as juridical subjects, and the social world as legally constituted. Again, in contrast to research which focuses upon state law, and persistently describes the ineffectiveness of law to change and control behaviour, Silbey describes the power of law to constitute social identity. She describes the ways in which 13-year-old students in a relatively affluent suburb use the American Constitution to support their belief that all forms of social deviance, other than specifically criminal actions, are permissible and ought to be protected by law; they assert their desire to be different by claiming a legal and constitutional right which, they say, authorizes resistance to convention, and by implication resistance to adult norms. These adolescents mobilize their conceptions of law, and law's authority, in their struggle to forge independent personal identities. The children's conception of the rights they claim bears little resemblance to the constitutional doctrine they study; it collapses the delicate distinctions among religious affiliation, sexual preference, and political belief which mark professional constitutional discourse. Nonetheless, the children find support for the difficult experiential and emotional voyage towards adulthood by asserting a universal juridical personhood protected by their conceptions of the American constitution. For these children, law is empowering.

Of course, there is a danger here that the effort to trace the powers of law in places outside the state will simply produce a new alliance, this time an alliance between the sociology of law and the surveilling, normalizing agencies of the psy-complex (Smart, 1987). Yet a sociology of law liberated from the state might through its identification of alternative legalities serve to legitimate such alternatives and, in so doing, ally itself with the multiple centres of resistance engendered by the multiple loci of power in modern society.

A sociology of law dominated by state law, however, ignores or misstates the role and importance of alternative legalities or legal pluralism (Griffiths, 1981). Where gaps are identified between the substance of state law and the governing pattern of social behaviour, they are, in one view, assumed to be normatively empty, indicative of nothing but technical problems in the clarity or communication of legal rules (see Wasby, 1970; Casper and Brereton, 1984; Pressman and Wildavsky, 1973; Heumann and Loftin, 1979). Another view recognizes that such gaps are often indicative of the existence of norms at variance with state legality. Some seek to legitimate such normative life (see Macaulay, 1963 and Moore, 1973), while others associate themselves more fully with the normative agenda of the state and lend sociological expertise to the task of overcoming that resistance (Blumberg, 1967; Wald, 1967; Muir, 1973; Dolbeare and Hammond, 1970).

For some sociologists of law, however, legal pluralism is more than a source of idiosyncratic evasion; instead, it is a potential source of political resistance to the hegemonic project of state legality. Deploying the concept of legal pluralism in its classical sense, under colonial conditions, these scholars recognize and valorize the indigenous cultures and normative orders of colonized peoples (e.g. Malinowski, 1926; Kuper and Smith, 1969; Hooker, 1975; Chanock, 1985; Comoroff, 1985). For them, legal pluralism suggests a way of acknowledging the particular character and important role of law in stateless societies. Here, legal pluralism challenges ethnocentric perspectives that define law in terms of the complex, segmented and institutionalized legal systems of modern Europe, and which while celebrating themselves also denigrate tribal, local or communal normative ordering as non-law. This Eurocentric vision had been used to legitimate the imposition of colonial law upon peoples for whom any law could be viewed in this way as a gift. The concept of legal pluralism deployed in this classical sense seems to sensitize observers to the varieties of forms of legal ordering and the varieties of forms of law. At the same time, it also sensitizes observers to the domination and subordination attached to the gift of European law.

Merry (1988) describes a more general and contemporary use of legal pluralism which refers to situations of diverse normative ordering and the interconnectedness of social orders. Here, researchers move away from colonial empires, describing plural legal orders within state systems. Legal pluralism is used to refer to ethnic separatism, or situations where groups within the same polity are bound, or claim to be bound, by different laws, or situations where different groups are affected differently by the same laws. Legal pluralism in this usage emphasizes the interaction of state and non-state normative orders, describing the ways in which 'state law penetrates and restructures other normative orders through symbols and through direct coercion and, at the same time, the way non-state normative orders resist and circumvent penetration' (Merry, 1988: 16). Thus Stuart Henry (1983) describes the way in which cooperatives compete and battle with state law in Britain; and Robert Cover (1983) analyses cases of religious objection to federal regulation of school systems, and colleges as situations of competing legal orders.

In these latter uses, legal pluralism denotes not only the intersection of colonial and customary law, but also the interaction of diverse, competing and resistant normative orders. As in the colonial context, the effort seems to challenge the notion of dominant or state law as the only law, to challenge the state's monopoly of justice claims and, at the same time, to dissociate justice claims and normative discourse from the coercion and violence of the state. An attention to legal pluralism seems to valorize law at the margins while highlighting the role of law in domination by accentuating the resistance organized at the periphery.

As Peter Fitzpatrick states,

> Legal pluralism, in sustaining the idea of a persistent plurality of legal orders has proved an enduring . . . affront to unitary state-centered theories of law. Yet its own relation to the state, and to state law, has been distinctively ambivalent. Some of its adherents attribute no special pre-eminence to the state or even see it as subordinate to other forms. . . . Other adherents prematurely reduce or subordinate plurality to some putative totality, usually the state or state law. I want to argue that both these stands are 'right' . . . state law does take identity in deriving support from other social forms . . . but in the constitution and maintenance of its identity, state law stands in opposition to and in asserted domination over social forms that support it. What is involved overall is a contradictory process of mutual support and opposition. (1984: 2)

The hegemonic reach of state legality, while it frames all social relations, does not constitute their totality. The paradox of liberalism is that its ideology limits its own hegemonic project and thus gives some deference to those places and spaces in the vast interstices of social and legal life where competing normative orders may generate or encourage resistance to state legality (Fitzpatrick, 1984, 1986).

While both law and norms work to produce order, to relegate relations and practices to the realm of the taken for granted, neither is, nor can be, completely successful. Indeed the way dominant power and policy élites work in a liberal state, through the legitimating forms of law, provides points of resistance and opposition (Thompson, 1975; Hay et al., 1975). Moreover, even in conceptions of power which seek to trace its operations beyond the boundaries of the state resistance is arguably always present. As Foucault (1978: 95–6) puts it, 'where there is power there is resistance . . . power relationships . . . depend on a multiplicity of points of resistance. These play the role of adversary, target, support or handle . . .'. Although contained within power, resistances are 'inscribed . . . as an irreducible opposite' (Foucault, 1978: 96). The 'tool kit' of habits, skills, cultures and roles from which people construct patterns of action provides room for challenge and opposition even as it imposes constraints (Swidler, 1986).

Recent work by Kristin Bumiller (1987) exemplifies the way sociologists of law can give voice and credibility to those who question, in a fundamental way, state legality and existing practices and institutions. She provides an example of how it is possible to talk about state legality without adopting the perspective of state officials. Bumiller studied persons who reported that they had suffered some form of insidious discrimination based on age, sex, or race. She reports that they refuse to turn to law in order to avoid the tendency of legal processes to individualize grievances and to require them to speak through a professional, a lawyer. She argues that these tendencies and requisites rob victims of a sense of being in control of their own lives and isolate them from their communities and cultures at a time when they are most in need of support. Her respondents resist a double victimization: first in becoming 'an object' of discrimination and, secondly, in becoming 'a case' in law.

Bumiller argues that the source of this double victimization is deeply embedded in the values and assumptions of liberal legalism. She seeks to call into question the idea of legal intervention itself rather than to recommend one or another particular instance of such intervention. She calls upon her readers to identify with the victims rather than the powerful and to imagine new ways of organizing social life to avoid discrimination and new responses to it. But, most of all, she makes sense of the refusal of victims to give in and to take what the law makes available. She finds in their narratives a powerful, alternative vision of persons and society. In so doing, she questions the capacity of liberal legalism to do much more than inflict further damage upon persons already victimized.

In another study, Carol Greenhouse (1986) describes the resistance to law by an entire community. Greenhouse studied a community of Southern Baptists and showed how their religious beliefs provide a basis for ideas about how conflict or potential conflicts should be overcome or avoided entirely. For the Baptists of Hopewell, Georgia, a white, moderately affluent, newly suburban town, conflict, or its absence, is an indicator of conformity to a Christian life. Ideas about conflict and Christianity are intimately connected with ideas about justice and law. Hopewell's Baptists avoid conflict; they also avoid the law. They do so because to invoke the law, to litigate, to seek the law's dispute-resolving, remedial, or retributive mechanisms necessarily requires invocation of, and by implication deference to, its authority. But such authority is exactly what this community seeks to avoid. 'The people in Hopewell', Greenhouse writes, 'do not consider order to be a matter of complying with rules, nor do they consider that human intervention can accomplish any constructive purpose' (1986: 25). Instead, they believe that social order rests upon a vital individualism that denies any forms of human authority, which is considered inappropriate and illegitimate. Social order depends upon voluntary acts of association and cooperation which challenge and cancel efforts to be unequal. Harmony and equality, the antitheses of conflict and authority, mark the ideal society for Hopewell Baptists. Quarrels, conflict, and resort to authority are sinful, evidence of a fall from grace. Thus while the state is not unimportant in the life of this community, it is anathema to its moral life.

Greenhouse provides a rich description of a community which not only resists the law, and not only imagines another way of living, but demonstrates in its daily life the terms of an alternative social order without the authority of state law as the foundation for that order. It is a community in which 'the cultural conception of order does not consist first or only of rules but . . . of social classifications understood in normative terms'. 'The norms', which form the basis of social order, 'are not commands, or requirements, but explanations and justifications' (Greenhouse, 1986: 25; see also 1982). Hopewell Baptists do not comply or fail to comply with normative rules, as law would suggest; rather they mobilize moral discourses, and embody those discourses in their social roles and conventions. Thus, élite status in the community is marked by the ability to avoid or resolve conflict, 'to stand outside competition, and to symbolize the common desire for communal harmony' (Bailey, 1971: 21; quoted in Greenhouse, 1986: 26). Greenhouse, like Bumiller, illustrates the way sociologists of law can help to notice social practices which question in important ways the naturalness or necessity of state law and its institutions.

Conclusion

Some might ask, what would empirical scholarship on law look like if it resisted scientific attitudes and went beyond state law? We have noted, first and foremost, that we think that sociolegal research would be enriched by more critical attitudes toward one's own data and greater consciousness about the process of construct-ing accounts of the narratives which constitute and comprise our experience of social relations. This is an argument for greater 'self-consciousness about values and contested social visions' (Trubek, 1986: 33). This means being willing to articulate and examine one's own values as part of one's research activities. Perhaps more importantly it means social research which seeks not only to identify and examine rival hypotheses and multiple narratives, but also attempts to keep multiplicity alive, rather than to test and reject – to silence – all but one interpretation and then to present it as *the* interpretation.

Scientism invites arrogance in interpretation (if not in policy recommendations) in which the observer allegedly stands outside the systems of meanings presented. We seek to implicate the observer. This means an even more complicated, subtle investi-gation of the malleability of fact and control of information in which observers are engaged in, or victimized by, the processes they observe. It means that one displaces the aspiration for truth and for an epistemological conquest of the social world with an aspiration for participation, albeit participation at a distance, in the construc-tion of narratives about social life. Finally, it means that the distinction between policy and politics is fundamentally untenable; it is no longer possible to speak to policy élites by claiming the authority of a disinterested science. One cannot speak apolitically about politics.

Secondly, we have noted that sociolegal research needs to explore legality beyond the state, to notice the ways in which control and authority are constructed in a multiplicity of social relations. The focus upon state law assumes and participates in a conception of the social order as a closed system, which imputes to existing social practices a spurious inevitability. Opening the space of law to a terrain not fully colonized by the state not only provides a more subtle and elaborate picture of legality and its connections to power, but it also suggests the possibilities of more varied and abundant locations of resistance. If, as Foucault suggests, there is no central institutional location of social power, if power 'comes from below' through acquiescence in its exercise and through the multiplicity of force relations, then there are no closed systems, no inevitable necessities except as are created through that acquiescence. Each act of consent is potentially an act of resistance, reformation or liberation. Sociolegal research needs to look beyond state law for the ways in which law manufactures consent and generates resistance.

The break from scientism will enable and legitimate research which is intensive and self-conscious, which sees things in their singularity rather than assimilating them to general categories. This turn to the particular will celebrate the varying forms of law instead of regarding variety as itself antithetical to the commitments of the rule of law. A social research which uses multiple lenses will itself more likely observe a more richly textured legality, the spaces as well as the thread, and more likely imagine an alternative legal fabric.

If we take as our subject the constitutive effect of law and the oppositions nurtured by legal pluralism, we cannot be content with literary theory applied to legal doctrine. We must instead study families, schools, workplaces and social movements to present a broad picture in which law may seem at first glance virtually invisible. We will find in these efforts instances which both confirm and contradict the dominant political and legal discourse; we will also find instances which will require us to re-imagine that discourse in a different way. We would then understand law not as something removed from social life, occasionally operating upon social forms, struggling to regulate and shape them, but as inseparable from, and fused with, all social relations and social practices.

To avoid overestimating the effectiveness and stability of legal forms, as we have heretofore overstated the ineffectiveness of law, it is necessary to look neither solely at the efforts at legal instrumentality and change, nor solely at the hegemonic realm of conformity, but at the ways in which issues, people, problems move from one domain to the other. With renewed attention to the role of intellectual resources, the stock of established expertise and symbols (Block and Burns, 1986; Swidler, 1986) available not only to agents of the state but to citizens as well, we can observe and participate in struggles to break from the hegemonic realm and to precipitate fundamental legal change.

Notes

Research for this chapter was supported, in part, by the Overacker Fund of Wellesley College.

1   As Kant (1949: 132) put it, 'Enlightenment is man's exodus from his self-incurred tutelage. Tutelage is the inability to use one's understanding without the

guidance of another person. This tutelage is self-incurred if its cause lies not in any weakness of understanding, but in indecision and lack of courage to use the mind without the guidance of another. Dare to know.'

2   Descartes (1958: 130–1), often thought to be an exponent of abstract, pure reason, saw the Enlightenment as making possible 'A practical philosophy, by means of which, knowing the force and the action of fire, water, of the stars, of the heavens . . . we may . . . employ them in all the uses for which they are suited, thus rendering ourselves the masters and possessors of nature.'

3   Not everyone who does sociological research seeks as an audience those who make or administer the law; there are several prominent examples and arguments to the contrary. (See Black, 1976; Friedman, 1986.)

References

Abel, Richard (1980) 'Redirecting Social Studies of Law', *Law and Society Review*, 14: 805.

Bailey, F.G. (1971) *Gifts and Poison: The Politics of Reputation*. Oxford: Basil Blackwell.

Black, Donald (1976) *The Behavior of Law*. New York: Academic Press.

Block, F. and Burns, G.A. (1986) 'Productivity as a Social Problem', *American Sociological Review*, 51: 767.

Blumberg, Abraham (1967) 'The Practice of Law as a Confidence Game', *Law and Society Review*, 1: 15.

Bok, Derek (1983) 'A Flawed System', *Harvard Magazine*, 38.

Bumiller, Kristin (1987) 'Victims in the Shadow of the Law', *Signs*, 12: 421.

Casper, Jonathan and Brereton, David (1984) 'Evaluating Criminal Justice Reforms', *Law and Society Review*, 18: 121.

Chanock, Martin (1985) *Law, Custom and Social Order: The Colonial Experience in Malawi and Zambia*. Cambridge: Cambridge University Press.

Chomsky, Noam (1967) *American Power and the New Mandarins*. New York: Pantheon Books.

Cohen, Felix (1935) 'Transcendental Nonsense and the Functional Approach', *Columbia Law Review*, 34: 809.

Comoroff, Jean (1985) *Body of Power: Spirit of Resistance: Culture and History of a South African People*. Chicago: University of Chicago Press.

Cover, Robert (1983) 'The Supreme Court 1982 Term. Foreword: Nomos and Narrative', *Harvard Law Review*, 97: 4.

Derrida, Jacques (1978) 'Structure, Sign and Play in the Discourse of the Human Sciences', in *Writing and Difference*. Chicago: University of Chicago Press.

Descartes, Rene (1637, 1958), *Discourse on Method*, in *Philosophical Writings*, ed. and tr. Norman Kemp Smith. New York: Modern Library.

Dolbeare, Kenneth and Hammond, Philip (1970) *The School Prayer Decisions*. Chicago: University of Chicago Press.

Dror, Yehezhel (1975) 'Applied Social Science and Systems Analysis', in Irving Louis Horowitz (ed.), *The Use and Abuse of Social Science*, 2nd ed. New Brunswick: Transaction Books.

Ehrlich, Eugen (1936) *Fundamental Principles of the Sociology of Law*. Cambridge, MA: Harvard University Press.

Engel, David (1980) 'Legal Pluralism in an American Community', *American Bar Foundation Research Journal*, 1980: 425.

Engels, Friedrich (1959), 'Socialism: Utopian and Scientific', in *Marx and Engels*, ed. Lewis Feuer. Garden City: Doubleday.

Feeley, Malcolm (1983) *Court Reform on Trial*. New York: Basic Books.

Fitzpatrick, Peter (1984) 'Law and Societies', *Osgoode Hall Law Journal*, 22: 115.

Fitzpatrick, Peter (1986) 'Law, Power and Resistance', unpublished manuscript.

Foucault, Michel (1972) *The Archeology of Knowledge*. New York: Pantheon Books.

Foucault, Michel (1978) *The History of Sexuality*, Vol I. New York: Random House.

Foucault, Michel (1980) *Power/Knowledge*. New York: Pantheon Books.

Freidson, Elliott (1972) *Profession of Medicine*. New York: Dodd, Mead.

Friedman, Lawrence (1986) 'The Law and Society Movement', *Stanford Law Review*, 38: 763.

Gans, Herbert (1975) 'Social Science For Social Policy' in Irving Louis Horowitz (ed.), *The Use and Abuse of Social Science*, 2nd edn. New Brunswick: Transaction Books.

Greenhouse, Carol (1982) 'Looking at Culture, Looking for Rules', *Man*, 17: 58.

Greenhouse, Carol (1986) *Praying For Justice*. Ithaca: Cornell University Press.

Griffiths, John (1981) 'What is Legal Pluralism?', unpublished manuscript.

Hay, Douglas, Linebaugh, Peter, Rule, John, Thompson, E.P. and Winslow, Carl (1975) *Albion's Fatal Tree*. Harmondsworth: Penguin.

Henry, Stuart (1983) *Private Justice*. London: Routledge and Kegan Paul.

Heumann, Milton and Loftin, Colin (1979) 'Mandatory Sentencing and the Abolition of Plea Bargaining', *Law and Society Review*, 13: 393.

Hobbes, Thomas (1839) *English Works*, ed. William Molesworth. London: John Brown.

Hooker, M.B. (1975) *Legal Pluralism: An Introduction to Colonial and Neo-Colonial Laws*. Oxford: Clarendon Press.

Kant, Immanuel (1949) 'What is Enlightenment', in *The Philosophy of Kant*, ed. and tr. Carl Friedrich. New York: Random House.

Kuper, Leo and Smith, M.G. (1969) *Pluralism in Africa*. Berkeley: University of California Press.

Lasch, Christopher (1977) *Haven in a Heartless World*. New York: Basic Books.

Lasswell, Harold and McDougal, Myres (1943) 'Legal Education and Public Policy', *Yale Law Journal*, 52: 203.

Lefstein, Norman, Stapleton, Vaughn and Teitelbaum, Lee (1969) 'In Search of Juvenile Justice', *Law and Society Review*, 3: 491.

Lindblom, Charles and Cohen, David (1979) *Usable Knowledge*. New Haven: Yale University Press.

Llewellyn, Karl (1930), 'A Realistic Jurisprudence – The Next Step', *Columbia Law Review*, 30: 432.

Llewellyn, Karl (1931), 'Some Realism about Realism', *Harvard Law Review*, 44: 1222.

Llewellyn, Karl (1940) 'On Reading and Using the Newer Jurisprudence', *Columbia Law Review*, 40: 581.

Llewellyn, Karl (1960) *The Common Law Tradition – Deciding Appeals*. Boston: Little, Brown & Co.

Llewellyn, Karl (1962) *Jurisprudence: Realism in Theory and Practice*. Chicago: University of Chicago Press.

Locke, John (1890) *Essay concerning Human Understanding*. London.

Loftin, Colin, Heumann, Milton and McDowell, David (1983) 'Mandatory Sentencing of Firearms Violence', *Law and Society Review*, 17: 287.

Macaulay, Stewart (1963) 'Non-contractual Relations in Business', *American Sociological Review*, 28: 55.

Malinowksi, Branislaw (1926) *Crime and Custom in a Savage Society*. Patterson, NJ: Littlefield Adams.

McDougal, Myres (1941) 'Fuller *v*. The American Legal Realists', *Yale Law Journal*, 50: 827.

Merry, Sally (1988) 'Legal Pluralism: A Review Essay', *Law and Society Review*, 22: 689.

Moore, Sally Falk (1973) 'Law and Social Change: The Semi-autonomous Field as an Appropriate Subject of Study', *Law and Society Review*, 7: 719.

Muir, William (1973) *Law and Attitude Change*. Chicago: University of Chicago Press.

Pressman, Jeffrey and Wildavsky, Aaron (1973) *Implementation*. Berkeley: University of California Press.

Putnam, Hilary (1985) *Realism and Reason*. New York: Cambridge University Press.

Quine, W.V.O. (1960) *Word and Object*. Cambridge, MA: MIT Press.

Rajchman, John and West, Cornell (eds) (1985) *Post-analytical Philosophy*. New York: Columbia University Press.

Reisman, David (1941) 'Law and Social Science', *Yale Law Joural*, 50: 636.

Rich, Robert (1977) 'Uses of Social Science Information by Federal Bureaucrats', in Carol Weiss (ed.), *Using Social Research for Policy Making*. Lexington: D.C. Heath.

Robertson, John and Teitelbaum, Paul (1973) 'Optimizing Legal Impact', *Wisconsin Law Review*, 1973: 665.

Rorty, Richard (1979) *Philosophy and the Mirror of Nature*. Princeton: Princeton University Press.

Rorty, Richard (1982) *The Consequences of Pragmatism*. Minneapolis: University of Minnesota Press.

Ross, H. Laurence (1973), 'Law, Science and Accidents', *Law and Society Review*, 2: 3.

Sarat, Austin (1985) 'Legal Effectiveness and Social Studies of Law', *Legal Studies Forum*, 9: 23.

Sarat, Austin and Felstiner, William (1986) 'Law and Strategy in the Divorce Lawyer's Office', *Law and Society Review*, 20: 93.

Sarat, Austin and Felstiner, William (1988) 'Law and Social Relations: Vocabularies of Motive in Lawyer/Client Interaction', *Law and Society Review*, 22: 737.

Scheingold, Stuart (1974) *The Politics of Rights*. New Haven: Yale University Press.

Schlegel, John (1980) 'American Legal Realism and Empirical Social Science-II,' *Buffalo Law Review*, 29: 195.

Silbey, Susan S. (1987) 'Children Studying Law', Paper presented at the 1987 Annual Meeting Law and Society Association, Washington, DC.

Silbey, Susan S. and Sarat, Austin (1987) 'Critical Traditions in Law and Society Research', *Law and Society Review*, 21: 165.

Skolnick, Jerome (1966) *Justice without Trial*. New York: John Wiley & Sons.

Smart, Carol (1987) 'Articulating Law: Family Law and the Exercise of Power'. Unpublished manuscript.

Spragens, Thomas (1981) *The Irony of Liberal Reason*. Chicago: University of Chicago Press.

172   *Susan Silbey and Austin Sarat*

Strauss, Robert (1957) 'Nature and Status of Medical Sociology', *American Sociological Review*, 22: 200.
Swidler, Ann (1986), 'Culture in Action: Symbols and Strategies', *American Sociological Review*, 51: 273.
Thompson, E.P. (1975) *Whigs and Hunters*. New York: Pantheon.
Trubek, David (1984) 'Where the Action is: Critical Legal Studies and Empiricism', *Stanford Law Review*, 36: 575.
Trubek, David (1986) 'Max Weber's Tragic Modernism and the Study of Law in Society', *Law and Society Review*, 20: 573.
Trubek, David and Esser, John (1987) '"Critical Empiricism" in American Legal Studies'. Unpublished paper.
Trubek, David and Galanter, Marc (1974) 'Scholars in Self-estrangement', *Wisconsin Law Review*, 1974: 1062.
Unger, Roberto (1975) *Knowledge and Politics*. New York: Free Press.
Wald, Michael (1967) 'Interrogations in New Haven', *Yale Law Journal*, 76: 1519.
Wasby, Stephen (1970) *The Impact of the United States Supreme Court*. Homewood: Dorsey Press.
White, Stephen and Reim, Michael (1977) 'Can Research Help Policy?', *The Public Interest*, 134.
Yngvesson, Barbara (1985) 'Legal Ideology: Community Justice in the Clerk's Office', *Legal Studies Forum*, 9: 71.
Zeisel, Hans (1982) *The Limits of Law Enforcement*. Chicago: University of Chicago Press.

PART THREE

POLITICS FROM THE FIELD

9

Social Research and the Rationalization of Care

Mary Simms

The 'New Right' would appear to have little in common with the Women's Movement but they would agree that 'the personal is political'. This chapter, by focusing on the 'community care' of the aged in Britain, considers the contribution the personal – the everyday work knowledge of 'social' professionals (for example, community nurses and social workers) – makes to the 'official rationality' – the political. In the context of both the restructuring of public expenditure and the reconstruction of hospital medical care, it examines the development of the ideologies of 'consumer choice' and 'personal responsibility' as 'social' legitimations for 'community care'. As community care, it is argued here, represents an aspect of the broader process of rationalization, it signifies the retrenchment of public care and the restriction of consumer choice *within* the public sector. This poses the question of how social scientists might limit their own contribution to rationalization in order to influence the development of choice.

What is 'community care'?[1] This question has been posed numerous times by lay people, politicians and social scientists, but only a partial answer has been forthcoming: 'community care = family care = female care' (Finch and Groves, 1980). As Johnson (1978) has argued, theoretical deficiency, both in the area of 'community care' and in social gerontology (the study of ageing and the aged), has arisen out of the 'policy orientated' focus of research. Thus the research 'problem' typically conforms to 'the problem' of old age as expressed by successive governments in official documents. Although the degree of emphasis and focus of this 'problem' varies, it is typically set against a demographic and economic backcloth (that is, the growing number of elderly people over 75 years of age in the population and the 'costs' this implies in terms of public expenditure).[2]

Thus, in the 1950s the development of geriatric medicine spawned epidemiological studies concerned with the measurement of clinical morbidity, and variables such as nutrition and incontinence and their relationship to social variables (see Johnson, 1978). This interest and indeed the development of geriatric medicine paralleled the then Conservative government's concern over the growing cost of the National Health Service, particularly the cost of the chronic care of the aged in hospital (Phillips Report, 1954; Guillebaud Report, 1956; Boucher Report, 1957).

By the late 1950s and early 1960s, while research interest continued to focus on 'sociomedical' issues, it was increasingly directed towards social factors leading to hospital admission. Now the parts playing by primary health care, social service care and the family in the care of the aged became incorporated within the sphere of research interest (Abel-Smith and Titmuss, 1956; Shenfield, 1957; Townsend, 1957; Townsend and Wedderburn, 1962–3). Government concern over the cost of the hospital care of the aged, particularly that of chronic care, continued to be expressed. During this period geriatric medicine continued to develop and the chronic care of the aged was progressively excluded from hospital medicine's sphere of interest, being defined instead as a 'social' problem. This development was signified by government policy on hospital 'rehabilitation' combined with 'community care' (see *Hospital Plan for England and Wales*, 1962; *Health and Welfare: The Development of Community Care*, 1963).

The restructuring of public expenditure from the late 1960s has been paralleled with the publication of government reports, the main theme of which is the prevention of 'need' for public residential care. Conversely, these advocate the greater involvement of the more 'economic' public domiciliary and 'private' carers, (that is, both formal and informal voluntary, and market purchased carers), in the community care of the aged (for example the Seebohm Report, 1968; DHSS, 1976a; 1976b; 1977; 1978; 1981a; 1981b; Griffiths Report, 1988; Wagner Report, 1988). Moreover, research produced during this period typically continues the 'anti-institution' theme generated by the theoretical work of Goffman (1968) and the empirical works of Sheldon (1961) and Robb (1967) in the 1960s. Thus it is assumed that care provided inside public residential institutions is 'inhumane' while care provided outside them by public and private carers – in 'the community' – is 'humane' (for example Davies and Challis, 1980; Willcocks et al., 1983; 1987).

The process of 'community care' represents a manifestation of this segmentalization of the care of the aged. Thus, in the 1950s community care denoted *care, other than the acute* (e.g. chronic care), *provided outside hospitals*. By the late 1960s and early 1970s community care denoted *care provided outside public residential institutions*, and from the mid-1970s community care has been employed to refer to *care provided outside public residential institutions increasingly by private carers*.

The process of community care therefore involves the transfer of responsibility for aspects of the public care of the aged (for example, chronic care), away from central government-funded and predominantly male, hospital 'medical' care, to professional and non-professional, predominantly female, 'social' carers funded to a greater extent by local authorities, and on to 'private', again predominantly female, formal and informal, voluntary, and market-purchased carers. This process has been manifested in the establishment of formal channels of *collaboration* between hospitals and local authorities at the time of the reorganization of the NHS, when Joint Consultative Committees and Joint Care Planning Teams were set up, and joint funding arrangements were implemented.[3] Parallels can be drawn between this development in Britain and the 'decentralization' of financial responsibility for 'social problems' like the care of the aged, described by political economists in the United States (see Estes, 1979; and Minkler, 1983). As Minkler states:

> In the United States, a key response to the sagging economy and the need for less costly 'solutions' to social problems has been to attempt to shift responsibility for many social problems from the federal to the state and local levels, and ideally to push them out of government and onto a supposedly vast and willing private and/or voluntary sector. (1983: 160)

This individualization and retrenchment of public care has been legitimated by the related ideologies of 'personal' and 'family responsibility' for ill health and care, and 'consumer choice', and on the grounds that public residential care is inhumane.

It follows that this relationship between social research and the rationalization of care has not only militated against the development of theory but it has contributed to the retrenchment of aspects of public care, thereby restricting 'choice' for the aged and their families *within* the public sector. Drawing from the accounts of community nurses and social workers this chapter considers the contribution these social professionals have made to this process. In this context the political question posed is, 'How might social scientists limit their contribution to this process in order to facilitate the expansion of choice through the development of public-sector care?'

The personal is political

While the production of policy-orientated research proliferates in the 1980s, there are important examples of theoretical trail-blazing. This takes the form of the political economy theory represented by the work of Walker (1981), and Townsend (1981) in the British context and Estes (1979) and Minkler (1983) in the United States, and the feminist position of Finch and Groves (1980; 1983) and Finch (1984). However, while providing important insights into the politics and economics of social policy, these are set apart from human construction. Conversely, the economics and politics of policy become factors which 'determine' or 'construct' dependency *within* the aged or 'pull' female carers 'back into domestic caring roles' (Finch and Groves, 1980: 503). It follows that the politics of 'community care', and social policy generally, become reified at this theoretical level, that is these products of human activity are apprehended as 'non-human, non-humanizable, inert facticities' (Berger and Luckmann, 1967; 106). In short, to these structuralist theories, while the macro is political – the personal is not.

Conversely the interpretative sociology of Weber (1949), Schutz (1962; 1967; 1970a; 1970b), Berger and Luckman (1967), Berger et al. (1974) and Berger and Kellner (1981), assumes social structure, social policy, the 'official rationality' to represent a product of the rationalizations of individuals and groups. Therefore theory must be grounded at this level of meanings. Thus, it is assumed that just as different groups participate to varying degrees in the formulation of community-care policy, so they contribute to the practice of this policy. Just as the 'political' is not something 'out there' but a part of our own rationalizations manifest in our everyday courses of action, so the economic is an aspect of everyday life which influences and constrains actions, in turn those actions contribute to the official rationality.

While the interpretative perspective places preeminent importance on grounding theory at this level of meanings, it is assumed that the meanings of some groups have a greater influence on the meanings and actions of others and thus make a greater contribution to the official rationality. As Giddens states: 'Even a transient conversation between two persons is a relation of power to which the participants may bring unequal resources . . . meanings which are made to count expressing "asymmetries of power"' (1976: 53). In the area of the health care of the aged, these groups (for example, doctors, nurses, social workers, social scientists) – the middle classes – have gained a monopoly over certain sections of specialized knowledge/power through a process of 'exclusionary social closure' (Parkin, 1979). However, this limited circle of eligibles or 'professions' by no means forms a homogeneous group, and power differentials exist both *within* and *between* them, arising out of the monopolization of different *types* of knowledge. These professions in turn, albeit to varying degrees, make the 'most direct contribution to the rationalization of culture' (Giddens, 1976: 115). (Note that the term 'profession' is employed here in the broader sense outlined by Strong (1979) which includes social scientists.)

Relationships, segmentalization and social process

These asymmetries and symmetries of power constituting social relationships provide the key to understanding changes in rationalizations, the development of social processes, and changes in the official rationality. While Schutz devoted little time to explicit discussion of power differentials, this was implied in sections of his work. Thus, he stated that relevances (knowledge) could be '*imposed*' onto individuals/groups in the course of relationships 'by their fellowmen' (Schutz, 1970a: 119). In another text this relationship between power knowledge and social process has been taken further:

Imposed on us as relevant are situations and events which are not connected with interests chosen by us, which do not originate in acts of our own discretion and which we have to take just as they are, without any power to modify them by our spontaneous activities, except by *transferring the relevances thus imposed into intrinsic relevances.* (Schutz, 1970b: 114; my emphasis)

As new relevances are imposed on to, for example, a community nurse by a general practitioner, this disrupts the sedimented knowledge of the former and her knowledge is subsequently reconstructed. This reconstruction takes the form of the extension of knowledge to incorporate former 'medical' relevances and the 'covering over' of aspects of knowledge formerly 'intrinsic' to nursing care. As Schutz illustrates:

The phenomenon of 'covering', of the disappearance of the former topical relevances behind the newly emergent ones . . . will become of particular importance for the theory of social action, which will be characterized by the fact that to the actor, the other's (my fellowman's) intrinsic relevances are imposed, they delimit the freedom of displaying and following up his own system of intrinsic relevances. In any sense there is an element of surprise inherent to the newly emergent and unanticipated relevances which supersede and cover the former set . . . Where a topic is dropped in the sense of being covered over by another one, it was essential that the newly emergent problem was connected with the first in such a way that the former either extended or restricted the plan of the latter. (1970a: 113–17)

As the nurses' 'commitment' to aspects of care declines in this way, this care is imposed on subordinate professionals (that is, social workers), and non-professional public and private carers. This segmentalization of knowledge/care, and thus the changing boundaries of professional and non-professional care, medical and social care, and public and private care, creates social processes like so-called community care, and thereby changes in the official rationality.

The degree to which knowledge/care is segmentalized indicates, as the accounts of community nurses and social workers illustrate below, the development of the process of community care and the changing 'politics' of these carers. This development emerged in the second part of interview accounts in replies to questions focusing on their relationships with the (more powerful) medical profession, and (less powerful) public and private non-professional carers. These replies indicated medical pressures for change, and the subsequent reconstruction and further segmentalization of care. This served to demonstrate the necessity of understanding the work, its changing quality, and the politics of individuals and groups in the *context* of their relationships with significant others. This provides a picture of the changing face of care, of social processes and ultimately the changing official rationality which is largely inaccessible to more segmented analysis.

This process of the reconstruction and segmentalization of knowledge also occurs in the course of social scientists' relationships with other, more powerful professions. A manifestation of this is sociology 'in' medicine, for example, the adoption of doctor-defined 'problems' and an acceptance of medically defined deviation as 'fact' rather than adopting a sociology-of-knowledge approach to medical knowledge (see Freidson, 1970). The policy implications of this development are discussed later.

In a more direct way, as Oakley (1981) and Cornwell (1984) have illustrated, relationships established between the researcher and those interviewed in the course of fieldwork can influence the development of accounts and ultimately of theory. Thus Cornwell's study of working-class health beliefs was distinguished by the development away from initial public accounts to later private accounts, a development partly accounted for by the gradual and partial dissolution of the asymmetrical researcher–subject relationship. Although my study of community care was restricted to single but lengthy interviews with carers, the development of the accounts of community nurses and social workers indicated a progression away from official to unofficial meanings. This contrasted with the accounts of hospital medical carers, which typically stayed at the level of the official. This progression, while associated with symmetries of power *within* the researcher–subject relationship (for example shared class, gender, and interest in 'the social'), was also, as previously stated, stimulated by questions on these professionals' relationships with more and less powerful groups.

Thus, due in this case to the symmetrical power relationships established between researcher and subjects, the accounts of social professionals developed. New relevances were consequently imposed on my consciousness (that is, knowledge deviating from that expected), thereby extending my theoretical constructs and introducing new but connected lines of inquiry.[4] This progression in accounts was therefore vital for understanding the reconstruction and further segmentalization of care in the 1980s, and for the development of the theory and politics of community care.

It follows that it would be both contrary to the main tenets of interpretative sociology and theoretically unproductive to predefine the boundaries of 'the field' (that is, significant groups and lines of inquiry), in the way that statistical sampling dictates in survey research. Conversely, following the logic of 'theoretical sampling' (Glaser and Strauss, 1967), the boundaries of the field rested on developing hypotheses and theory, and could be contracted or extended according to theoretical relevance. An analysis of government reports and social research provided the initial sampling and question framework for semi-structured tape-recorded interviews involving professional and non-professional carers, and chronic-care elderly people. Interviews took place during the period 1983 to 1985, in two localities: an inner-city and a semi-rural area. Drawing from the accounts of community nurses and social workers working in the semi-rural locality, the social construction of the theory, practice, and politics of part of the process of community care is described. This focuses on the reconstruction of 'choice' as a legitimation for community care and therefore for the retrenchment of aspects of public care. Fictitious names are employed throughout.

The social professionals

The ideology of 'choice'
At the outset of interviews, community nurses and social workers in the semi-rural locality emphasized the importance of choice in the context of a recognition of a plurality of cultures. Thus, an emphasis was placed on the nurses not imposing their own culture on to patients, but instead adapting to cultural differences. This profess-

ionalism in its social manifestation was typically contrasted with the growing absolutism of hospital care. As Mandy Chance, a community nurse manager, illustrated:

> In the community you can't go up to a patient and say, 'Right, you go in that bath; you do this, you do that'. Quite often in the hospital you say, 'You've got to have a bath', and they come and have it. I mean you can't treat patients like that. I mean, you're in their home, you must always remember that in the community, you're a visitor in their home, you can't force them. You wouldn't force them in hospital, but there's a certain – if they're in hospital you can say, 'Oh, it's your treatment. You have to have a bath.' You go up to a patient and they say 'I don't want a wash today', I just have to sort of say, 'Well, let's do your hands and face today'. You do that and you say, 'Well, I can do a little bit more', and you work your way around them.

Social workers also emphasized the importance of 'choice' to the professionalism of social work. As Joy West, a hospital social worker illustrates below, this involved adopting a mediative position between, the increasingly absolutist medical scientists, and the less powerful patient/client:

> You still get it as much as you try to break it down, particularly with the elderly: 'Doctor says' . . . We go spare at times because we go up or we get a referral to go and see a person and you do an introduction and you ask them about going into a Home and they say immediately, 'The doctor says it would be better if I . . .', and you see it's there then. And you say, 'Well, would you like to go home or into a Home.' And they say, 'Well, really I would like to go home but the doctor says . . .'. If you like, part of the change in that phrase has been done because they see that person as a powerful person, and if doctor says I've got to go then I've got to go . . . So you go back to the consultant and you say, 'You know Mrs B really does want to go back home'.

As interviews progressed, nurses and social workers described changes in the knowledge and practice of geriatric medicine, signified by the increasing restriction of hospital medical provision to acute care, and a decline in commitment to chronic care. Manifestations of this further segmentalization of care were 'borderline' and 'crisis' boundary discharges of chronic-care patients, and the planned closure of chronic-care wards and hospitals. As the professional boundaries of geriatric medicine were reconstructed to exclude chronic care, the process of community care advanced to refer to *chronic care provided outside hospitals by subordinate public and private 'social' carers.* Within this context community nurses, and especially social workers, described the implications of this retrenchment of public care for the chronic-care aged in terms of the curtailment of the *choice* to receive long-stay care in a hospital bed.

The reconstruction of community nursing and social work

As accounts unfolded, the influence of the reconstruction of hospital medicine on the subordinate, predominantly female 'social' professionals became evident. This was manifest in the further restriction of the professional interest of nurses to acute 'nursing' care (for example, dressings and treatments), the majority of which is concentrated in the middle-aged. In turn, Part III, Section 2 (i) of the National Assistance Act (1948), makes local authority social services departments responsible for the care and attention of the aged when it was 'not otherwise available to them'. When social workers were first questioned about the criteria for entry to local authority residential Homes or Part III Homes (that is, 'Part III fit'), they assumed that this was a 'factual' and non-contentious issue (that is, 'If they're ill and in need of any sort of medical attention then it's a hospital and medical responsibility'.). However, as questions continued, the changing professional boundaries of 'medical', 'nursing' and 'social' need became evident, with the consequent ambiguity of the concept 'Part III fit', and the gradual inclusion of chronic care within the boundaries of social work:

> *MS*: It seems to me that the person who requires chronic care is caught between hospital–medical need and need for residential care.
> *Morris Green*: Yes, he or she is in limbo. It is an unfortunate thing that happens time and time again . . . If you take double incontinence, for example, they (geriatricians) wave a lot of that aside. They say, 'Oh, he's doubly incontinent but we can manage with toilet correction and rehabilitation'. . . . Now years ago they wouldn't have discussed that case . . . So we're letting up a little bit and it's not only from the physical aspects of care, it's also from the mental – we've let up there.

Social workers with relatively long histories of work in this area pinpointed the most visible change in admission procedure to residential Homes as occurring from the late 1970s onwards. Thus, when Jane Murray, a field social worker, started working with the aged in the early 1970s, she described the typical admission as bordering on 'olympic athlete' standard who would be expected to spend the remainder of their lives, (at least ten years) in the Home. Joy West also noticed when returning to her work after a short break from 1977 to 1978, that the admission of elderly incontinent patients or clients to local authority Homes represented a significant departure from former practice. Therefore, a manifestation of the reconstruction of the rationalizations of social workers and therefore of 'need' for social service care, was that priority was given to the chronic-care aged, to former 'medical' criteria of need.

As accounts unfolded, a range of degrees or a continuum (that is greater–lesser) of commitment to 'social' care, and a decline in this commitment, became evident. The latter emerged in questions focusing on preventive health care, public residential care, and private, market-purchased care, and was signified by a movement away from an acknowledgement of cultural pluralism to a more absolutist position and by a decline in commitment to public care. This development was important as it indicated the further segmentalization of care and thus the development of community care. Moreover, it signified the retrenchment of public care and therefore the reduction of choice *within* the public sector. As community care was legitimated on the ground of choice, this development in accounts precipitated a reappraisal of the politics of community care within this broader-meaning context.

The further segmentalization of community nursing

'Community care' is chronic care provided outside hospitals by subordinate public and private carers. In replies to questions on preventive health care, nurses typically described their implementation of central government policy (DHSS, 1976b; 1977) and the Regional Health Authority guidelines relating to 'health education'. This involved encouraging individuals and their families to take responsibility for health care, by 'promoting changes in lifestyles'. The aim of this was to avoid the development of acute 'medical' problems and therefore hospital admission. As Mrs Collins, a nurse manager stated:

> *MS*: Do you think your work is partially preventive?
> *Mrs Collins*: Yes, I think we are doing it all the time. It doesn't matter whether you are dealing with a leg ulcer or with a diabetic, you find you are automatically giving them advice. Whether they take it or not – that is another matter. But if someone has a fall you say, 'Well you *shouldn't* have that mat there, you *should* do away with that mat and loose bits and things. You *should* be careful getting in and out of the bath, and can you get in and out of the bath all right? Are you eating a good diet and are you going to the toilet, and why don't you try having so and so?' And I think you find without thinking about it, these things come out. And you come out and think, 'Heavens, you've given all that advice to prevent things from occurring in the future and how to help improve their health and safety generally with all the things that are available for them today . . . It's not the problem they've got at this particular moment, it's their *whole life and lifestyle*. (my emphasis)

Health education, 'lifestylism' (Rodmell and Watt, 1986) or 'healthism' (Crawford, 1980) signified the further segmentalization of nursing care. Through this process the whys and hows (for example: Why did I develop an acute problem? Why did I need medical treatment? And how do I prevent an acute problem?), become reduced to immediate individualistic relevances (that is, diet, loose rugs, cleanliness, smoking, etc.), in short, 'lifestyle'. This removes responsibility from the collectivity for aspects of ill health and care (e.g. chronic care), and subsequently places it with individuals and/or their families thereby retrenching public care. Moreover, this development signifies a further decline in the recognition of cultural pluralism and growing professional absolutism more typical of the model of hospital care described and criticized by nurses at the outset.

Within this broader meaning context it appeared that the ideology of choice as initially defined by nurses conflicted with the practice of health education, the aim of which was to change lifestyles in accordance with what was deemed agreeable to the middle-class professional. This practice therefore assumed that the population of this locality was homogeneous rather than pluralist, that there were no economic or social constraints on the actions of sections of the population, and that all people concerned *should* (i.e. have no 'choice' other than to) conform to professional advice. This stage in the segmentalization of care was consequently manifest in a double-bind situation referred to as the 'cultural pluralism–moral absolutism dilemma'. Thus on the one hand the nurse could not 'impose' herself, her culture onto the patient, but on the other hand she was unable to 'change lifestyles' without doing so.

A further decline in commitment to social care was indicated by the development of 'victim blaming'. Thus some nurses were beginning to 'blame' patients for the development of an acute 'nursing' or 'medical' problem if they had failed (either through choice and/or due to economic constraint) to change their lifestyle in accordance with professional directives. They would then be temporarily removed from this cultural context, in order to receive the necessary type of acute care in the more absolutist context of the hospital.

Nurses' replies to questions focusing on the role of market-purchased care again indicated the further segmentalization of care, signified by the increasing acceptance of the part played by the private sector in 'community care'; a development legitimated on the grounds of choice. Again, this development was understood in the context of restrictions on public expenditure and changes in medical constructions of 'need' for hospital care. Thus the middle ground on the continuum of commitment to social care/public care, was occupied by nurses committed to a mixed economy; the coexistence of public and private care. For example, Mandy Chance, a nurse manager, argued that private nursing Homes were 'a great help' as they provided convalescent care for the elderly (boundary) hospital discharge. She felt that this extension of care into the private sector should continue, with the qualification that private Homes were adequately supervised. One extreme on this range of commitment to social care (that is, lesser commitment), was represented by Linda Smith. Consistent with her approach to preventive health care, she argued the case that people should be personally responsible for their own health care, and not the State:

> *Linda Smith*: A lot of them, I'm thinking about younger nurses doing their training and coming up, rather than in my age range, are in the union and things like that and the union seems to have an indoctrinating influence on them. Private, they think, is bad, because it's taking everything away from the masses. I don't think it is because it's an extra that if you can afford to pay for you are not depriving others who need to use the NHS . . .
>
> *MS*: Perhaps they would argue that not everyone has the freedom to choose in this country, there is a growing number of unemployed and they haven't got the freedom to choose?[5]
>
> *Linda Smith*: They've got the freedom to choose more than if it was a completely run country like others where you can't choose anything . . . You don't have to be without money these days because it's not that people haven't got money. Like the lady who wouldn't go into hospital because she would lose her social security [referred to earlier in a question on preventive health care]. She's got the money, she just doesn't spend it as she should do. I mean she has no money over her rent and rates. All she has to find is something for her heating and food virtually. Because she doesn't go out, she's not well enough to go out, so she shouldn't spend anything going out and she has the extras of social security that come in. I just don't think she spends it properly. They need more educating how to spend their money, how to use the money that they've got . . .

Therefore as nurses' accounts unfolded they indicated a further decline in commitment to social care and thus the further segmentalization and retrenchment of public care. This was manifested in the process of community care, which now referred to *chronic care provided outside hospitals by subordinate public and private carers*. The reconstruction of the ideology of choice has paralleled this reconstruction and individualization of responsibility for health and care. Thus, at the outset of interviews choice was employed in the context of an acknowledgement of cultural pluralism. As interviews progressed the growing moral absolutism of community nursing emerged and choice was then employed in the context of an assumption of cultural homogeneity. Thus, it was assumed that all people were free to 'choose' healthier lifestyles, or to choose *between* public and private care. However, as public care is segmentalized and retrenched and the process of community care develops, 'choice' for the aged is reduced. This was linguistically signified by nurses: for example, the aim of preventive health care was to 'keep' the aged in 'the community' – outside hospitals, and it was felt that the aged 'should' change those aspects of their 'lifestyles' which might influence the development of an acute problem. If they 'chose' not to, then they would be 'blamed' for the development of an acute problem.

Consideration will now be given to the development of the politics of community care in the accounts of social workers, before turning to the implications of this research for the theory and methodology of social research.

The further segmentalization of social work

'Community care' is care provided outside public residential Homes by subordinate public and private carers. As former 'medical' criteria (that, is chronic care), has taken priority in the hierarchy of need for social service care, former 'social' criteria have been further subjugated. Thus, while the elderly previously living alone were found to be given priority over those living with relatives for residential places, Willcocks' (1982) study of residential care found this section of the elderly population to be taking up a *larger percentage* of the places in Homes.[6] It follows, that the 'choices' available *within* public care, for the lonely but physically fit aged and the chronic-care aged living with relatives, were subsequently reduced.

When bringing this additional interpretationally relevant material to bear on the concept of choice as first described by social workers, it appeared that this was typically referred to in the context of the aged remaining *outside public Homes*, either in the hospital, or more typically, in 'the community'. Thus, social workers argued that the gradual assimilation of chronic care within the professional jurisdiction of social work, and the subsequent superordination of medical criteria of need for local authority residential care, led to the subjugation of the 'choices' available for those clients requiring chronic care who wished to remain *in their own homes*. As Karen Salter, a field social worker illustrated:

> We spend a lot of time fighting for people's rights, protecting them . . . I mean he [the coroner], and one of the geriatricians at the local hospital have both clearly stated that they are appalled that elderly people are allowed to live like that in the community, they should have no choice. They shouldn't need to sign a document to say that they are agreeable.

The geriatrician actually said to me the other day when we were arguing, 'She cannot return home, she has to go into Part III, she is too much at risk, Part III'. I went to see the old person, she said she didn't want to go into a Home: 'I want to go back home.' I knew she couldn't manage, I knew we could maintain her in her home up to a limited degree. We talked about it two to three weeks on the go, she never changed her mind. We ended up, the consultant and I, over a desk haggling over it, the consultant saying in the end, 'Take her. You don't need her signature.' I said, 'No, I'm not taking her against her will.' That's the other thing that frightens me about the elderly; it won't be long before the law is changed and we become the SS not the Social Services. That's what worries me, that people like the coroner will get their own way and the law will be changed and they will be signed away because they are too much of a nuisance in the community. And that will be a very sad day because we are talking about basic human rights there . . .

Thus Karen Salter describes a further decline in hospital medical commitment to 'social' knowledge/care and growing professional absolutism (that is, the patient/client 'shouldn't need to sign a document to say that they are agreeable' to go into a public Home). Thus the protection of the 'rights' and 'choices' of the elderly client is referred to in the context of the aged remaining *outside public residential Homes*. Rarely was 'choice' employed to refer to the 'choice' of the aged to be admitted to local authority Homes or the evident reduction of choice *within* public care for the aged 'socially' in 'need' of this care.

While the degree of commitment to social care/public care within social work in this semi-rural locality was typically greater than that found in community nursing, choice was also employed by some social workers, to legitimate the further inclusion of private-market purchased care in community care. Again, this development was understood in the context of restrictions on public expenditure and the reconstruction of hospital care. For as local authority social services departments have gradually gained responsibility for chronic care, some of the aged considered to lie on the boundaries of medical–social need – 'in limbo' – were being admitted to private nursing homes. While social workers typically explained this limited liaison with the Heads of private Homes through recourse to the financial restrictions on local authorities, 'choice' was employed by a few to legitimate this development. The aged, it was now argued, as it was in the Seebohm Report (1968), should have the freedom to choose, not simply between centrally funded and local authority funded care, but between public and private market-purchased care.

Therefore, as social workers' accounts unfolded they indicated the further segmentalization and retrenchment of care, manifested in the process of community care (that is, care provided outside public Homes, increasingly by private carers). As in the accounts of community nurses in this semi-rural locality, the reconstruction of the ideology of choice had paralleled this reconstruction and individualization of responsibility for care. Thus, as interviews developed, choice was typically employed in the context of the aged remaining *outside* public Homes, and choice *between* public and private care. However, as care is further segmentalized and the process of community care develops, choice for the aged within public care is reduced. Thus, as former 'medical' criteria (for example, chronic care) subjugate former 'social' criteria of need for social service care, the choices of the chronic-care aged with family carers or the physically fit but lonely elderly person, within the public sector, are restricted. This development was linguistically signified by social workers; thus the aged were typically 'kept' or 'contained' in 'the community' – outside public Homes.

Rationalization and the politics of 'community care'

The accounts of community nurses and social workers illustrate that the process of community care is constituted by the segmentalization of the care of the aged. This individualization and retrenchment of public care, as the diagram below illustrates, has been paralleled by the reconstruction of the politics of 'the social'; the ideologies of 'personal responsibility' and 'consumer choice' legitimating this development. Moreover, this process of community care, and to a lesser degree the changing politics of the social, represent products of working relationships with other more and less powerful groups, which are in turn constrained by the changing economics of care (Figure 1).

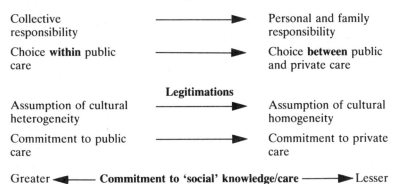

Collective responsibility	⟶	Personal and family responsibility
Choice **within** public care	⟶	Choice **between** public and private care
Legitimations		
Assumption of cultural heterogeneity	⟶	Assumption of cultural homogeneity
Commitment to public care	⟶	Commitment to private care

Greater ◀— **Commitment to 'social' knowledge/care** —▶ Lesser

Figure 1   *The process of community care and the changing politics of 'the social'*

Until now, description of community care has drawn from the accounts of social professionals in a semi-rural locality. However, the accounts of community nurses in an inner-city locality indicated that the process of community care was less advanced there. For example, inner-city community nurses typically described the adverse effects (for example, shortage of time for discussion or reassurance), that the further segmentalization of nursing care had upon the aged. Also an assumption of cultural pluralism underpinned their replies to questions focusing on preventive health care and market-purchased care. Thus, the influence of economic and social factors on health and the subsequent constraints this might place on the ability of patients to change their 'lifestyles' in order to prevent the development of acute problems, was emphasized, and 'victim blaming' was not evident.

Moreover, while many inner-city nurses had experienced limited involvement with private-sector care due to the retrenchment of public care, they were typically opposed in principle to its expansion as it was 'profiting' and was not accountable to the State which, it was argued, paved the way to abuse. Finally, choice was typically rejected as a legitimation for the expansion of private care. Instead, inner-city nurses argued that more resources should be introduced into the Welfare State to increase the choices *within* public care, and choice for all rather than a few. In short, collective provision was considered the *morally justified* reward for collective contribution to production in previous years.

When looking at the process of community care in the context of changes in medical knowledge, it can be seen to represent an aspect of the larger process of the rationalization of culture which is manifested in health care by the process of medicalization (Cornwell, 1984). Illich (1977) describes persuasively, if overstatedly (see Cornwell, 1984), the expansionist face of medical science in the medicalization of life thesis. He argues that this process involves the increasing tendency for social deviance to be labelled a medical–scientific problem. The importance of Illich's thesis lies in his observation that as medical science develops, areas of life are labelled medical problems which removes moral accountability from lay people. Such expansion was evident in the initial development of the specialty of geriatric medicine in the 1950s, and in its continued growth.

However, Illich fails to acknowledge the segmentalization of care accompanying medicalization. This oversight appears to be related to the assumption of 'medical imperialism' (Strong, 1979) which underpins his thesis (Cornwell, 1984). In consequence he fails to consider the parts played (albeit to varying degrees) by others constituting the hierarchy of care and therefore their *active* participation in the medicalization of care. This oversight limits substantially the explanatory value of the medicalization thesis. Thus, as hospital medical knowledge has increased and care has become further segmentalized the jurisdictions of subordinate 'social' professionals have extended to incorporate aspects of former 'medical' care (for example, chronic care). Social service departments have in turn become financially and morally account-able for chronic care which has become superordinate in criteria of 'need' for social service care. Conversely, the commitment of social workers to aspects of former social knowledge/care has declined, and the process of community care has developed. This medical-ization and segmentalization of care then continues to influence all groups in the hierarchy of care, from public medical to public social to private family carers. In short, Illich's thesis of medicalization was modified by this study to incorporate *all* of the hierarchy of care.

As knowledge is hierarchically organized, rationalization is progressive. Thus, as the accounts of community nurses and social workers illustrate, while the predominantly male, hospital-based medical profession make the biggest contribution to this process (and within this hierarchy, surgery, and to a far lesser extent psychiatry and geriatric medicine), the social, predominantly female professions make a lesser contribution, and so on down the hierarchy. Moreover, in areas of social and economic deprivation such as the inner-city locality, rationalization was found to be less advanced across all groups, than in the semi-rural locality.

The concept of progression, as Cornwell (1984) has illustrated, is evident in Habermas's theory of the rationalization of culture. Habermas (1971), drawing from the works of Weber and Marcuse has argued that rationalization is the key process involved in 'modernization'. This is constituted by the social extension of sub-systems of purposive–rational action signified by the institutional-ization of scientific and technical knowledge. When this new type of power-legitimating tradition interacts with the traditional 'action-orientating' legitimations derived from religious, moral and meta-physical beliefs, the latter lose their 'cogency' and break down (Habermas, 1971: 99). Through description of the reconstruction of rationalizations constituting the rationalization of care a plurality of legitimations have been revealed. Thus, both traditional, or 'human-itarian', and modern or 'utilitarian' types of legitimations, were found to coexist, the former being progressively subjugated by the latter. Thus the reconstruction of the politics of 'the social' was understood in the context of the rationalization of culture/care.

Rationalization and the politics of social research

The rationalization of culture is manifest in social science research into public care provision, as in the execution of this care itself, in the segmentalization of knowledge and a declining commitment to context for understanding need for public care. This is signified by the growth of 'causal', aetiological, and policy-orientated research, or 'abstracted empiricism' (Wright Mills, 1970) as described at the beginning of this chapter.

Such abstracted empiricism typically focuses on one area of care (for example local authority residential Homes, family care, the elderly), in isolation to its *relationships* with other areas of care (for example hospital medicine, community nursing, social service care, and market-purchased care) and in isolation to the changing politics and economics of this care. It subsequently fails to explain changes in the knowledge, politics, and practices of these various areas of care, and subsequently within the elderly population. Thus, while studies (for example Willcocks, 1982) have observed that the degree of infirmity of residents in public residential Homes has progressively increased over the last ten to twenty years, no *explanation*, other than that of demography, has been proffered. Furthermore, no explanation has been proffered for what appear to be contradictory sets of statistics relating to residential care, namely the *increase* in the number of people in local authority Homes (from 152 000 in 1978 to 172 000 in 1983), and the effective *fall* in the provision of places in Homes since 1978 (Grundy and Arie, 1982).

By adopting an interpretative approach to the community care of the aged and looking at changes in the knowledge of professional groups, including that of medical specialties, an explanation for the above findings may be proffered. Thus, drawing on the accounts of community nurses and social workers described above, the rising degree of frailty among residents of Homes and consequent decreasing length of stay could explain the greater 'turnover' of places in the Homes. The latter can, in turn, be seen to be related to changes in medical knowledge and therefore criteria of need for hospital care.

The rationalization of knowledge can also lead, as the accounts of community nurses in the semi-rural locality illustrated, to victim-blaming. Thus abstracted empiricism might lead to local authorities in areas of acute economic and social deprivation being blamed for poor conditions in their residential Homes, and this would in turn contribute to the rationalization of public care on humanitarian grounds. Similarly, social scientists might ask, 'Why do some elderly people fail to take responsibility for their own health care?'

Empiricists attempting to answer this question by focusing on the aged in isolation to the broader context of care would end up 'blaming' the elderly people concerned.

Abstracted empiricism has consequently generated absolutist recommendations and ultimately policy initiatives which are incompatible with the lives and 'choices' of sections of the population. Thus abstracted empirical studies of local authority residential Homes have contributed to the theme underpinning current government policy that care provided *outside public* residential Homes – community care – *is essentially* more humane than care provided within them. Such research has contributed to the rationalization of the care of the aged, the retrenchment of public care, and thus the reduction of consumer 'choice' *within* public care. As Silverman has argued earlier in this volume, and as the accounts of community nurses and social workers bear witness to, there is no 'discourse of truth', 'community care' and 'choice' are neither essentially 'good' nor 'bad' and 'they have no meaning apart from the way in which they are articulated in a given historical and institutional context'.

However, as this chapter has shown, the rationalization of knowledge is progressive, certain truths or rationalizations articulated by certain groups, and within these groups by certain individuals, making a greater contribution to the official rationality or truth than others. Moreover, it has become fashionable for those making the biggest contribution to the official rationality and/or who support it, to consider themselves as 'non-partisan', 'independent' or 'objective', while they chastise people opposed to this rationality as being 'political', 'partisan' or 'romantics'. The New Right's criticism of the Prince of Wales' expressed concern with unemployment, the inner cities, and the preservation of the environment illustrates the politics of the personal. To quote Norman Tebbit's defence of this criticism: 'We're in a period of eight, ten, perhaps twenty years of Conservative Government and therefore any criticism of the world as it is sounds like a criticism of the Government' (*The Guardian*, 11 April 1988).

This chapter has illustrated the politics of the personal through description of the relative contribution the social professionals make to the rationalization of care – the official rationality. This has involved adopting a theoretical and methodological position which stands largely in opposition to the rationalization of social science as manifested in the reductivism of abstracted empiricism. This position has involved the thematization of the knowledge and thus practices of groups of carers and social scientists and the way this is influenced by their relations with one another. This has produced theory of the social process of community care and therefore explanation of statistical correlations relating to areas of the care of the aged inaccessible to more segmented analysis. In turn it has illustrated that 'need' for public care is not purely an artefact of 'natural' demographic changes such as the growing number of elderly people over the age of 75 in the population, but that it is also constituted by social processes like rationalization.

An understanding of contemporary social processes consequently enables social scientists to help project future trends in care provision. Thus it has been argued that chronic care is no longer considered a 'medical' problem, but instead a 'natural' part of old age which can be provided by subordinate public and private carers in 'the community'. There is also a growing, and I would argue a related, tendency within social gerontology to stress the 'normality' of old age and as a consequence to underemphasize the needs of the chronic-care aged for public care, particularly that of residential care. This rationalization and individualization of responsibility for health and care could advance to the stage when *no* public care for the aged would be considered a 'medical' or a 'social' responsibility. The medical professionals could argue that *all* problems in old age are a natural or normal part of ageing, and the social professionals could complete this legitimation on the grounds that it is the 'choice' of the elderly person to receive no public care.

An answer to the question I posed earlier – how are social scientists to lessen their contribution to the rationalization of care in order to influence the creation of real choice – is therefore through an appreciation of context for understanding need. Thus through analysing the process of community care in the context of working relationships between different groups of carers, and between these carers and myself as a social scientist, it was seen to be constituted by the reconstruction of need, the erosion of aspects of public care and the reduction of 'choice' within the public sector. This development of accounts/theory therefore led to a re-examination of the assumption that community care is essentially more humane than public residential care.

Thus, in order to create choice, social scientists need to understand the social construction of the official rationality as formalized in social policy, at the micro-level of groups of individuals and their relationships with one another. The rejection of epistemological hierarchies such as Parsons' science/non-science distinction (see Cornwell, 1984: 19), and its focus on the changing knowledge and practices of individuals and groups in the course of social relationships, make interpretative sociology best suited to this end. Such research provides greater understanding of the contri-

bution medical and social scientists make to the process of rationalization and therefore to the restriction of consumer choice. It
consequently provides insight into areas where change is necessary
if greater choice is to be developed, and is more likely to generate
policy recommendations aimed at collectivities (for example,
through increased public provision), rather than at individuals
abstracted from context in the guise of 'personal responsibility' for
health and care. For example, Cornwell's study of the development
of working-class health beliefs in the context of their relationships at
work, within the family and community, and with health professionals, led her to conclude in regard to health education/promotion
and preventive work:

> Changes in commonsense ideas and theories about health and illness
> (and thus in health-related behaviour) are not likely to occur in the
> absence of changes in other areas of people's lives. It may therefore be
> more important to change people's position in relation to employment,
> for example, or to change the sexual division of labour, than constantly
> to direct attention to health attitudes and beliefs. (Cornwell, 1984: 206)

Rodmell and Watt come to a similar conclusion about health
education: 'Making "healthy choices easier choices" (Dennis et al.,
1982) is likely to require significant transformations of the social
conditions under which any choice is made' (Rodmell and Watt,
1986: 5).

Similarly, in regard more generally to community-care policy, this
could only be a humane initiative if every level of public care, from
chronic care in residential Homes through to support, both
financially and practically for family carers, was available and
adequately funded. When 'choice' for public residential care would
not be restricted to the chronic-care aged without family care unable
to purchase care from the market place. This restructuring of public
expenditure, however, requires a political solution which will only
arise through the accumulation of evidence in the course of
everyday lives which indicates the importance of public provision
for the facilitation of choice. Social scientists can contribute towards
this process through interpretative understanding of the way social
relationships influence the politics of field research and care.

Notes

This chapter is based on a study, 'The Aged "in Limbo": Accounts of "Community
Care" in the 1980s'. The author wishes to thank David Silverman and David Smith
for their comments on this research at various stages, and the ESRC for its financial
support.
1   Although the study from which this chapter is drawn focuses on the 'com-

munity care' of the aged, the thesis developed could also be applied to the other 'priority groups' (that is, the mentally and physically handicapped, the mentally ill, and children).

2   Macintyre (1977) has focused on the 'problem' of old age as it has been defined in government reports. Employing Waller's (1936) 'organizational' and 'humanitarian' classifications of social problems, Macintyre illustrates that organizational concerns (for example, the cost of providing for the growing, and economically nonproductive, aged population), typically subjugate humanitarian concerns (for example, concerns with the quality of the lives of the aged) in government policy.

3   See *National Health Service Re-organisation* (1972) and the National Health Service Act (1977) 22 (1).

4   A development referred to by Merton (1949) as the 'serendipity pattern'.

5   This 'devil's advocate question' (Schatzman and Strauss, 1973: 81) marked an important stage in the development of the research relationship. Not only did it help to round out my understanding of Linda Smith's position, but it provided further evidence of the degree to which the segmentalization of nursing care had advanced in this locality, and of its changing politics. Such a development of accounts and theory would have been unobtainable to normative research procedures.

6   Willcocks states: 'What is of particular interest in the previous living arrangements of our sample is the extent to which a 'change in place of origin' has occurred over time. Those elderly who had been living alone in the community are now taking up proportionately more places, and a commensurate 'loss' is experienced by those living with relatives . . . It would appear then that the family is now less likely to be relieved of the burden of caring. Amongst outstanding residents (in care for ten years or more), 40 per cent of women and 29 per cent of men had been living alone prior to admission; amongst newcomers (residents for less than one year) this rises to 57 per cent and 55 per cent' (1982: 5).

References

Abel-Smith, B. and Titmuss, R. (1956) *The Cost of the National Health Service in England and Wales*. Cambridge: Cambridge University Press.

Berger, P.L. and Luckmann, T. (1967) *The Social Construction of Reality*. London: Penguin.

Berger, P.L., Berger, B. and Kellner, H. (1974) *The Homeless Mind*. London: Pelican.

Berger, P.L. and Kellner, H. (1981) *Sociology Reinterpreted: An Essay on Method and Vocation*. London: Pelican.

Boucher Report (1957) *Report on Services Available for the Chronic Sick and Elderly*. Reports on Public Health and Medical Subjects, No. 98. London: HMSO.

Cornwell, J. (1984) *Hard-earned Lives: Accounts of Health and Illness from East London*. London: Tavistock.

Crawford, R. (1980) 'Healthism and the Medicalization of Everyday Life', *International Journal of Health Services*, 10 (3).

Davies, B. and Challis, D. (1980) 'Experimenting with New Roles in Domiciliary Service: The Kent Community Care Project', *The Gerontologist*, 20 (3).

Dennis, J. et al. (1982) 'Health Promotion in the Reorganised National Health Service', *The Health Services*, 26 November.

DHSS (1976a) *Priorities for Health and Personal Social Services in England: A Consultative Document*. London: HMSO.

DHSS (1976b) *Prevention and Health: Everybody's Business: A Reassessment of Public and Personal Health*. London: HMSO.

DHSS (1977) *Prevention and Health*. Cmnd 7047. London: HMSO.

DHSS (1978) *A Happier Old Age: A Discussion Document on Elderly People in our Society*. London: HMSO.

DHSS (1981a) *Growing Older*. Cmnd 8173. London: HMSO.

DHSS (1981b) *Care in the Community*. Cmnd 8084. London: HMSO.

DHSS (1983) *Explanatory Notes on Care in the Community*. London: HMSO.

Estes, C.L. (1979) *The Aging Enterprise*. San Francisco: Jossey-Bass.

Finch, J. and Groves, D. (1980) 'Community Care and the Family: A Case for Equal Opportunities', *Journal of Social Policy*, 9 (4).

Finch, J. and Groves, D. (1983) *A Labour of Love: Women, Work and Caring*. London: Routledge & Kegan Paul.

Finch, J. (1984) 'Community Care: Developing Non-sexist Alternatives', *Critical Social Policy*, 9 (Spring).

Freidson, E. (1970) *Professional Dominance: The Structure of Medical Care*. Chicago: Aldine Atherton.

Giddens, A. (1976) *New Rules of Sociological Method: A Positive Critique of Interpretative Sociologies*. London: Hutchinson.

Glaser, B.G. and Strauss, A.S. (1967) *The Discovery of Grounded Theory: Strategies for Qualitative Research*. Chicago: Aldine Atherton.

Goffman, E. (1968) *Asylums: Essays on the Social Situation of Mental Patients and Other Inmates*. Harmondsworth: Penguin.

Guillebaud Report (1956) *Report of the Committee of Enquiry into the Cost of the National Health Service*. Cmnd 9663. London: HMSO.

Griffiths Report (1988) *Community Care: Agenda for Action*. London: HMSO.

Grundy, E. and Arie, T. (1982) 'Falling Provision of Residential Care for the Elderly', *British Medical Journal*, 284: 799–802.

Habermas, J. (1971) *Toward a Rational Society: Student Protest, Science and Politics*. London: Heinemann.

Health and Welfare: The Development of Community Care (1963) Cmnd 1973. London: HMSO.

Hospital Plan for England and Wales (1962) Cmnd 1604. London: HMSO.

Illich I. (1977) *Limits to Medicine, Medical Nemesis: The Expropriation of Health*. London: Pelican.

Johnson, M. (1978) 'That was Your Life: A Biographical Approach to Later Life', in V. Carver and P. Liddiard (eds), *An Ageing Population*. London: Hodder & Stoughton in association with The Open University Press.

Macintyre, S. (1977) 'Old Age as a Social Problem: Historical Notes on the English Experience', in R. Dingwall, C. Heath, M. Reid and M. Stacey (eds), *Health Care and Health Knowledge*. London: Croom Helm.

Merton, R.K. (1949) *On Theoretical Sociology*. New York: Free Press.

Minkler, M. (1983) 'Blaming the Aged Victim: The Politics of Scapegoating in Times of Fiscal Conservatism', *International Journal of Health Services*, 13 (1).

National Health Service Re-organisation (1972) Cmnd 5055. London: HMSO.

Oakley, A. (1981) 'Interviewing Women: A Contradiction in Terms', in H. Roberts (ed.) *Doing Feminist Research*. London: Routledge & Kegan Paul.

Parkin, F. (1979) *Marxism and Class Theory: A Bourgeois Critique*. London: Tavistock.

Phillips Report (1954) *Report of the Committee on the Economic and Financial Problems of the Provision for Old Age*. Cmnd 9333. London: HMSO.

Robb, B. (ed.) (1967) *Sans Everything – A Case to Answer*. London: Nelson.

Rodmell, S. and Watt, A (ed.) (1986) *The Politics of Health Education: Raising the Issues*. London: Routledge and Kegan Paul.

Schatzman, L. and Strauss, A.L. (1973) *Field Research: Strategies for a Natural Sociology*. Englewood Cliffs, NJ: Prentice Hall.

Schutz, A. (1962) *Collected Papers*, Volume 1. The Hague: Nijhoff.

Schutz, A. (1967) *The Phenomenology of the Social World*. Evanston: Northwestern University Press.

Schutz, A (1970a) *Reflections on the Problem of Relevance*. New Haven: Yale University Press.

Schutz, A. (1970b) *On Phenomenology and Social Relations*. Chicago: University of Chicago Press.

Seebohm Report (1969) *Report of the Committee on Local Authority and Allied Personal Services, 1968*. Cmnd 3703. London: HMSO.

Sheldon, J.H. (1961) *Report of the Birmingham Regional Hospital Board on its Geriatric Services*, Birmingham Regional Hospital Board.

Shenfield, B.E. (1957) *Social Policies for Old Age: A Review of Social Provision for Old Age in Britain*. London: Routledge & Kegan Paul.

Strong, P.M. (1979) 'Sociological Imperialism and the Profession of Medicine: A Critical Examination of the Thesis of Medical Imperialism', *Social Science and Medicine*, 13a: 199–215.

Titmuss, R. (1968) *Commitment to Welfare*. London: George Allen & Unwin.

Townsend, P. (1957) *The Family Life of Old People*. London: Routledge & Kegan Paul.

Townsend, P. and Wedderburn, D. (1962–3) *The Aged in the Welfare State: Interim Report of a Survey of Persons aged 65 and over in Britain*. London: G. Bell.

Townsend, P. (1981) 'The Structured Dependency of the Elderly: A Creation of Social Policy in the Twentieth Century', *Ageing and Society*, 1, (1).

Wagner Report (1988) *Residential Care: A Positive Choice*. London: HMSO.

Walker, A. (1981) 'Community Care and the Elderly in Great Britain: Theory and Practice', *International Journal of Health Services*, 11 (4).

Waller, W. (1936) 'Social Problems and the Mores', *American Sociological Review*, 1: 924–33.

Weber, M. (1949) *The Methodology of the Social Sciences*. New York: Free Press.

Willcocks, D. (1982) 'Gender and the Care of the Elderly in Part III Accommodation'. Paper presented at the British Sociological Association Annual Conference 1982.

Willcocks, D., Peace, S. and Kellaher, L. (1983) 'A Profile of Residential Life: A Discussion of Key Issues Arising out of Consumer Research in One Hundred Old Age Homes', in D. Jerrome (ed.), *Ageing in Modern Society*. London: Croom Helm.

Willcocks, D., Peace, S. and Kellaher, L. (1987) *Private Lives in Public Places: A Research-based Critique of Residential Life in Local Authority Old People's Homes*. London: Tavistock.

Wright Mills, C. (1970) *The Sociological Imagination*. London: Pelican.

10

Ethnography addressing the Practitioner

Michael Bloor and Neil McKeganey

Funding agencies for sociological research often expect sociological researchers to address themselves to audiences of policy makers and administrators. This is a situation which contrasts sharply with most clinical research, where the main audience for research reports remains a practitioner one, perhaps reflecting the considerable autonomy which clinicians enjoy in altering their existing practices in the light of new developments.

This chapter is concerned with the relevance of qualitative sociological research to a *practitioner* audience, rather than a policy-maker audience. It draws on our research in therapeutic communities (Bloor et al., 1988) to show how qualitative research can be 'evaluative' (in the broad sense of the term) and can be a spur to practitioners to alter practices. We will report in detail and with illustration on how comparative data on practice differences between a range of similar institutions, by the mere fact of the juxtaposition of contrasting practices, imply an evaluative judgement between one set of contrasting practices and another: comparative description implies evaluation and promotes alterations in practice. We begin with a clarification of our use of the term 'evaluative'; we then move on to a brief description of the comparative study; and to a detailed illustration of two sets of contrasting practices which would suggest to practitioners alterations in practices.

Approaches to evaluation

It is possible, in theory, to distinguish several different approaches to evaluation. For example, there is what one might term the 'attribute approach', whereby a service or a type of institution is defined as possessing certain core or essential attributes: individual institutions or instances of service provision are then evaluated on whether or not they possess these core attributes. In the case of therapeutic communities there is no one model of practice. This alerts us to the wider epistemological difficulty that there are no unproblematic grounds for deciding on the core features of any service or institution (Rawlings, 1981).

However, much the most important approach to evaluation is the controlled trial, mainly used in clinical epidemiology, but widely promoted as an appropriate research model for the evaluation of a wide range of services (see, for example, Cochrane, 1972). Illsley (1980) has argued convincingly that there are serious limitations to the applicability of this research model to health services research. He points out that the minimal conditions for such research – standardized inputs, a control population, uncontroversial outcome measures, large throughputs of clients for statistical analysis, and so on – are not to be found in most practice situations. So 'if evaluation is equated with this single methodology . . . then practitioners, policymakers, and administrators will rarely find it possible to conduct evaluative work' (Illsley, 1980: 115).

We would go one stage further than this and point out that the un-standardized nature of most types of service provision, therapeutic communities included, means that there are no a priori grounds for modifying practice in one community in the light of evaluative research conducted in a second community. Even where researchers and practitioners are able laboriously to create the necessary experimental conditions in a single study-setting for such an evaluative study, the fact that the service in question is not standardized (is subject to clinical autonomy, to individual styles of working, to changes in personnel and to changes over time) means that there is no earthly logical reason for a practitioner to modify his or her practice in the light of research findings in another community, because his or her own practices (which will almost certainly differ from those of the evaluated community) have not been assessed. Some practitioners may indeed modify their prac-tices as a result, but they will have responded to scientism rather than science.

If we resist the equation of evaluation with the methods of clinical epidemiology and accept a broader definition for the term, then a range of approaches to evaluation becomes possible. It will be evident, on reflection, that evaluation in a broad sense actually takes place all the time in day-to-day practice. In the course of his or her everyday activities a practitioner forms a judgement about the successfulness of his or her current approach to treatment in the case of a particular patient or client and decides to modify that treatment accordingly. Again, a particular administrative procedure appears not to be working properly and is changed. These *everyday* evaluative decisions cannot be replaced by a technical procedure, expropriated by a controlled design: these delicate, balanced, disputatious, and sometimes arbitrary judgements occur on an everyday basis as a necessary part of service provision. But research can inform these judgements, can contribute to evaluation in this broad sense.

Our own descriptive approach can contribute to evaluation in this sense. Our comparative study was primarily descriptive in intention: we sought to describe within a comparative framework the range of therapeutic community practices. But comparative description, the juxtaposition of practices, is obviously relevant to evaluation, and naturally informs evaluative judgements.

The comparative study

With our Dutch colleague, Dick Fonkert, we have undertaken fieldwork by participant observation in eight different therapeutic communities representing a range of practice. Normally, this kind of intensive fieldwork is only feasible in one or two settings, but by making the eight settings the focus of six different individual studies, it has been possible to re-use the participant observation data so collected for retrospective comparison across a range of practice. Findings from the six individual studies have been published previously (Bloor, 1980a; 1980b; 1981; Bloor and Fonkert, 1981; McKeganey, 1982; 1983a; 1983b; 1984a; 1984b; 1984c; Bloor, 1984; 1986a; 1986b; 1986c; 1986d; McKeganey 1986; and McKeganey and Bloor, 1986). The individual communities studied were as follows:

1 *Parkneuk Community*, a communally organized foster-family type of community for mentally handicapped and disturbed children;
2 the *Day Hospital* at Aberdeen's Ross Clinic, providing day care for personality-disordered or neurotic patients;
3 a *Camphill Rudolf Steiner Community* for mentally handicapped and disturbed children;
4 a *Concept House* in Holland for the residential treatment of drug addicts;
5 *Ashley House* and
6 *Beeches House*, two contrasting halfway houses for disturbed adolescents;
7 *Ravenscroft* and
8 *Faswells*, two contrasting small residential psychiatric units.

It will be clear to therapeutic-community practitioners and others that this list in no way encompasses the wide range of communities that are available. We have not, for example, included a therapeutic community day centre or a penal institution run along therapeutic-community lines (Barratt, 1978; Boyle, 1977). We offer no apologies for this since the number of communities in our present list was only achieved with considerable difficulty and since we felt it was important to include some documentation of variations in practice within communities of the same broad type.

There is a sense in which comparative ethnography is not ethnography at all; the strength of ethnography may be represented as its ability to depict a mix of cultural practices in a particular and unique constellation, in a particular and unique context. And yet any ethnography (whether it focuses on a single context or not) employs the comparative method – it juxtaposes one observation against another, it contrasts and highlights some practices in relation to others, and so on. In the broad sense in which we have used the term 'evaluation', qualitative studies are implicitly evaluative – evaluative judgements are native to the research method.

This being the case, one of the things we have sought to do in the conclusion to our comparative study has been to make these implicit evaluative judgements explicit. We have listed some seven practices which *appeared* when juxtaposed with experience of other communities, to promote therapy in the settings in which they were found. We emphasize 'appeared' here because we have no wish to claim a 'scientific' validity for these judgements, indeed we view the evaluative judgements of the researcher to be essentially similar to those everyday evaluative judgements made by practitioners which we described earlier. Our procedure has been to present *our* evaluations to practitioners in order that they may inform their (that is, practitioners') evaluations. One role for field research as we see it is to provide descriptive materials which can function as comparative or contrasting settings for practitioners to assess, and perhaps modify, their own practices.

In our comparative study we concluded our ethnography by listing seven practices which, by drawing upon our comparative materials, appeared to us to promote therapy in their native settings. These practices are listed below in no particular or hierarchical order:

1 making fellow residents responsible for keeping residents in treatment;
2 ways of increasing residents' awareness of the changeability of the community structure;
3 the 'after-group' as a way of promoting resident reflectivity;
4 the attendance of residents at staff change-over meetings;

5 the 'tight-house' as a way of countering institutionalism;
6 resident selection of participating staff;
7 the offering of alternative sources of satisfaction to junior staff.

Considerations of space preclude us from describing any more than the first two of these practices here (for a complete description see Bloor et al., 1988).

Collective responsibility for keeping residents in treatment
None of our communities were custodial institutions and so all of them were, to varying degrees, vulnerable to premature departure by residents. As in any course of treatment, those who discontinue treatment prematurely can be expected to derive less benefit than those who remain for the full course. We shall contrast the practices surrounding 'defaulting' in two different communities: the psychiatric day hospital at Aberdeen's Ross Clinic, and 'Ashley' – a halfway house for disturbed adolescents.

First, we present very brief descriptions of the two communities as they appeared at the time the fieldwork was undertaken (one of them has undergone substantial changes since that time). The day hospital was set in the grounds of a large psychiatric hospital and normally provided day care to approximately thirty patients diagnosed as neurotic or personality disordered. Although most of the patients attended the hospital on a day basis there was a minority of in-patients. The staff complement consisted of four psychiatrists and one occupational therapist – each of whom also had treatment responsibilities outside the unit – and four full-time psychiatric nurses. All treatment took place in groups – a community meeting each morning, twice-weekly activity groups for such things as gardening and cooking, twice-weekly occupational therapy sessions, daily small groups, and a weekly encounter group. The treatment approach at the day hospital, as in most therapeutic communities found in British psychiatric hospitals, owed a great deal to the treatment regime developed by Maxwell Jones at Henderson Hospital (see Rapoport, 1960). The average length of stay of patients who did not default from treatment was about three and a half months.

Ashley was a large old house in an English provincial city, run by a well-known charitable trust. The house had space for fourteen adolescent residents; those who did not default normally stayed for around four months. Referrals came mainly from the social work and probation services, many of the residents having experienced difficulties coping with adverse family circumstances or with adjustment following stays in custodial or psychiatric institutions.

The staff complement consisted of a warden, a deputy, and four other staff (including a trainee and a full-time student volunteer). Some of the most senior residents were employed (part- or full-time) or in full-time education, but for the majority there was a daily programme of groups and activities (including cooking the meals and cleaning and decorating the house). Staff did not oversee resident activities, rather they 'orchestrated' the house by encouraging residents to take greater individual and collective responsibility for their own actions and those of their fellows.

This house culture of collective responsibility could be observed in the following fieldnote reporting on a discussion in one of the morning coffee groups where several residents strove alongside a staff member (Frank) to persuade a glue-sniffing resident (Gayle) to take a more positive view of the house instead of wanting to return to her borstal:

> Frank tried hard to elicit some response from Gayle who sat at the table slumped in gloom. He was backed up by Elaine and Victor (residents). She was asked several questions about her borstal and how it was different from the house. Gayle said she had her own room in the borstal: Frank remarked that Elaine had had their room to herself before Gayle arrived, and Elaine came in to reminisce that she'd been violently opposed to sharing her room before Gayle arrived and that she'd been quite willing to leave Gayle alone last night when she said that she wanted to be by herself. Gayle said that she hadn't any friends here. Elaine said, aggrieved, that she was her friend . . . Frank asked Victor to repeat what he'd told him about the post-sniffing downer being worse the higher the buzz off the glue, which led to a wish for release with more glue, which led to a worse downer, and so on. Victor obliged (and after the group he sat on in the dining room talking to Gayle). Frank asked Gayle what activities she liked to do: she mentioned cycling, whereupon Frank said that was the activity that was planned for this afternoon. She also mentioned playing the piano: this led to a flurry of interest – Betty could also play, Gayle could play 'The House of the Rising Sun', Frank used to have a girlfiend who played that tune on the organ. The house used to have a piano: they could be picked up quite cheaply second-hand, mebbe the house could get another.

But Gayle was a newly arrived resident. Residents of longer standing who had been incorporated into the adolescent peer group were not pressured by their peers to remain in treatment. Two weeks prior to the discussions with Gayle, another coffee group had been taken up with the topic of the departure of a more senior resident (Dougie); two of the residents who had been most vocal in encouraging Gayle to stay (Victor and Betty) dissociated themselves from staff attempts to discuss Dougie's imminent departure:

> Two of the residents discussed the matter. Both Victor and Betty

thought it was up to Dougie what he did. Victor said it didn't matter to him. Betty said the staff were 'nagging' Dougie.

The aim of therapeutic communities is nothing less than the resocialization of residents. Whilst some residents may be expected to default from treatment on first arrival, others may only consider departure after they have been in the community some weeks and they develop a true grasp of the enormity of the changes expected of them. At Ashley this latter category of residents would find no peer group disagreement with their decisions to leave. Indeed, the surreptitious attempts of one resident to catch the postman in order to intercept his giro (welfare cheque) were well known to his fellow-residents. And when he did eventually steal away from the house another resident volunteered to help him carry his luggage to the bus station.

The day hospital faced the problem of premature departure in a particularly acute form, since any patient who wished to default needed to do nothing more than simply stay away from the day hospital the next morning. Perhaps in response to this especial difficulty, the day hospital operated in a way that was unique among the therapeutic communities we studied, in that it made fellow-patients responsible for keeping patients in treatment.

Patients who defaulted could expect a delegation of their fellow-patients (sometimes with a staff-member in attendance) to visit them at their homes, urging them to return. The pressure so exerted could be considerable and some defaulting patients resorted to subterfuge to avoid such visiting delegations: one patient who had already defaulted once before and returned was thought to be refusing to answer the door on a second occasion when patients visited him, and another patient secretly left the country.

Relatedly, staff were aware that patients (some of whom were para-suicides), who came under considerable pressure in the course of the groups, would be comforted and kept company outside the groups:

> This afternoon considerable pressure was put on Dawn: she had spoken of her feelings of hopelessness and depression, her failure to 'work' in the group, and her feeling that she ought to leave the day hospital. Several staff members had already left for prior appointments. Edith (staff) said she had seen Dawn glance at the clock several times: now was her chance to end it (the group). Her voice breaking, Dawn picked up her bag, she said she'd end it alright, and rushed out of the room. Edith did nothing to stop her. At Harry's (patient) bidding, Olive (patient) went after her, caught her up in the toilets and made her promise to come again tomorrow. Once before she'd dashed off and her fellow-patients set off after her. Indeed, this dashing after bolting patients is a

fairly common occurrence – Edith could predict that Dawn would be looked after.

This watchfulness over fellow-patients could and did extend well beyond the hours of the day hospital into the long watches of the night. Strange friendships and alliances were formed in which a shared experience of the emotional intensities of the day hospital was perhaps the only common denominator among parties separated by age, class, and circumstances. Patients who succeeded in terminating their treatment without the prior knowledge and approval of staff and patients were regarded by their fellow patients as betrayers.

In effect, the patient culture at the day hospital helped to maintain patients in a stressful treatment situation from which otherwise it would have been all too easy to escape. This aspect of the patient culture was acknowledged and supported by the staff. Most therapeutic communities are non-custodial institutions and therefore they face a potential problem of numbers of residents departing prematurely, as did Ashley, the halfway house described earlier. It is therefore possible that the day hospital practice, of making patients collectively responsible for keeping each other in treatment, could be adopted more widely.

Devices for increasing residents' awareness of the changeability of the community structure
With the sole exception of the concept house all of our communities were formally democratic institutions in which both the government and the governance of the community were open to debate and modification. This is not to say that the communities were wholly democratic. Rather, democracy is one of the creative myths of therapeutic community practice (Morrice, 1972); by participating in the democratic forms within the community, and by encountering and displaying the limits to that democracy, residents not only reveal aspects of their own difficulties but also learn new and less pathogenic ways of responding to their own, and others', thwarted expectations. By contrast any perception on the part of residents that the structure of the community was fixed and immutable, or that the government and governance of the community were the sole responsibility of senior staff, might well lessen the involvement of residents in those democratic forms, and in the process reduce the opportunities for therapeutic work which their participation might otherwise have provided.

Our research has alerted us to two devices which may counter such a tendency and which may increase residents' involvement in the democratic forms within a community, namely a collective visit to a second community where the organization is very different, and the Beeches 'Think Day'. Before illustrating these two devices it will be helpful to provide a short sketch of the two communities involved.

Faswells community, like the day hospital, was located within the grounds of a large psychiatric hospital. However, unlike the Ross Clinic, Faswells' host institution was depressingly traditional. Set on the outskirts of London, its high perimeter wall and huge gates were a dull reminder of its custodial past. Physically the community was housed in a rather shabby bungalow, the central corridor of which led to a large lounge and two large single-sex dormitories. At the time of our research there were fifteen patients within the unit, quite a few of whom had been residents for between one and two years. Most of the residents were diagnosed as neurotic or personality disordered and the therapeutic programme of small and large group meetings was similar to that at the day hospital.

Beeches community was somewhat similar to Ashley in that it too was located in a large house which provided residential care for a comparable client group – though a greater proportion of the Beeches residents were classifiable as educationally subnormal. Staffing in both houses was similar, though at Beeches there was a qualified teacher. However, the aspect which most distinguished those two halfway-house communities was the extensive planning of activities that was a feature of the Beeches programme. By creating an elaborate social structure of planned activities around residents, staff sought, through a process of regulation and repetition, to develop new patterns of behaviour in residents. This detailed overseeing of residents' activities would be gradually reduced over the course of the resident's stay which in theory, though only rarely in practice, could be between one and two years.

Although, as we have said, therapeutic-community staff place a good deal of emphasis upon residents' involvement in the various democratic forms within an individual community, it will be obvious that the actual extent of residents' participation at any one time will vary, depending upon a range of situational factors. Within Faswells residents were expected to participate fully in the therapeutic discussion of their own and each others' problems as these were revealed in the course of the various large and small groups and art and music therapy sessions. Residents were also expected to take on the responsibility for chairing the large group meetings and cleaning the common areas of the community. At the time of the fieldwork in Faswells, however, the residents' involvement in many of these activities was very limited:

Today's large group meeting was one long joke. For nearly the entire 45 minutes of the meeting the residents sat in a state of barely suppressed laughter and giggled asides. The nursing staff sat unsmiling and Clive (resident) sat for the entire meeting with a shopping bag on his head. The end of the meeting was eagerly awaited with various of the residents counting down the seconds to the close of the meeting which was in fact called two minutes early.

It will be worth providing some contextual information on the events surrounding this meeting. Throughout the previous week in Faswells there had been growing disquiet amongst staff that many of the Faswells residents had ceased to derive any benefit from their involvement in the community. This disquiet manifested itself most recently in the drawing up by staff of rules for day membership (no attendance after 5 p.m., no visiting during the weekend) and the listing of those members involved. As might have been expected, the drawing up of this list led to a good deal of resentment amongst residents. This was apparent at an earlier large group meeting:

Staff announce the rules for day membership and list the various residents who they say should begin to make plans for leaving. Mark (one of the residents listed) leaps to his feet and shouts out 'All this with rules is effing ridiculous – this place is a therapeutic community not an effing fascist state!' Sharon (resident) chimes in: 'You're all effing mad. If this goes through, I'm leaving!' She storms out of the room followed by Raymond (another resident on the list) and Ellen (a newly arrived resident).

Although Faswells staff were concerned at the reaction of the longer-term residents they were most worried by what they saw as the tendency amongst newly arrived residents to reproduce the other residents' resentments, and to limit their own involvement in the various group meetings accordingly.

However, matters changed dramatically some weeks later following a collective visit by staff and the various new residents to a second community that was very different to Faswells. The impact of this visit could be seen most clearly in relation to the organization of meal times. Within Faswells mealtimes were very low-key affairs with residents simply collecting their food from the kitchen and then dispersing individually or in pairs to the various side-rooms. In the second community, by constrast, a good deal of importance seemed to be placed on staff and residents eating in a relaxed and caring communal atmosphere. On their return to Faswells many of the residents and staff commented on how impressed they had been by this aspect of the second community and resolved to organize their own regular communal meal. This visit to a second community also precipitated a number of discussions amongst residents about how 'caring' a community Faswells had become. During one large group meeting for example the following exchange was recorded:

Jim [resident]: Rachel, you are on the 24-hour report for missing the afternoon meeting.

Rachel [newly arrived resident]: I didn't come because the afternoon meetings are a joke.

Jim: Couldn't you do anything yourself to make them less of a joke?

Rachel: I've thought about that but it's a bit like pumping up something that's already dead.

Sarah [newly arrived resident]: I don't know about you but I find it really hard to speak. When I came here people would put me down for speaking, saying I hadn't been here long enough to know what was happening so now I just feel really inhibited.

Jim: I don't think it's fair for you, Rachel, to say the meetings are a joke – if they are then you have some of the responsibility for that 'cause I've never heard you speak in a meeting yet.

The discussion continued in this fashion until it was agreed that Rachel should take over the role of chairperson when Jim stepped down in a few days' time.

The residents' involvement in such discussions was particularly valued by staff since it provided numerous opportunities for them to confront residents about various aspects of their behaviour which were thought to parallel the difficulties that initially led them into psychiatric treatment.

In communities where therapy occurs through inducting residents into an organized programme of activities that enables the resident to learn new ways of behaving (as at Beeches), rather than through confronting residents (as occurred in the Day Hospital and at Faswells), the residents' involvement in democratic discussions was valued both as a way of channelling residents' grievances about the community in a constructive direction and as a way of showing that residents were coming to accept the social reality of the community. If residents perceive the community to be recalcitrant to democratic change then the effectiveness of the instrumental regime is naturally reduced, and secondary adjustment (Goffman, 1968) and deviant subcultures will probably develop.

The Beeches Think Day was a neat rebuttal of the charge of oligarchy and a practical demonstration of the mutability of the community structure. The event began with the elicitation of topics from residents that they would like to discuss. A long list was quickly drawn up, including some from staff; topics ranged from the suggested abolition of the no-violence rule to the setting up of a house darkroom for photography. Members were asked to divide themselves into groups of four with a minute-taker and a chairman; staff ensured that no group was composed wholly of residents:

Isobel (staff) coordinated the groups' topics so that they didn't overlap. We then had about 10 minutes to discuss each topic but our group spent

about half its time on the item that most interested them – the 'residents'
private room'. I divided the discussion of this into different sections:
what the room was meant to be, what the rules would be, where it would
be and what equipment would be in it. Mark (resident) took the minutes
and I chaired the discussion. My contribution was meant, according to
the warden, to facilitate the residents' expression of their ideas and to
guide their ideas. Thus in talking about the no-violence rule we
discussed Lenny's (resident) suggestion that people who got into fights
should be just left to themselves – staff should not intervene and there
should be no consequences for violence; I asked what they thought
would happen in the house if fights were left to go their own course – did
they think there would be more bullying in the house? did they think
there would be more damage? All agreed that there should be no change
to the violence rule and we duly recommended this. Each group
reported back their recommendations which the community then
discussed.

By their very participation in this exercise residents were led to
subscribe to the democratic ethos of the house, to the legitimacy of
the house structure, and to the consensual and mutable character of
the house rules. We are not, of course, suggesting that the Think
Day ensured that the Beeches regime was unequivocally democratic; there were limits to that democracy – the residents' request
for a private room, for example, was not accepted by staff, though
others of the residents' recommendations were accepted and led to
immediate changes in the organization of the house. Rather, the
Think Day helped to construct the Beeches regime as a democracy
in the eyes of the residents.

Both of these devices – the visit by Faswells staff and residents to
a second community, and the Beeches Think Day – seemed to
increase the residents' involvement in the democratic forms of each
community and thereby expanded the range of opportunities for
therapeutic work in each setting. There may be some value then in
therapeutic community practitioners adopting similar devices in
their own communities.

Conclusion – addressing practitioners

Part of the final chapter of our comparative study (Bloor et al.,
1988) has been devoted to drawing practitioners' attention to a list
of practices (currently found in just one or two communities) which,
because of our comparative experience, we felt might be usefully
introduced elsewhere. Of course, we were careful to qualify our
recommendations – the circumstances of no two communities are
the same, and simple transplantation might not be possible.
Moreover, any given practice might carry disadvantages as well as

advantages – it was clear, for example, that the day hospital practice of making fellow patients responsible for keeping each other in treatment carried the risk of 'attention-seeking' defaulting, with patients staging departures precisely in order to become the focus of other patients' concern.

In addition we have also outlined our recommendations elsewhere – in a paper to an international conference of practitioners, and in an article in the foremost practitioners' journal (Bloor and McKeganey, 1987). We have also sought to feed our work back to the individual communities participating in our research. At the close of his fieldwork in Ashley for example, Bloor provided staff with a similar comparison to the one drawn in this chapter:

> I had previously said that I would give the staff some feedback on my thoughts about the house before I left – not a 'scientific' statement, but simply an informed observer's reflections. I'd given some thought to this in advance and had decided to concentrate on one problem I thought was perhaps inadequately attended to – premature departure by residents 'frightened' of the changes expected of them – and a possible solution – a stronger resident culture. I spent an evening talking about this with the warden last night . . . and she brought it up in the staff group this afternoon.
>
> It led to a lot of discussion: general agreement that the problem was there.
>
> At the end of the (weekly) community meeting [the warden] said that she'd like (after her return from holiday) a special meeting of the community to discuss the problem of people leaving.

Of course we are in no position to judge the impact of these recommendations and it would, in any case, be premature to attempt to do so. Even if our efforts (improbably) led to wholesale changes of practice, extrapolation to other areas of sociological research should be cautious. Therapeutic-community practitioners have an untypical regard for social science, their criticisms of traditional institutional regimes owing much to sociological texts like Goffman's *Asylums* (1968), and an early anthropological account of Maxwell Jones' Henderson Hospital therapeutic community (Rapoport, 1960) has become a sort of staff training manual.

However, we believe our general argument has some validity, regardless of the success or otherwise of our particular recommendations in this study. Our general argument is as follows: There are a number of different potential audiences for qualitative sociological research. To achieve changes in practice it is not always a necessity to address oneself to audiences of policy makers and administrators; in many areas of the health and social services practitioners retain the autonomy to alter their own practices in the light of new developments. Indeed it is this very heterogeneity of practice which serves to vitiate the impact of controlled trials and experimental research methods. Qualitative sociological researchers may invite practitioners to assess the working practices they have described in the light of their own current practices and judge for themselves whether the adoption of new practices is indicated. Such practitioner assessments will occur more readily when the researcher presents his or her findings in a comparative framework, particularly if a range of practices is presented so that various related but different working practices can be compared. By making explicit those implicitly evaluative decisions that are native to qualitative research methods (comparisons of like cases, the search for 'deviant' cases, and so on), and by addressing his or her findings to a practitioner audience, the researcher is in effect inviting practitioners to verify their own analysis by their adoption of new working practices.

The politics of sociological research are in a state of flux. Elsewhere in this volume, Silverman has drawn on the work of Foucault to show that the researcher who calls for a more patient-centred medical practice may be unwittingly contributing to the extension of professional surveillance of patients. And we have already discussed the deficiencies of experimental designs addressed to policy makers. Our suggested approach – ethnography which addresses practitioners – lacks the obvious political dimension of research addressed to policy makers. However, the political impact of such research can be considerable as researchers make a contribution to what Lipsky (1980) has termed the 'street level' of practitioners' work.

While we are aware that our suggested approach is open to criticism (for example, in the form of the old rhetorical question 'Whose side are we on?'), we are not aware that the approach has been suggested previously in the terms we have set out here. The reason for this may simply be that sociological studies of everyday practice are still something of a rarity. In medical sociology, for example, sociologists have often gained access to doctor–patient encounters, but they have normally concerned themselves with describing practitioners' conduct rather than practitioners' work – they have normally sought to describe, for example, doctor–patient communication, or social control, rather than to describe history-taking, examination, and medical decision making (McKeganey, 1989). We should therefore end our argument by pointing out that any attempts to further exploit the evaluative potential of ethnography for a practitioner audience must be paralleled by a growth of ethnographic studies which focus on practitioners' work, not practitioners' conduct.

Note

We wish to thank Dick Fonkert for access to his data on the Dutch concept house which formed one of our eight component studies. Michael Bloor wishes to acknowledge the support of the Medical Research Council, and Neil McKeganey acknowledges the support of the Economic and Social Research Council. We are grateful to Sarah Cunningham-Burley for comments on an earlier version of this chapter.

References

Barratt, B. (1978) 'The Therapeutic Community Today in the Penal Services', paper given to the Anglo-Dutch Workshop on Therapeutic Communities, Windsor.

Bloor, M.J. (1980a) 'The Nature of Therapeutic Work in the Therapeutic Community', *International Journal of Therapeutic Communities*, 1: 80–91.

Bloor, M.J. (1980b) 'The Relationship between Informal Patient Interaction and the Formal Treatment Programme in a Psychiatric Day Hospital using Therapeutic Community Treatment Methods', Occasional Paper No. 4, Institute of Medical Sociology, University of Aberdeen.

Bloor, M.J. (1981) 'Therapeutic Paradox – the Patient Culture and the Formal Treatment Programme in a Therapeutic Community', *British Journal of Medical Psychology*, 54: 359–69.

Bloor, M.J. (1984) 'A Comparison of Two Contrasting Halfway Houses for Disturbed Adolescents', Occasional Paper No. 6, Institute of Medical Sociology, University of Aberdeen.

Bloor, M.J. (1986a) 'Contrasting Therapeutic Community Practices in Two Halfway Houses for Disturbed Adolescents: a comparative sociological study', *International Journal of Therapeutic Communities*, 7: 5–24.

Bloor, M.J. (1986b) 'Problems of Therapeutic Community Practice in Two Halfway Houses for Disturbed Adolescents', *Journal of Adolescence*, 9: 29–48.

Bloor, M.J. (1986c) 'Social Control in the Therapeutic Community: Re-examination of a Critical Case', *Sociology of Health and Illness*, 8: 305–23.

Bloor, M.J. (1986d) 'Who'll Make the Tea?' *New Society*, 75: 185–6.

Bloor, M.J. and Fonkert, J.D. (1981) 'Reality Construction, Reality Exploration, and Treatment in Two Therapeutic Communities', *Sociology of Health and Illness*, 4: 125–40.

Bloor, M.J. and McKeganey, N.P. (1987) 'Outstanding Practices, evaluative aspects of a descriptive sociological study of eight contrasting therapeutic communities', *International Journal of Therapeutic Communities*, 8: 273–85.

Bloor, M.J., McKeganey, N.P., and Fonkert, J.D. (1988) *One Foot in Eden: A Sociological Study of the Range of Therapeutic Community Practice*. London: Routledge.

Boyle, J. (1977) *A Sense of Freedom*. London: Pan.

Cochrane, A. (1972) *Effectiveness and Efficiency*. London: Nuffield Provincial Hospitals Trust.

Goffman, E. (1968) *Asylums*. Harmondsworth: Penguin.

Habermas, J. (1972) *Knowledge and Human Interests*. London: Heinemann.

Illsley, R. (1980) *Professional or Public Health?* London: Nuffield Provincial Hospitals Trust.

Lipsky, M. (1980) *Street Level Bureaucracy*. New York: Russell Sage.

McKeganey, N.P. (1982) 'The Social Organisation of Everyday Therapeutic Work in a Camphill Rudolf Steiner Community', PhD thesis. University of Aberdeen.

McKeganey, N.P. (1983a) 'The Social Organisation of Everyday Therapeutic Work – Making the Backstage Visible', *International Journal of Therapeutic Communities*, 4: 85–101.

McKeganey, N.P. (1983b) 'The Cocktail Party Syndrome', *Sociology of Health and Illness*, 5: 95–103.

McKeganey, N.P. (1984a) 'No Doubt She's Really a Little Princess: A Case Study of Trouble in a Therapeutic Community', *Sociological Review*, 32: 328–48.

McKeganey, N.P. (1984b) 'Rudolf Steiner's Anthroposophy and Curative Education: The Possibility of an Adequate Ethnography', *International Journal of Sociology and Social Policy*, 4: 1–14.

McKeganey, N.P. (1984c) 'A Comparison of Therapeutic Work in Two Therapeutic Communities located in Psychiatric Hospitals', Occasional Paper No. 7, Institute of Medical Sociology, University of Aberdeen.

McKeganey, N.P. (1986) 'Accomplishing Ideals: The Case of Hospital-based Therapeutic Communities', *International Journal of Therapeutic Communities*, 7: 85–100.

McKeganey, N.P. (1989) 'On the Analysis of Medical Work: General Practitioners, Opiate-abusing Patients and Medical Sociology', *Sociology of Health and Illness*, 11: 24–38.

McKeganey, N.P. and Bloor, M.J. (1986) 'Teamwork, Information Control, and Therapeutic Effectiveness: A Tale of Two Therapeutic Communities', *Sociology of Health and Illness*, 9: 154–78.

Morrice, J.K. (1972) 'Myth and the Democratic Process', *British Journal of Medical Psychology*, 45: 237–46.

Rapoport, R. (1960) *Community as Doctor*. London: Tavistock.

Rawlings, B. (1981) 'Two Practical Concerns for Therapists: The Problems of Real Therapeutic Communities and Success Rates', in P. Atkinson and C. Heath (eds), *Medical Work: Realities and Routines*. London: Gower.

11
Studying Policies in the Field

Peter K. Manning

Fieldwork, although it involves observation of behaviours and the relevance of the constraints of both the material and natural world for social life, is primarily the analysis of discourse. The stock-in-trade of the fieldworker are written descriptions of verbal accounts of socially evaluated events and behaviours within designated social worlds. A social world frames and orders discourse, whilst the cognitive domains partition and differentiate social worlds. Social worlds and domains are preconstituted and reconstituted by typifications and typifications of typifications in part represented in language. The collection of domains ordered and assembled for purposes of persuasion and legitimation, for connotative power, may be called ideological discourse. Ideological discourse takes shape within organizational contexts, and is used to represent the public face or front of organizations. In a quote that is thematic of the concerns of this chapter, Foucault describes the consequences of the emergence of medical discourse in France near the end of the eighteenth century, noting (1973: 38–9) the '. . . deeply rooted convergence between the requirements of a *political ideology* and those of medical technology . . .' which served to constitute the social space of the hospital and constitute the specific laws of disease. A map, metaphorically speaking, was drawn up by locating the item of interest, the symptom, as a part of an ensemble, disease, and placing disease as a part of a larger plan of the pathological world. In this way, the facts, values, beliefs and tacit assumptions of organization members are mapped by policy discourse. Policy discourse is also a partial indication of such broader matters of politics and ideology referred to by Foucault.

The politics of field research lies not just in the field, but also in the systematic analysis of the discourse that formulates the field of meaning itself. The constitution of a field is in part done by analysis of organizational discourse. For this task, the study of signs, and signs about signs, or social organization, is required. Such analysis draws upon *semiotics*, or the science of signs (Saussure, 1966;

Culler, 1975; Hawkes, 1977; Eco, 1976; and Manning, 1987a), as well as traditional field data. This chapter identifies linguistic and cognitive meanings of the term, 'policy' in HM Nuclear Installations Inspectorate (NII) in Britain, as well as processes of definition, formulation and implementation of policy.

Semiotics

The relationship between expression and content, which together constitute the sign, can be indexical (or natural such as a footprint indicating a man's movement), pragmatic, what is useful, or 'arbitrary', for example metonymic (a whole stands for the part, such as when the experience of a song represents the lyrics, or when a part stands for the whole, such as when a song stands for a romantic relationship), or metaphoric. The process of linking or connecting expression and content is social and depends upon the perspective of the observer. Peirce (1958) has argued that any sign is incomplete because it requires an *interpretant*. The interpretant links the expression and content. Since the interpretant changes, signs change meaning as they change interpretants. There is no reality lying under or behind a sign, no 'real world' against which any sign can be checked. The interpretant of a sign is another sign, and that sign is validated as it were by yet another sign and so on. The connections made between signifier and signified and amongst signs are mental, and depend upon the attribution of meaning. This, it is well known, is often accomplished by means of metaphor. Metaphoric meanings, such as those associated with the British flag, army and the lion, courage, patriotism, and Empire, are 'surplus meanings', or connotations attached to the various signs clustered together to represent British people to themselves in the larger world political economy. The study of such 'surplus meanings' (Barthes, 1972) associated with connotations that surround 'policies', also directs attention to ideological or traditional understandings that audiences attach to the varieties of policy represented in discourse, the functions of those ideologies within organizational contexts, and the setting-specific meanings they encode.

A semiotic analysis of policy requires an identification of the paradigms or associative contexts within which referents of the signifier, 'policy' can be located, and within the contexts, the range of denotative meanings or syntagms noted. 'Policy' studied semiotically also seeks to discover the code that orders or provides the principles that make coherent the interrelated names, labels, or signs to which members bring their political and social concerns, and from which they, in turn, reproduce a sense of order (see

Manning, 1987a, 1987b, 1988a). Such an investigation seeks to explicate the interactive relationships between policy, discourse and organizationally sanctioned practice. Practice fashions discourse, just as discourse fashions practice. Unlike conversational analysis which is restricted to 'middle management of conversations' (Levinson, 1983) such as patterns of turn-taking and topic-switching, semantically oriented semiotics applied to discourse analysis examines texts and accounts as wholes and as component features of an emergent web of performative utterances, promises, and tacit directions. The objects of analysis may be segments of everyday speech, documents, interviews, tapes of media or texts, but the aim is to capture the whole as it is composed internally as a set of signs representing (a) text(s) in format, and externally as a representation of a segment of culture. Discourse analysis of policy directs our attention to several additional matters.

Figures of speech – metaphor, irony, synecdoche, and under-statement – are semantic matters that link writing styles to meaning (see Levinson, 1983). These are often organizationally based, or a part of the commonsense knowledge of organizational members, and as such, a part of the organizational culture. Analysis is guided by the forms of discourse chosen in the 'writing phase', and could be guided by tropes, or perspectives on the field which constituted the facts, defined their relevance, and assembled them into orderly frameworks. Primary of these is metaphor, or a way of seeing, a turn of mind so to speak, and varieties of tropes such as synecdoche and metonymy. Metaphors, implicit or explicit, guide many aspects of field work and the analysis of fieldwork data (Manning, 1979). Consider these examples of metaphoric guidance of analysis. Irony, seeing something as it is not, transforms and converts mere appearance into reality. Irony is the master trope of organizational analysis since it sees the organization as maintaining a degree of rational control over its environment by the specification of determinant rules, procedures and goals. 'Organization' defined in discourse terms, is seen as a set of signs about signs (another way of rendering this is to recognize that organizations are social worlds), stands in contrast to 'environment': it represents a rational island in the midst of irrational counterforces (compare Manning, 1979: 662). Ironic analysis draws on Kenneth Burke's fundamental notion of 'perspective by incongruity' (1962). It is likely that sociological discourse is almost inevitably ironic, even when it is apparently factual and flatly descriptive (compare Geertz, 1988).

Unfortunately, analysis of tropes or figures of speech tends to produce rather 'frozen' renditions of events and processes. Semiotic analysis must address the question of *semiosis*, or changes in meaning. Clearly, understanding the process of change in meaning within an organization is essential to developing a rich and even partially animated understanding of policy. Changes in paradigms, in their contents, or in their interpretants can be socially located and differences in meaning compared in order to demonstrate consequences of transformation in meanings (see Manning, 1987b).

Many forms of writing and policy discourse exist (Geertz, 1988; Van Maanen, 1988). Such variation is a key to careful investigation of the shaping, defining and constructing the emergent meaning of the social objects constituted by policy. Observation, documents, and interviews may be required to establish the links between organizational discourse, paradigms, or associative contexts within which ideas cohere, and the external environment of the organization.

Discourse analysis of policy is not actor oriented. Because the focus is upon the codes which provide voices and forms of expression, especially metaphors, the interest is not in actors' feelings, roles or selves. The discourse perspective surfaces a broad question of comparative sociology begged by Geertz: the relative importance of the subjectively articulated position of the native observer, or the 'native's point of view' (Geertz, 1974). Personal styles, or biography (Gertz, 1988), and factual knowledge are less relevant to policy analysis than an understanding of the social grounds for 'knowledgeability', or a semi-shared tacit sense of the correct, the trustworthy, adequate and workable that links formal schemes such as organizational objectives, standard procedures and policies with practical actions (Giddens, 1984).

The connections for which knowledgeability is a gloss are those between what might be called 'talk and the world' (see Goffman, 1974: ch. 13). *Content*, or substance of policy and associated practices constrain and shape any fieldwork-based analysis.

Discourse analysis must place discourse within the context of political interests and values, and note the selective vision that perspectives provide on the world. Just as models or maps of disease differentially direct attention to certain facts, symptoms and diseases, discourse screens and amplifies meaning. Discourse empowers and gives vision: it also disempowers and blinds. In the following section, some organizational influences on policy discourse are noted.

Method and setting

A fieldwork study of HM Nuclear Installations Inspectorate (NII) was carried out in England, primarily between 1983 and 1986.[1] The overall aim of the research was to integrate notions of policy with the social organization of the Inspectorate, and involved gathering some 21 lengthy interviews and fieldwork during two intensive periods in the NII between March 1984 and March 1986.[2]

The Nuclear Installations Inspectorate

The NII came into being in April, 1960 with the passage of the Nuclear Installations (Licensing and Insurance) Act of 1959, in part as a result of the serious fire and release of radioactivity at the Windscale fuel reprocessing plant in 1957 and the publication of the Fleck Commission Report in December, 1957 (Patterson, 1983). Crises have shaped the Inspectorate, and continue to reshape priorities and the allocation of resources.[3]

With the passage of the Health and Safety at Work Act in 1974, establishing the Health and Safety Commission and consolidating the several inspectorates under one umbrella, the NII was shifted from the Department of Energy to the Ministry of Employment, Trade and Industry, Executive. Its considerable energies are divided between maintaining production and a viable electrical industry and ensuring cooperative environments in which safety is the mutual concern of workers and management. Based in London from the outset, in May of 1986 all the branches, save the fuel-reprocessing branch (always in Bootle, near Liverpool, and not far from the Sellafield/Windscale site), were moved to Bootle. The Chief Inspector, his staff, and the policy branch, remain in London.

The NII is headed by a Chief Inspector and his deputy, and is composed of some 103 persons allocated almost equally into five branches. The first branch is devoted to operating plants; the second monitors the planning and building of plants approved and in process; the third regulates fuel reprocessing, and the fourth has responsibilities for future plants. The newly created fifth branch (begun in early 1986), is smaller than the others, about six people, and is charged with the development of policy. Each is headed by a branch head, and contains three–four sections, each with a head. Internally, the operational four branches are divided function-ally between 'field inspectors' and 'specialists' (mathematicians, chemists, electrical engineers, physicists), although this is not a rigid distinction, since many of the experts have been field inspectors and the field inspectors are also experts. They are white scientists and engineers, all but one of whom is male.

The organization responds to and evaluates requests from the industry (composed of semi-governmental bodies, two electricity-producing organizations, licensees who can be granted licences to generate power in the UK – the South of Scotland Electricity Generating Board (SSEGB) and the Central Electricity Generating Board (CEGB) – and one fuel-reprocessing/waste disposal corporation, British Nuclear Fuels. Although the responsibility for the safety of the operating plant lies with the licensee, NII judges the adequacy of the arguments (called the 'safety case') for the safety of facets of the planning, design management and operation of the installation. The NII engages in a series of on-going bargaining and negotiation sessions concerning the nature, quality, and indicia of 'safety'. One of the dominant themes in self-description of the mandate of the NII is that they serve as the 'conscience' of the industry in a neutral, objective and fair way. Their decisions cannot be appealed against, and they have absolute authority to take swift action to close a plant, fine the operators, delay return to power after routine maintenance, and the like.

Inspectorates as an organizational type

Inspectorates are established as a result of political forces, and emerge at given historical periods. These shape the mandate and licence at least as much as decisions taken or developments subsequent to the establishment of the agency by administrative law, specific legislation or executive action.[4]

Several general points about inspectorates as types of organization should be noted. They can be seen as having been established to monitor and regulate phenomena that are infrequent in occurrence, are relatively important when they do occur, and where the society has taken a decision to make a commitment to the encouragement and protection of the market in which such goods, services or activities are exchanged, regardless of the regulatory costs associated with the governmental intervention. The regulation of safety is not a function easily sustained by 'market forces', as it is a 'collective good' (Samuelson, 1954; Feeley, 1970), requiring governmental protection. The aims of regulation in this case are to meet the aims of legislation establishing the function, produce an outcome or state of affairs, prevent harm or restore the status quo ante. Monitoring and inspection are used, and the administrative definitions of acceptable compliance are paramount (see Hawkins, 1984).

The structure of inspectorates is based on the assumption of the need to *monitor events* and react to events. Hence, the decentralized and 'bottom-heavy' nature of the distribution of personnel, high discretion at the bottom, and belief in the personal, interactive and 'hands-on' nature of the work. Style, persuasion and interpersonal competence, as well as any abstract skills which the job may require, are valued (see Hutter, 1986; Hawkins, 1984). Coordination of collective action comes about through generalized rules and procedures, guided principally by wisdom accumulated and distilled from experience. Inspectorial work focuses upon *cases*, or individual problems seen in context. Situational logic is employed. This means that the incident or event is seen within the context of current matters at hand, and long-term plans and policies are more or less background to such considerations. As the relevant facts are gathered, patterned, and become the basis for a decision, they are fitted within the decision field. This sort of logic contrasts with the logic of long-term rationality which emphasizes the achievement of distant goals even at the cost of the solution of short-term problems. The enforcement mode adopted by Inspectorates in general, the *conciliatory style* of implementing governmental social control (Black, 1976: 5), is shaped by general policies as well as the familiar and routine relationships between the persons responsible for decisions in the organizations regulated and the inspectors, branch and section heads. In this sense, the working principles that guide regulation in Britain, 'reasonable practical means' tests and 'best practicable means' tests, are glosses on detailed understandings of given plants, reactors, managers and the licensees' representatives (see O'Riordan et al., 1985). These practices produce what Reiss (1983b: 815) calls '. . . a body of standards virtually unique to a given situation – standards that the agency more or less holds to enforcing its mandate'. The NII, especially in the process of licensing, maintains flexibility to decide matters in each case without being bound by rule, provided only that its decisions are consistent with its mandate to insure safety (paraphrase of Reiss, 1983b: 815; see also, Hawkins, 1984;· Hutter, 1988).

The transformations of policy in NII

Transformation refers to a systematic change in a social form, or the perceptual structure within which information is contained. Form implies that some shared conception of rules exists which makes forms sensible and meaningful. Changes in the form of a phenomenon appear at known points in a social system. The transformation of social forms such as social policy is not limited to known forces, because all social systems are open and produce and receive new information. In order to understand notions of policy and their transformations, a few fundamentals should be stated at the outset.

It is important to underscore that associations with the word 'policy' did not easily spring to mind in the Inspectorate, even when asked about. When pressed, respondents could give examples. Most frequently mentioned were: the twenty-year (notional) review of the 11 Magnox reactors, the Sizewell Inquiry and matters arising therefrom, and the governmentally mandated move of the NII to Bootle (about 150 miles from London). The policy of greatest interest to branch Heads and the Chief Inspector of the NII was prospective guidance based upon two pamphlets written by HM Nuclear Installations Inspectorate, *Safety Assessment Principles for Nuclear Power Reactors* (1979) and *The Work of HM Nuclear Installations Inspectorate* (1982). Interviewing also established what informants thought policy was *not*. They viewed two types of policy as largely irrelevant to the mandate of NII. These were: *safety* policy, which meant 'the three Cs': cancer, casualties and catastrophes'; and *health* policy, which surrounded issues of chronic risks to groups such as dust, mercury and asbestos and occupationally related risks such as those intrinsic to work with lead. The central policy unit of the Health and Safety Executive (HSE) was seen as primarily a matter of 'law and information'. The word evoked process, and development, and a low level of realization amongst the 'field forces' in many respects.

At least eleven denotative meanings of the term 'policy' were elicited, ranging from very broad characterizations such as 'talk' or 'consultation', to very specific, almost operational definitions such as 'what policy branch do'. Six clusters of these denotative meanings, metaphoric associations, were discovered, connoting flux, coping, response, formalized approaches to problems arising, constraints on choice and the activities of units within the NII. The most common notion of policy saw it as a temporally bounded emergent process of negotiated outcomes embedded in the context of written documents with understood or implicit meaning constraining actions and choice. Functional roles and the authority shaped actions. In some sense, informants opposed dynamic and static versions of policy connected loosely as the mandate of the NII. In its several times, places and voices, policy was not seen in terms of influence on outcomes, but as a series of transformations arising either within or from developments without the organization. This suggests that it is important to examine the policy processes and the locations of policy transformation.

Three kinds of policy transformation occur in the NII: *vertical transformations*, or the changes when information moves from inspectors *up* to their supervisors (and the reverse of that), and data that arise in the higher administrative cadre, either within the Inspectorate or policy section of the HSE, Management Board, or from the Chief Inspector, and which come *down*; *horizontal transformations* or changes that occur when ideas or data move across branches (especially in this case, from policy branch to other branches); and *interorganizational transformations* or changes that occur as a result of interorganizational negotiations with licensees or potential licensees.

Two varieties of vertical transformation are of interest from the point of view of semiotic analysis.

1 The central presumptive notion of an inspectorial system is that problems arise, and are reported 'up' by inspectors. In practice, inspectors see themselves as autonomous, and feel that reporting up suggests that they cannot cope with an issue themselves. They eschew it and as a result, typically, matters stop when a 'good enough' answer emerges. Most matters are handled at the level at which they originate. Groups or families of problems, not individual items, arise, and are defined by the means available. These 'families' are general matters of management that affect several power stations, or reactors of a particular type. Resolutions are case-based, and these resolutions are organizational routines (Feldman, 1988). Problems are resolved by these routines and in particular instances, rather than as generic issues.

2 The nature of the flow of policy from the top down is not well understood or even recognized by members at various levels within the NII. From the bottom, the flow appears to be from bottom up, and there is little understanding of an overall authoritatively sanctioned approach. In this context, generalized approaches are associated with imposed issues and problems which arise *externally* to which the Inspectorate must respond in an accountable fashion. This means that internal matters that emerge, arise, or rise to the top are not defined as policy-related, but as more day-to-day decisions to be taken.

Horizontal transformations, on the other hand, are better understood throughout the organization. There are four aspects of the horizontal transformation of policy within the NII.

1 The *case-by-case focus of work* The licensing mode of regulation assumes that the eventual outcome of the process will be a licence; the questions are only the time that will be involved and the time and money required to reach some kind of mutually acceptable consensus on the nature of operating requirements of the reactors, or the licence conditions. This means that questions of the safety case prepared will be centred on the particular case at hand and its features such as the emergency planning, the site selection, the reactor design, the staffing plans, the decommissioning plans and the features of the sequence of steps required to bring a reactor up

to power and on line. The work on a site is organized horizontally in the sense that assistance may be required from a specialist assessor in another branch.

2 The *division of labour* alters meanings. Inspectors, as opposed to the specialist assessors, are assigned to sites, one for each of the operating power stations. These assignments focus their attention upon the particular site and their relations there. As the specialists are to address questions sent to them by the inspectors, such as the safety of welds, the causes of overheating, problems in leaking cooling systems or the like, there is a somewhat natural tension between the inspectors and the specialists.

3 The *organization of the five branches*, shaped by the accidents and inquiries that precipitated the passage of the Acts of 1959 and 1974 that brought the Inspectorate into being, reflects many of the above-mentioned tensions. Nuclear Installation Inspectorate branch organization seems to embed several quite different principles, and to produce semi-autonomous segments striving to maintain uncertainty and independence. They are based variously upon: distinctions between *staff and line* (branches 1–4, and 5, the policy branch); *temporality* (branches 1 and 2 which focus on commissioning sites and operating sites and 4 which notionally deals with future reactors and has been over the last few years entirely given over to response to the Sizewell Inquiry); and *function* (branches 1, 2 and 4 focus on generating electricity by means of nuclear power, branch 3 on fuel reprocessing, and 5 on policy). Loose alliances are formed between branches around problems of mutual interest. This web of alliances and weak ties within and across the branch organization leads to a number of conflicts and structural adjustments. Centralized control and uniform direction of activity were elusive. The extant unity arose from a task-driven and workflow-created shared sense of purpose within branches. This was commonly produced by the inspectors and the licensees' routine maintenance schedules.

4 *Decentralized decision-making was valued*. The sources of families of problems requiring general guidance policy are diverse, and case-by-case decision making predominates in any inspectorate. In any case, the capacity of branch Heads to guide precisely the actions and decisions of their inspectors is as limited as their vision and access to information 'on the ground'. As NII has grown and diversified, branch autonomy increased while the exchange of information across branches is less frequent than it was.

The shaping of policy in NII is intimately linked with the close *interorganizational relationships* between the NII and the licensees (see above). These exchanges shape the volume of work, and the division of labour within the Inspectorate, as well as those matters seen as policy issues: they are the context for negotiating a licence.

The NII is in a reactive or responsive position *vis-à-vis* the licensees because with respect to the licensing process, but not with respect to subsequent work of inspection and review, NII responds to licensees' requests. What many suggested was a kind of policy-making activity in which NII had an emergent and historical quality, in part captured metaphorically in the unfolding, negotiated, step-by-step process by which a licence is granted. Each licence issued since 1979 made more concrete the precedents established by the NII. In some sense, these were also thought of as 'standards'. The word did not refer to standards in the sense of absolute rules or levels of required performance. They were rather standards in the sense of written examples, or 'packages' of types of requirements set out in the licensing conditions. Thus, the importance of projected precedent to be set by the licensing of the proposed first British PWR. It was hoped by administrators that these precedents would pattern subsequent licensing procedures for the projected four or five PWRs hinted at by the CEGB. This strategy of prior review and evaluation is designed to ensure that the designated issues of concern to the NII are addressed prior to the initiation of a plan. But in practice, the planning, the vetting, and the negotiation of conditions stated in the licence are simultaneously being organized. Routines and solutions, well worked out within the organization, meet the problems, while some solutions found their problems (compare Feldman, 1989).

A number of influences emerging from interorganizational negotiation shape policy. First, the workload and the amount of paper generated is overwhelming. The database for a given safety case is daunting, and can run to volumes and shelves of documents. No single individual does, or could, read and digest this material. One must trust most of what is submitted by the licensee and assume it is done well and competently. It is conventional wisdom within the inspectorate that one cannot read and evaluate every-thing. Within the limits of time and energy, NII people sample and evaluate, but they are unable to check completely the data submitted for many of the safety cases. Secondly, bargaining is political and moral, rather than surrounding 'purely scientific' questions of press-ure circuit design, ergonometrics and the like. The fundamental questions asked in the course of bargaining are matters of values, morals and politics thinly dressed with the limp excuses of 'business' and pseudo-economic language. There is considerable disagreement, for example, over the level at which one should use redundancy rather than multiple-function back-up systems; the value of retrofitting old systems, and the relative danger of PWR as compared to Magnox or graphite-cooled reactors. These questions cannot be answered solely with scientific facts because the facts themselves exist in some value context. Costs of building and alterations are subject to fluctuations in international costs of fuel, interest rates, and even labour unrest in the coal industry. The shaping of policy-related action comes in a variety of meetings with the CEGB, and the results of these meetings may not be widely circulated. These are not, strictly speaking, rule governed.[5]

The NII responds not only to requests, but also to unanticipated events and accidents. Time is always seen as scarce and events emerge to gobble it unexpectedly. This explains the event-driven character of much of the activity of NII staff. In the normal course of events, in the ageing set of British reactors, leaks occur, industrial accidents happen on sites, the temperature in a reactor unexpectedly rises, coolant is lost from tiny, indiscernible pin-holes somewhere in the miles of plumbing, cranes fall and crush the floors of reactors, and fuel reprocessing plants, full of noxious chemical gases, spring leaks. Reactors are periodically shut down for maintenance and must go through an elaborate and supervised procedure, including a detailed report, before they can return to full power. Such shut-downs and returns to power, considered 'routine maintenance', are the most common causes of accidents in nuclear power stations, including the most famous of all, the Three Mile Island incident and the Chernobyl core meltdown. The sensitive nature of the operations and their public potential all serve to enliven the work and keep the air tense and anticipatory. The CEGB request for a licence for a PWR at Sizewell produced work that completely occupied Branch 4 for five years or more, most of the time of the Chief Inspector in his last two years of office (1984 to the summer of 1985), and periodically demanded the time of a large number of people in NII.

To observe that policy in NII is shaped by reactions to requests or is responsive is to recognize the centrality of external sources of the work. The normal state of overload of the staff within the Inspectorate, the event-driven nature of the issues that are defined as matters of policy concern, for example the twenty-year Magnox review, the Sizewell/PWR inquiry and related work, all dramatize the emergent or process-based nature of the outcomes of decisions seen to shape policy. The NII sees its mandate as anticipation of events, and of damage control of those that do occur.

Interorganizational tensions were also produced by some emergent internal contradictions of policy, such as placing enormous effort into the development of the safety case for the PWR when the outcome of the planning inquiry could have dealt the British nuclear industry a death blow. There were also tensions between the NII and the HSE surrounding the degree to which the HSE might exercise greater centralized control over NII operations. There were potential conflicts between the government's espousal of nuclear power and the Inspectorate's consideration of the PWR in 1984–86.

The idea that policy is discourse, an active formulation of meaning, seems a central association of signifier 'policy' as discussed by these informants in the NII. In discourse terms 'policy' is talk about a social world from a place in that world. It thus constitutes the several meanings of that world as it is spoken (Rock, 1987). 'Policy' is an emergent matter located within the tacit boundaries of assumed modes of discourse paradigms. It is an unfolding matter, an emergent, somewhat invisible, set of tacit assumptions about the meaning of a set of discrete decisions found in several locations. It is important to locate these general statements within the specific organizational context studied.

In the NII the case-by-case, bottom-heavy nature of inspectorial organizations reduced the likelihood of long-term planning and policy making. Matters mentioned as 'policy' relevant often arose as a result of political and economic developments outside the organization, and some of these involved rather immediate questions of the mandate of the organization and its survival. The processual and emergent faces of policy in NII are amplified by the decentralized character of the operations of the Inspectorate, the autonomy and discretion of the inspectors, the external source of much of the work and the various levels and styles of management found in the branches. The flowing and changing nature of the ideas means that its referents vary from branch to branch; from licensee to licensee with whom the NII negotiates; at various levels within the NII, and between the HSE executive and the NII as an Inspectorate within the HSE. In some sense, the search for policy meanings disappears into the setting-specific discourse at lunch tables, in hallways, in power stations, and in meetings.

Fieldwork settings and tropes

Policy discourse is situated discourse. Fieldwork is shaped substantially by the character of the setting, the constraints of access, factual or objective knowledge relevant to the research, the interpretative issues involved in data-gathering and analysis, the level of abstraction within which discourse is cast, and the metaphors that best capture the cultural context within which the research is done. These factors, in turn, shape the nature of policy discourse. In order to highlight this, I compare and contrast fieldwork done on the police in Britain with fieldwork in the NII (Manning, 1977, 1980, 1988a).

Police fieldwork
Two aspects of the setting are important: the *symbolic themes* or repertoires of the police and the structure of the organization. First, the themes are shaped by traditional organizational form, the occupational subculture and the common law tradition. Police are action oriented, and action and violence are both everyday occurrences and a feature of their stories, occupational culture and even the division of labour within the department. The police engage in fairly visible social-control functions, and at least part of their activity is verbal, observable in public and accessible to the senses. Police degrade what they see as abstractions and intellec-tualization, and overvalue (from the intellectual's or administrator's point of view) direct action to solve a problem. They view themselves as 'men of action'. They possess no general theory of policing or of human conduct, and their technology, part of which is quite sophisticated, is embedded nevertheless in traditional organiz-ational tasks and structure. They rely on commonsense judgement in face-to-face encounters with people. Their work is uncertain, demand sporadic, and outside their direct control. They are highly dependent on information brought to them by citizens. Police, for the most part, are educated at the high-school level, come from lower-middle-class origins, and bring a working-class style to the organization and the occupational culture of the officers below the rank of sergeant (see Manning, 1979, 1989). Second, *police organization* is highly bureaucratic, while work takes place within a decentralized command structure; the workforce is dispersed widely in a geographical area. The police possess high discretion, are rarely closely supervised, and value autonomy and personal authority. Their work, although visible to the public, is invisible to their supervisors (Jermeir and Berkes, 1979). Their primary locus of symbolic and self-affirmatory action is 'the streets'; they control people in situations where violence may be required.

Nuclear Installations Inspectorate
The symbolic *themes* one finds in the NII amongst the Inspectors, branch Heads, and Chief, differ from those found amongst the police. Inspectors in NII are thought-oriented, and most of what passes for action is reading, condensing, summarizing, minuting and

passing on internal memos, reports, and scientific documents. Inspectors spent notionally about 20 per cent of their time in the field, making site visits. However, they are primarily working at their desks, telephoning, attending meetings and conferences with colleagues within the NII and with the CEGB. Much of the work is 'invisible' to the naked eye – one sees paper move, words spoken, decisions discussed, gossip shared, but the movement of paper, the constant shuffle of files and records, is a blur. It is not easy to 'see' a decision being made. As civil servants with considerable higher education and training, NII people value abstraction, reasoned judgement, good sense, careful analyses and systematic evaluation. They seek clarity and precision in their own writing and speech and value it in others. They value understatement, subtlety, and irony, and rarely like overt confrontations, disagreements or direct sanctioning of others. The preference is for maintaining a constant dialogue which relies on good conscience, honesty and humour. Although they view themselves as scientists and engineers, they are translating scientific principles and ideas into working judgements about matters social, political, moral, economic and technical. One might call the problems 'sociotechnical' insofar as they are involved in the products of the interactions of human beings and technical systems such as the nuclear reactor and related various components, subsystems and systems. Here they stand between the scientific and the political or policy world of public safety. They see their work as 'scientific'. Yet, of necessity, science is a discourse or form for discussion, while the ultimate purpose and justification for the work is moral and political. In this way, they stand in relation to science as the police do to law. Organizationally, they are subject to the ebb and flow of work determined by the CEGB; the request for licences, the wish to modify a plant, or change the conditions of the licence, and they are dependent, furthermore, often for information, evaluations and scientific assessments produced by the scientists employed by the CEGB or their subcontractors. This is a constant source of irony to the Inspectors since they are asked to judge, often at short notice, the quality of a scientific assessment made by CEGB scientists about, for example, the merit of a new fire-control scheme or radioactive-emissions tracking system. The second thing to be considered is the characteristics of the NII as an *organization*. The NII is an inspectorate with the usual concentration of personnel on the bottom of the organization, high discretion, and decentralized authority. The decentralized nature of the NII, branches acting in large part as semi-feudal baronies, and relatively little communication between branches other than between 1 and 2, means that great discretion lies within the branches and at the individual level.

Great value is placed on autonomy and decisiveness, and little close supervision is carried out, although some section heads monitor the work-flow of their workers rather closely. The cumulative pattern of decisions is usually only known to branch heads when a crisis occurs, when a decision is needed, or when a complaint is lodged by the CEGB about some decision.

Differences compared
The situation with respect to constraints was different in the NII. There, the focus was on paperwork, on meetings and telephone calls and consultations, and the several relevant sites (some 18 reactors around England and Wales) were dispersed. Furthermore, the reactors themselves are patently inaccessible to the senses: some parts of reactors are accessible by cameras or X-rays or video cameras, and some parts can be seen, but most of the interior is permanently closed to view. Regardless of the scientific base, many decisions have to be made inferentially because one cannot see the part, the system is too complex, or in complex interaction with other systems. Some of the parameters at issue are estimates or guesses. (What is the probability of a rare event like the meltdown of a core, something that has happened once in the 50 years or so of nuclear technology experimentation?) In many important ways, NII works with reasoned approximations of many matters central to their mandate.

The interpretative issues also differ. The level of verbally explicit detail carried in the interviews was higher, and the phrases, terms, concepts, and reasoning were scientific in character. I was assumed to know more than I actually knew about nuclear reactors, although I was not patronized or treated as ignorant (I was, in fact, relatively ignorant). My position at the University of Oxford and the sponsorship by the HSE of the research were more of an advantage in establishing trust during the fieldwork than were my American positions when doing fieldwork with the American police. Many of the key questions about the safety of the reactor were cast into scientific terms. Non-technical issues, and even other questions about reactor safety or about safety more broadly defined, were not discussed (see Manning, 1988a).

The level of abstraction at which the questions of nuclear safety were debated, discussed and outlined, was consistent with a very high-level notion about the study of policy and the nature and content of policy. The similarities between police and NII are striking. The varied, concrete, elusive and changing meanings of 'policy' in policing were reproduced in NII. That complexity was expressed in technical terms rather than in somewhat more earthy, direct and concrete terms as was the case amongst the police.

The salience and significance of verbal discourse in social life varies. In the police studies, with the exception of work on the technology of organizing a response to public calls for assistance, these limits seemingly are not difficult to overcome, in large part because once access is negotiated at a given level of the organization, scenes can be observed, and key themes of the work can be analysed. Talk can be checked against action; tales with observed scenarios; contradictions between ideology and practice explicated and paradoxes noted.

Metaphors, one form of organizing talk, vary. The metaphors in policing are those of drama, conflict, distrust, action, control, struggle against evil (crime), and serving the interests of the high morality of the state, while those in the NII were of reasoned cognition, scientific concepts and analogies, sensible and careful planning, trust and mutual cooperation in the interests of achieving shared aims and objectives. There are few dramatic turning points for the NII because Britain's last world-class disaster was the source of their creation. The licensing process is a lengthy one, often taking years to complete. The events that punctuate the career of a plant are housed in a huge cabinet, and decisions minuted in files. There is little finality about any of the work done, because it is essentially negotiation. In short, it is not easy to study bureaucrats when the 'paper trail' itself is so vast as to be inaccessible, and the depictions of the process are caricatures unavailable to the senses. The use of policy was ironic in both NII and amongst the police, and the sources of the irony were similar: both organizations dealt with uncertain events out of their control for which they were socially accountable. The greater the explicit policy on anything, the greater likelihood of being held accountable. Mystification and opacity are the stock in trade here, and this, in turn, is related to the nature of policy discourse.

Discourse in the field

This review of policy tropes reveals some of the hidden assumptions in the social sciences about the nature and premises of policy. The NII does not have a specific written policy on any matter; nevertheless, it has mapped a way of talking to itself, a reflexive series of accounts that some have called culture (Swidler, 1984). It is a non-technical account of safety that takes shape and meaning in bargaining and negotiation with the licensees, which is semi-public, and which obscures the problematics of the technology itself. The discourse that has been described sits within a larger noetic field of assumed meanings, purposes and outcomes. In this sense, it is analogous to the discourse analysed by Foucault in the *Birth of the*

230 Peter K. Manning

Clinic (1973) in which he suggests that the development of the clinical gaze, his metaphor for the scientific study of the body, disease and death, produced a new way of seeing that was no longer metaphorical or analogical. His analysis of the discourse that dominated medicine prior to the great scientific inventions of the nineteenth century, shows how a new space was created inside the human body, in which disease was to be observed and studied. The old signified (or content), the body, now occupies a new place in scientific discourse, as now a signifier (expression) of a partitioned, ordered, empirically instantiated map. A new configuration of meaning and a spatial/temporal location for it was created. The radical shift in discourse involved in the establishment of what is now termed 'scientific medicine' is charted. This new scientific objectification of the body made it possible for doctors not only to gaze at but to gaze into a person's body, and to capture the nature and significance of this gaze in scientific discourse. In many ways, as Foucault shows, discourse blinds to certain matters and opens others to the gaze; as Kenneth Burke more modestly noted, 'a way of seeing is also a way of not seeing' (1962). In social policy analysis, we have not yet reached inside the body metaphorically.

The received view of policy in the social sciences, to a remarkable degree, contains hidden assumptions that can be analysed on the one hand in respect of the materials presented above and on the other in connection with the insights of Foucault. Each assumption should be examined in the context of discourse analysis of any given policy because these assumptions lie 'beneath' the surface features of any given policy. As long as policy is studied as rational means of achieving ends, it will omit fundamental irrationalities hidden by lies, self-deception, organizational strategies and tactics.

The first and most basic of these might be called the value-free illusion. This assumes the unquestioned capacity of human beings to free themselves of their own illusions and ideologies which define and make real the nature of the problems to be analysed and controlled. The second assumption might be called the illusion of social control through bureaucratic action. This assumption is made by all bureaucrats to a greater or lesser degree. It is easy to begin to believe that organizations have the capacity, will and authority to alter, control, modify, and improve a variety of multiply determined social arrangements. In some sense, this is a prerequisite for administrative action. The third is the position of such bureaux that 'things are different' as a result of the existence of bureaucratic actions. Not only are they different in some discernible way, the difference that they produce is more good than evil. It is assumed that they accomplish, on the whole, a degree of betterment in the quality of life. Very often, of course, the organization gathers no systematic evidence to establish the veracity of this ideologically driven assumption (Edelman, 1964; Meyer and Rowan, 1977). Yet another assumption concerns the quality of the control of the environment by organizational action. This might be called the efficacy tenet of organizational action that is often coupled with the rather American belief or assumption that action is preferable to inaction and that 'actions speak louder than words'. There is also an assumption that science shapes bureaucratic decisions, even if this science is a vaguely understood science of public administration.

With the exception of the last point, policy discourse in the NII illustrates these tenets.[6]

How is it that policy discourse has emerged in this form, transformed within NII, and now patterns governmental discussions?

Foucault's work on the clinic has general relevance to this question and the analysis of policy discourse. He has noted the importance of discourse and the *episteme*, ways of making certain matters public and visible and in this sense subject to public monitoring and control. However, science can obscure and make less visible practices and assumptions about phenomena not subject to actual empirical measurement and control. Foucault argues similarly about sexuality: as it has been viewed more rationally and become open to public discussion, it has become subject to more forms of regulation. It becomes an object for scientification and scientific reasoning, rather than being idiosyncratic, personal or even, at times, whimsical. Foucault also alerts readers to the predetermined nature of authoritative reasoning and structures of vision.

The NII has created a public discourse that conceals many of the problems and contradictions of nuclear safety-regulation. The focus of the NII on negotiating licences precludes consideration of the broader questions: is generating electrical power by means of nuclear reactors safe? Are different types of reactors 'safe' in varying degrees? How should safety be defined, measured and evaluated? How can it be proven that something is safe, when the concept of safety, at least in part, arises from the degree of personal security citizens feel about risks, what they take to be acceptable? Are there issues of safety and risk that cannot be resolved, given the recency of commercial nuclear reactors? What does the fact that most of the innards of reactors, miles of pipes, electrical wiring, sealed reactor cores are invisible mean for monitoring the safety and deterioration of operating parts?

The NII has formulated a scientific entity in policy talk that is unavailable to the gaze. It is based on a configuration resting on trust and non-empirical determinations of 'safety'. It builds on a series of unexplicated assumptions.

It is accepted that scientists disagree on the safety of various types of reactors and of various forms of safety systems, but this is viewed as resolvable in the event and in practice. Nuclear power is tightly coupled as a production process, and highly complex and interactive (Perrow, 1984), and massively dangerous in the event of an accident or release of radioactivity. The operations of reactors are not accessible to the naked eye – much must be taken on trust. This trust is located with the NII, much as priests and shamans take on the burden of illness and evil. Historic evidence about reactor safety, some fifty years old, is just now being widely shared. Many feel nuclear power is fundamentally unsafe (Perrow, 1984; Patterson, 1983).

National policies and regulatory structures vary cross-nationally, largely a result of the degree of 'capitalistic' competition permitted in building and operating reactors. France is highly controlling, nationalized and uses one basic design; the UK is controlled by governmental semi-nationalized industries and the NII; the United States and West Germany are the most 'capitalistic', permitting private monopolies supported and protected by governmental agencies, and widely diverse in respect of plans, reactors, and patterns of ownership and operation (Valentine, 1984).

National nuclear power policy in Britain is characterized more by drift and indecision than by precise goals, objectives and long-range planning (Williams, 1980). The NII policy is not, and perhaps could not, be based on the strict interpretation of scientific principles, law, or standards, and case-by-case procedures are used. The transformation of policy, from the bottom up, from the licensees and the government to the NII and, to a lesser degree, from the top down, means that policy is elusive.

Fieldwork analysis of policy which assumes the rational, value-free, and controlling aim of policy discourse remains problematic. The shifting meaning of policy and its oblique relation to the noetic field of nuclear safety (rather than the practice of inspecting and evaluating safety cases) means that fieldwork will be about discourse about safety, conceptions of safety, and relative/comparative notions of safety within and between branches and licensees. Foucauldian analysis suggests that constitution of the discourse is a precondition of organizational control over a domain. Science, in this case, engineering and nuclear physics, has been transformed into a language map of an invisible area of social life. The gaze into the reactor and its component parts and associated systems of safety and electricity production is not available to the fieldworker or the citizen. It exists in discourse, just as the reactor exists as material reality. Semiotic analysis directs attention to the gaps, rips and torn edges of the canopy of ideology organizations pull over themselves.

Notes

1 The study was part of a larger programme of research coordinated by the Socio–Legal Centre at Wolfson College, Oxford and supported by funding from the Health and Safety Executive. I held the position of Senior Scientific Officer at the Centre and was a Fellow of Wolfson College, Oxford, from March, 1984 to March, 1986.

2 The research included bibliographic historical research on the origins of nuclear power and the shape that that quest took in Britain specifically just before, during and after World War II. These patterned the growth of the regulatory structures for the production of nuclear-generated energy. Some comparative analysis of nuclear safety policies and approaches in France, the United States and Britain was explored (see, for example, Campbell, 1988; Valentine, 1984). Clippings from newspapers published in Britain and America on nuclear power and related issues such as waste disposal, fuel reprocessing, the economics of power production, and international developments in the nuclear power have been collected and filed since 1982. Documents and records produced by the Sizewell Inquiry (1983–85) and the Layfield Report (Layfield, 1987), were consulted. Fieldwork, including observations, interviews, attending meetings, joint conferences between NII and the Central Electricity Generating Board and plant management, a site visit to a power station on an inspection, and records analysis, was undertaken. Three of the then four branches of the Inspectorate were studied. Branch three, fuel reprocessing, was omitted.

3 These include the series of gas leaks and explosions at the Sellafield plant in early 1986; the anticipated move to Bootle which took place in 1986–87; and the hearings presided over by Sir Frank Layfield held in Snape Maltings on the east coast of England in 1983–85 precipitated in part by the Central Electricity Generating Board's (CEGB) proposal to build a pressurized water reactor (PWR) at the current Sizewell power station. During the study, the Sizewell hearings were virtually the dominant concern of the Inspectorate, and some proportion of the resources and personnel, variously estimated at between 25 and 60 per cent, were committed to preparing testimony, documents, and answering inquiries. The resultant Layfield Report (Layfield, 1987) recommended building the proposed PWR.

4 Interpretations of an Inspectorate's actions turn out to be quite different if one takes a political/Marxist perspective on origins and functions (Parks, 1970) rather than a symbolic/expressive (Gusfield, 1963, 1981) or functionalist (Reiss, 1983a, 1984) perspective.

5 Rules which guide the operation of nuclear power stations take several forms and arise from quite different sources. Some derive from international bodies, such as the rules about exposure to radiation; some are stated in the conditions of the licence; some are developed by the licensee to govern plant procedures, operations and management arrangements. Still other rules are created by the National Radiation Safety Board and a group composed of heads of power stations and research reactors.

6 The NII do not use science as the primary rhetoric, but rather civil service

language of modest, careful 'muddling through' complexity in good faith and humour. Science and scientific discourse take different forms and uses in Britain (compare Gusfield, 1981 with Jasanoff, 1986).

References

Barthes, R. (1972) *Mythologies*, sel. and tr. Annette Lavers. New York: Hill and Wang.
Black, D.J. (1976) *The Behavior of Law*. New York: Academic Press.
Burke, K. (1962) *A Grammar of Motives and a Rhetoric of Motives*. New York: Meridian Books.
Campbell, J. (1988) *Nuclear Power in Crisis: Institutional Imperatives and Public Policy Failure*. Ithaca: Cornell University Press.
Culler, J. (1975) *Structuralist Poetics*. Ithaca: Cornell University Press.
Eco, U. (1976) *A Theory of Semiotics*. Bloomington: University of Indiana Press. (Paperback edition, 1979.)
Edelman, M. (1964) *The Symbolic Uses of Politics*. Urbana: University of Illinois Press.
Feeley, M. (1970) 'Coercion and Compliance: A New Look at an Old Problem', *Law and Society Review*, 4 (May): 505–19.
Feldman, M. (1988) 'Understanding Organizational Routines: Stability and Change', Working paper No. 88/35. Norwegian Research Centre in Organization and Management, University of Bergen, Norway.
Feldman, M. (1989) *Order without Design: Information Production and Policy Making*. Stanford, CA: Stanford University Press.
Foucault, M. (1973) *The Birth of the Clinic*. New York: Vintage.
Geertz, C. (1974) 'From the Native's Point of View: On the Nature of Anthropological Understanding', *Daedalus*, 28: 27–45.
Geertz, C. (1988) *Works and Lives: The Anthropologist as Author*. Stanford, CA: Stanford University Press.
Giddens, A. (1984) *The Constitution of Society*. Berkeley: University of California Press.
Goffman, E. (1974) *Frame Analysis*. Cambridge, MA: Harvard University Press.
Gusfield, J. (1963) *Symbolic Crusade*. Urbana: University of Illinois Press.
Gusfield, J. (1981) *The Culture of Public Problems*. Chicago: University of Chicago Press.
Hawkes, T. (1977) *Structuralism and Semiotics*. Berkeley: University of California Press.
Hawkins, K.O. (1984) *Environment and Enforcement: Regulation and the Social Definition of Pollution*. Oxford: Oxford University Press.
HM Nuclear Installations Inspectorate (1979) *Safety Assessment Principles for Nuclear Power Reactors*. London: HMSO.
HM Nuclear Installations Inspectorate (1982) *The Work of HM Nuclear Installations Inspectorate*. London: HMSO.
Hutter, B. (1986) 'An Inspector Calls', *British Journal of Criminology*, 26 (April): 114–28.
Hutter, B. (1988) *The Reasonable Arm of the Law? Enforcement Procedures of Environmental Health Officers*. Oxford: Oxford University Press.
Jasanoff, S. (1986) *Risk Management and Political Culture*. New York: Russell Sage.
Jermeir, J. and Berkes, L. (1979) 'Leader Behavior in a Police Command

Bureaucracy: A Closer Look at the Quasi-military Model', *Administrative Science Quarterly*, 24 (March): 1–23.

Layfield, Sir F. (1987) *Sizewell B Public Inquiry: Summary of Conclusions and Recommendations*. Department of Energy. London: HMSO.

Levinson, S. (1983) *Pragmatics*. Cambridge: Cambridge University Press.

Manning, P.K. (1977) *Police Work*. Cambridge, Mass.: MIT Press.

Manning P.K. (1979) 'The Social Control of Police Work', pp. 41–65 in S. Holdaway (ed.) *The British Police*. London: Edward Arnold.

Manning, P.K. (1980) *The Narcs' Game*. Cambridge, Mass.: MIT Press.

Manning, P.K. (1987a) *Fieldwork and Semiotics*. Beverly Hills: Sage.

Manning, P.K. (1987b) 'The Development of Policy in the HSE', Conference paper presented at the Health and Safety Conference, Oriel College, Oxford, September.

Manning, P.K. (1988a) 'Organizational Beliefs and Uncertainty', pp. 80–98 in N. Fielding (ed.), *Actions and Beliefs*. Farnborough: Gower.

Manning, P.K. (1988b) *Symbolic Communication*. Cambridge, Mass.: MIT Press.

Manning, P.K. (1989) 'The Police Subculture', pp. 360–4 in W.G. Bailey (ed.), *The Encyclopedia of Police Science*. Dallas, TX: Garland Press.

Meyer, J. and Rowan, B. (1977) 'Institutionalized Organizations: Formal Structure as Myth and Ceremony', *American Journal of Sociology*, 83 (September): 340–63.

O'Riordan, T, Kemp, R. and Purdue, M. (1985) 'How the Sizewell B Inquiry is Grappling with the Concept of Acceptable Risk', *Journal of Environmental Psychology*, 5: 69–85.

Paris, D. and Reynolds, J.F. (1983) *The Logic of Policy Inquiry*. London: Longman.

Parks, Evelyn (1970) 'From Constabulary to Police Society', *Catalyst*, 6 (Summer): 76–97.

Patterson, W. (1983) *Nuclear Power*. 2nd edn. Harmondsworth: Penguin.

Peirce, C.S. (1958) *Collected Papers*. Cambridge: Harvard University Press.

Perrow, C. (1984) *Normal Accidents*. New York: Basic Books.

Reiss, A.J. Jr (1983a) 'The Policing of Organizational Life', in M. Punch (ed.), *Control in the Police Organization*. Cambridge, MA: MIT Press. pp. 78–97.

Reiss, A.J. Jr (1983b) 'Compliance without coercion', *University of Michigan Law Review*, 83(4): 813–19.

Reiss, A.J. Jr (1984) 'Selecting Strategies of Social Control over Organiational Life', in K. Hawkins and J. Thomas (eds), *Enforcing Regulation*. Boston: Kluwer-Nijoff. pp. 23–35.

Rock, P. (1987) *A View from the Shadows: Policy Making in the Solicitor General's Office*. Oxford: Oxford University Press.

Samuelson, P. (1954) 'The Pure Theory of Economic Expenditure', *Review of Economics and Statistics*, 36 (November): 387–90.

Saussure, F. de (1966) *Course in General Linguistics*, ed. C. Bally and A. Sechehaye, tr. W. Baskin. New York: McGraw-Hill. (First published, 1915.)

Swidler, A. (1984) 'Culture in Action: Symbols and Stratagems', *American Sociological Review*, 51 (April): 273–86.

Valentine, J. (1984) *Atomic Crossroads*. London: Merlin.

Van Maanen, J. (1988) *Tales of the Field*. Chicago: University of Chicago Press.

Williams, R. (1980) *Nuclear Power Decisions*. London: Croom Helm.

12
Interventions in New Social Movements

Elim Papadakis

The central theme of this chapter is the intervention in contemporary social movements by social researchers. Many of them are intellectuals who are sympathetic to the aims and goals of a social movement and who play a part in reinterpreting the meaning of its actions and in redirecting its path. This leads us into a discussion of the implications for the aims of participants in social movements of interventions by intellectuals and social researchers, particularly those who are used by (established) organizations to secure their own legitimacy. The critique by post-modernists or Foucauldians of the Enlightenment model of field research is central to this discussion, particularly since new social movements[1] have served as a source of inspiration for both sides of the debate.

Although some writers have sought to identify common goals within such diverse social protests, others have delighted in their heterogeneity and subversive quality. Habermas (1971; 1981a; 1981b), for instance, has identified, both in the student movements of the 1960s and in the new social movements of the 1980s, a potential vehicle for the completion of the modernist project, for an ethics based on communication, rational argument and intention. Movements that do not share his vision for the completion of the project of the Enlightenment are characterized as regressive. By contrast, Foucault and the post-modernists have not only celebrated the resistance by such movements to processes of rationalization but highlighted the manner in which they represent 'local revolts . . . along the disciplinary continuum' (Walzer, 1986: 65). The study of micro-power is linked to the micro-politics of new social movements.

Despite fundamental differences in their approaches, both post-modernists and Habermas have distanced themselves from Marxist theories of social change, from the working class as the main carriers of conflicts of the future and from the sphere of production. Both Habermas (who projects rational models for social change based on metatheoretical and universalist perspectives) and Foucault (who attacks any such attempts to create overarching and totalizing schemes for social relations) (see Lash, 1985) share a concern about social actors and subjectivity being rendered instrumental. It will be argued in this chapter that the attempt to combine metatheoretical accounts with critiques of intellectual élitism (through a focus on the construction of subjects in discourses) is the most salient aspect of discussions over the empowerment of subjects other than as objects of the professional gaze in sociological research. The opposition between modernist and post-modernist approaches may not be as pronounced if one shifts from abstract generalization to the everyday practice of new social movements. Although both Habermas and Foucault draw inspiration from new social movements, neither makes explicit how such forces will act to bring about social change (Lash, 1985).

The same cannot be said of individual researchers or organizations that, in response to the challenge from new social movements, have incorporated field research in their attempts to provide new policy directions. Going much further than the Enlightenment model of field research, the sociological interventions by Alain Touraine among social movement activists are intended to help people at the grass roots to launch a more successful and effective struggle for social change. In West Germany social researchers have been used both by the state and by new social movements to rearticulate the shift in mass attitudes over nuclear power, environmentalism, peace and alternative lifestyles.[2]

Analysis of these interventions will be used to assess the pertinence of the fears expressed by Foucauldian critics of emancipatory discourses and the normalizing role of the human sciences.

Sociological intervention in the French anti-nuclear protest

The work of Touraine has provided a point of contact, albeit in a highly ambiguous manner, between meta-theoretical accounts and diverse social movements and qualitative social research. Like Touraine (1971), some post-modernists place their work at the intersection of industrial and post-industrial society (see Lash, 1985). A close connection is hypothesized between the politics of new social movements and the development of new forms of power centred not so much around the forces of production but rather the control of knowledge and information. There is, however, a crucial difference. Touraine, in a similar vein to Habermas, is concerned with the clash between two social orders, with the discovery of a central conflict dimension (to replace that of the working class versus the bourgeoisie in capitalist industrial society). Post-modernists, on the other hand, would welcome the diversity of social conflicts and struggles, whilst eschewing attempts to impose alternative models of society.

Touraine (1981) has argued that his method of sociological intervention is the application of theories of social movements. It aims to distinguish between different *meanings* of social struggle in order to reveal the presence (or not) of a social movement. The role of the researcher is to encourage the reflexivity of social actors, to assist them with self-analysis, with interpreting the significance of their own action.[3] This novel method of research only strives for objectivity within a prescribed framework: it assumes that a social struggle can only be defined as a social movement if it entails a struggle against 'the holders of technocratic power', those who are at the forefront of developing new ways of managing the economy not only through control of processes of capital accumulation but also through control of knowledge and information. For instance, protesters against nuclear power are only engaged in a social movement if they can clearly define (1) an adversary ('technocratic power created by capitalism'), (2) the stake of the struggle (conflict over common cultural orientations, for instance, over ways of solving economic crises) and (3) the actors themselves (in whose name they are fighting) (Touraine, 1983: 176–7).

Whenever these struggles focus on community rather than modernization, opposition against specific nuclear power installations rather than on new ways of managing the economy, the nuclear industry rather than technocracy, fear rather than level-headed analysis of social action, defensive rather than offensive struggles, grass-roots fundamentalism rather than definition of adversaries, an ethic of conviction rather than of responsibility and crusades rather than strategies, they are distancing themselves from the goals of a modern social movement.

Sociological intervention goes much further than participant observation. The methodological/theoretical rationale for intervention is to achieve an 'adequate understanding of motives and meaning' of social conflicts which would otherwise remain 'deeply hidden from the mere spectator' (Bouchier, 1982: 297). The knowledge of the sociologist becomes inextricably linked with the politics of new social movements. The researcher plays an active role by promoting discussion among activists over the meaning of their struggle. The sociologist aims to assist the activists in 'elevating' the level of their struggle to that of a true social movement. Later, an assessment is made of whether a particular struggle contains the seeds of a social movement capable of challenging technocratic power. In the study of the anti-nuclear protest (Touraine, 1983), two groups were formed and invited to discuss their struggle with interlocutors of their own choice (including sympathizers and opponents, many of whom belonged to major political and industrial organizations). The researchers actively intervened to analyse the conditions and meaning of the struggle. Hypotheses were then presented to the activists. Acceptance of these signified the likely success of the social movement, rejection signalled the inability of the activists to elevate their struggle to that of a modernizing social movement.

Touraine strives to unite the work of the researcher and the object of study (1971: 233). He distances himself from the short-term goals of a particular campaign, whilst seeking (on the basis of sociological analysis and intervention) to influence its general direction as a social movement against technocratic power. The intervention in the anti-nuclear protest, he argues, led some militants to commit their struggle 'to a new direction', to 'a much clearer perception of the conditions that would allow that struggle to exist and develop'. He concludes that for the researchers 'this recognition both of their independence and of their usefulness corresponded so completely to their intention that they found in it the justification of their work' (1983: 171).[4]

Whatever the shortcomings of his methodology, Touraine has provided valuable insights into the attitudes of militants and the chances for success of their struggle. Does this also entail a positive contribution by researchers to the direction of a grass-roots campaign? The 'success' in persuading some activists to adopt a more analytical approach and to reflect on their action is only qualified. The method of intervention was challenged by many activists and some withdrew from the exercise altogether. This draws attention to the dangers of imposing a model for emancipation by 'enlightened' social researchers. It should be stressed that this discussion would not be possible if the researchers had not made public the sources and nature of the conflicts.

The researchers wanted to test their model of a social movement against the reality of the anti-nuclear protest. It is stressed for instance that the sociologist was not a 'benevolent ally' but an analyst 'urging each individual to explain his or her position' (Touraine, 1983: 58).[5] However, this detachment (in order to further the analysis), the reluctance by Touraine to turn himself into the leader of the group is undermined by the aggressive attempt to convert through 'self-analysis' 'those tendencies which seemed at variance with the research team's image of the movement' (1983: 131). The researchers perceived themselves as prophets of an incipient social movement (1983: 194) and sought to raise the consciousness of the activists (1983: 139).

One is reminded of the warning by Foucault against a shallow and dangerous approach to emancipation and rationality. Although they were in favour of self-analysis, the researchers were reluctant to evaluate or separate the groups' influence on the researchers and vice-versa. It would, they argued, be contrary to the spirit of the intervention 'since the work of the groups consisted simultaneously in self-analysis and intervention' (1983: 113). Touraine retained this ambiguity because of his over-riding preoccupation with the discovery of *the* social movement of post-industrial society.

Even participants who shared this goal accused the researchers of 'manipulation of language'. Others reproached them for pressuring the groups into adopting a 'particular image' of their struggle, of devising abstract objectives and programmes to the detriment of the 'lived experience of the movement and, above all of the group itself' (1983: 88). The researchers might have considered how much any social movement can afford to preoccupy itself at length with discourse, with self-analysis and interpretation. In addition, the temporary withdrawal by some women resulted from their perception of yet another attempt (by sociologists) to impose a 'male logic' (1983: 89). At one stage an entire group became so aware of the attempts to create divisions between them that they created an elaborate hoax to demonstrate their unity against the researchers.[6]

These negative reactions by the participants unsettled the researchers. The latter interpreted the behaviour of the dissenters in terms of their own paradigm of modernization, whilst acknowledging perceptions of manipulation. A contrast was evoked between 'cultural withdrawal' and the commitment to a 'political counter-project' (1983: 98), between rejection of industrial–technological society 'in the name of lived experience, balance and community' and the definition of 'a new society' (1983: 120), between anti-statism linked to communitarian values and 'the makers of programmes who seemed to be reformist political manipulators or disembodied theorists' (1983: 137).

Both Touraine and Habermas argue that modernizing tendencies can only be further developed through 'rational' discourse. However, this is not an end in itself. Rather it needs to be steered by an awareness of the social uses of knowledge. In this respect, Touraine identifies social movements as the central potential carriers of social change. Whereas in the past, social action was limited by 'meta-social guarantees of social order' (such as the 'order of things, divine law, or natural, historical evolution'), the capacity of modern societies to create, destroy and transform their environment has enabled social movements to play a much more active role in 'all aspects of social and cultural life' (Touraine, 1985: 778). Whereas in the past, social protest was confined to established institutions, 'in modern societies social movements are located precisely where change takes place' (Eder, 1982: 10).

This perspective was adopted by many of the anti-nuclear activists. However, in order to counter the criticism that the analysis merely reflected the situation of one particular group, comment was invited from other activists who had not been involved in the intervention. The activists on the whole regarded the analysis as a 'useful way of conceiving the problems of the movement' and of bridging the gap between theory and practice (Touraine, 1983: 148). There is, however, a certain Foucauldian irony in the adoption by a major umbrella organization, the Network of the Friends of the Earth, of the terminology of the sociologists. At their 1979 annual congress, they outlined their commitment to conflicts of the future over the control of information and the technocracy (1983: 167). A major grass-roots organization was adopting an interpretation which, according to the paradigm of modernization constructed by Touraine, ran counter to the orientation of many grass-roots activists.

The researchers reported that one group of activists had taken new initiatives and committed their struggle to 'new directions' because of the intervention. Both researchers and participants 'affirmed that the knowledge it had brought, had given the militants, who had never ceased to act according to the aims of their struggle, a much clearer perception of the conditions that would allow that struggle to exist and develop' (Touraine, 1983: 171). However, a second group of activists rejected this Enlightenment model and accused the researchers of producing a biased report which had failed to analyse their 'real experiences', their attempts 'to get a real democracy working and set up certain structures, certain kinds of representation, new forms of information' (1983: 151).

The researchers could hardly refute the charge. In a model drawn up by them to plot the positions of the participants in relation to the 'highest level' of social conflict, those who had rejected the 'social management' of social movements were placed furthest away. The views of these participants on the nature of power, on the locus of social struggles, bore a strong resemblance to post-modernist concerns. To them 'the search for a social adversary can only conceal an inability to challenge oneself' (Touraine, 1983: 44). They felt that power was located 'not in the capitalist system but in individual psychology' (1983: 133), and called for each individual to 'challenge his or her own way of living or thinking' (1983: 73). These views on the nature of power and the locus of social conflict are post-modern to the extent that they show an understanding of how power is a strategy for constituting subjects. However, the focus on self-actualization also corresponds to the message of the new professionals of the psyche – counsellors, psychotherapists and other enforcers of disciplinary practices.

Touraine is aware that to focus on the modernism of the anti-nuclear protest 'might favour the action of a new managing élite' unless it is linked to a broader 'struggle against the holders of technocratic power' (1983: 121). The shared cultural orientations of the anti-nuclear protest and the technocrats provides the basis for conflict rather than 'a modernizing reformism favouring the interests of a new ruling class' (1983: 177). The critique of the anti-nuclear protest has to be 'more modernizing than the policy of the ruling class and the State, but in the opposite direction' (1983: 177). The notion of the self-management of new social movements is contrasted to the manner in which older social movements (particularly the labour movement) have been turned into 'instruments of management or co-management'. None the less Touraine has not provided a convincing model for preventing the emergence of new structures of power and domination via an élite that seeks to impose its perception of the highest level of social struggle on the remainder of the community.

The Greens in West Germany[7]

I now draw out in more detail the implications of interventions by social researchers in contemporary social movements. The focus is on the Greens in West Germany who are perceived both by many of their sympathizers and by established organizations as potentially a profound threat to prevailing structures of power and authority.

The complex intermeshing of theoretical assumptions and research interventions can be linked to responses both by sympathizers to some of the aims of contemporary social movements and by modernizing élites and professionals in state employment to problems arising in areas such as the environment and the provision of welfare services.

Four levels of intervention (which are often linked with field research) can be identified. First, the close ties between intellectual inspirers or theorists and participants in the new social movements, represented above by Touraine, are an important characteristic of the development of the Greens. Indeed, the distinction between theorists and participants is often difficult to uphold. Secondly, the attempt by the Greens to challenge prevailing structures of domination, to counter technologies of monitoring and surveillance and to broaden their social bases of support has led to a complex series of 'dialogues' between new social movements and established organizations. This has highlighted both the advantages and the pitfalls of 'communicative rationality' insofar as this concept can be operationalized. Thirdly, and related to these dialogues, supporters of the Greens in the alternative self-help movement have been at the forefront of experiments in the provision of welfare which in some respects embrace the critique and implicit rejection by Foucault of the modern social state. In other respects, these experiments have led not so much to a rejection of, but to the installation of a different form of, state intervention in people's daily lives. In other words, some of these challenges have been successfully accommodated by a modernizing welfare state. Lastly, both the state and new social movements have made use of interventions by researchers and, despite resistance among some groups, the majority of supporters of new social movements appear to accept them.

The suspicion of interventions by the intelligentsia
Modernizing counter-élites, defined by knowledge and a certain level of education (see Touraine, 1971) have, with limited success, influenced the direction of new social movements. None the less, many Green activists would reject the style of the intervention carried out by Touraine in France. 'Prominent personalities' are seen to have a destructive effect on the attempt by the movements to create credible alternatives to prevailing political structures. The usefulness of intellectual inspirers is questioned by activists who draw the distinction between the capacity of such people to generate publicity for the movement and the practical skills required by militants engaged in a locally based social struggle.

There are innumerable problems facing theorists who seek to assist new social movements.[8] The gap between attempts to identify universal elements in diverse and complex social struggles (see Brand, 1986) and actual practice has led to a questioning of the role of intellectualist interventions. Boggs (1986), who regards the Greens as a prototype of post-Marxist radicalism, stresses their anti-Jacobinist orientation. None the less, the Marxist inheritance still exerts some influence:

> In their most mature expression, these movements constitute counter-hegemonic struggles in the Gramscian sense to the degree they can lead to an alternative ideological framework that subverts the dominant patterns of thought and action, that challenges myths surrounding the vulnerability of the status quo. (Boggs, 1986: 5)

This is an accurate account of a predominant tendency within the Greens. However, it ignores the powerful anti-intellectualism that has prevailed among some sections and the purposeful opportunism involved in accepting some but not other aspects of emancipatory discourses.

This was particularly evident among the so-called Spontis who emerged in the wake of anti-nuclear and environmentalist protests in the mid-1970s and exerted a powerful influence on a burgeoning counter-cultural movement. The Spontis expressed most acutely the reaction against the Marxist orientation of the New Left, against the 'repression of instincts', 'abstract theorizing' and the emphasis on analytical approaches to social problems. The neo-Nietzschean critique of knowledge and rationality posits a mythological basis for social life, the formation of 'anti-authoritarian collectivities' in which recognition is given to the 'differences of others' (see Papadakis, 1984: 36–8). State power is conceived of in highly subjectivist terms rather than in formal abstract categories.

Their position (see Röttgen and Rabe, 1978) is close to that of Foucault and the post-modernists. Rather than consensus they would focus on dissensus (Lash, 1985: 17). For Foucault plans for reform are of little use unless they emerge from the activists engaged in a social struggle (see Silverman, 1987: 203). He is deeply suspicious of the 'emancipatory discourse' (D'Amico, 1986). Attempts to devise or imagine alternative social systems are regarded as an extension of 'participation in the present system' (Foucault, 1977: 230, quoted in Minson, 1986: 140).

Such an approach is anathema to Habermas who has argued that by equating rationality with the preservation of economic and administrative systems of action, in other words state power, new social movements may often reject reason itself (Habermas, 1981c: 140). Whereas Habermas identifies the 'emancipatory potential' of, for instance, the feminist movement and its role as a carrier of universal values (1981a: 34), a Foucauldian approach to issues such as the socialization of child care and domestic tasks would highlight 'how a certain socialization and various measures of "women's liberation" provided some of the conditions of the emergence of the involuted private modern family' (Minson, 1986: 143; see Donzelot, 1979: 221). More specifically, the extension of state child-care facilities in the German Democratic Republic has not weakened 'commitment to the nuclear family as . . . a relay of "social" disciplinary norms' (Minson, 1986: 142). Yet a simplistic adaptation of emancipatory models can often lead to a superficial assessment of such progressive measures (see for example Bassnett, 1986).

By juxtaposing modern and anti-modern tendencies and by

hypothesizing an essential difference between a (progressive) modernizing and (regressive) cultural orientation, both Habermas and Touraine side-step the issue of how power is exercised at the micro level.[9] The underlying rationales for much of the action of social movements that do not conform to their models for emancipation tend to be discounted.

Sections of the Greens have attempted to turn away from élitist, prescriptive approaches to social emancipation. The search by Touraine for a new central conflict in society and for a new carrier for this conflict would be anathema to many. Whether this is a sign of their inability to create such a central class, or of their reluctance to act as an authoritarian vanguard, sections of the Greens, in a manner similar to Foucault, have suggested that the working class will have to formulate its own response 'from below' (see Papadakis, 1984: 216–17). Post-Marxist analyses also point to the 'pluralization of social life-worlds: the separation of public and private spheres, the growth of local autonomy, and the dispersion of various centres of life activity such as work, family, community and culture' (Boggs, 1986: 30). The attempt to transcend Marxism also implies a rejection of revolutionary intellectual élites, of social manipulation through claims of 'absolute knowledge of social totality' (Boggs, 1986: 59–60).

What requires further explanation is how these new orientations will shape field research. From a Foucauldian perspective, post-Marxist analyses need to incorporate a more thorough critique of emancipatory discourses and the normalizing role of the social sciences.

The suspicion of interventions through dialogue
The involvement by the Greens in local politics and their close links to a vast network of self-help community projects was perceived by the dominant parties as a major threat to their legitimacy. Strategies were developed to accommodate 'new politics' issues and to gain some advantage from the innovations of the self-help movements. Politicians and professionals in the state apparatus who could understand these changes were in demand and, if necessary, academics were recruited to advise on these initiatives (see below on the implications of interventions through dialogue). The architect of the Social Democratic strategy for 'dialogue' with the new social movements was Peter Glotz, who rose from the position of Senator in West Berlin to General Secretary of the party. Glotz saw himself as the mediator between two cultures which were drifting apart. He was concerned about the impact of these developments on his own party and wanted to find a basis for consensus and

greater communication between established cultures and left-wing subcultures (see Glotz, 1979: 1982).

Glotz correctly anticipated the growing dilemma for his party in trying to unite a productivist ethos with an ecological orientation, in trying to articulate the concerns of its more traditionalist working-class bases of support and those of the upwardly mobile white-collar and professional middle classes. In discussions with participants in new social movements, he admitted that social democracy had neglected new political issues (such as the environment, peace and alternative lifestyles) and spiritual and ethical questions.

Among the initiatives supported by Glotz was the funding by the government of self-help projects. According to one senior public servant advising the West Berlin government on health-care projects, the alternative movement, though not necessarily offering solutions to social problems, was able to draw attention to them (interview, May 1982). These initiatives support the observation by Arney and Bergen that 'the field of medical power has changed to become incorporative and rapidly responsive to developments around it' (Arney and Bergen, 1984: 167). They can also be linked to the attempt by the state (especially under pressure from conservative parties and business interests) to reduce its own financial contribution to the public provision of welfare (see Grunow, 1986).

The Greens became deeply suspicious of the strategy of dialogue. In the words of one activist, discussions with the state

> make sense to find out what the other side wants, what tricks it is using . . . and then to expose all this . . . Among us dialogue is instantly associated with the danger of being bought off and corrupted. You assume a great deal of self-confidence if you believe that you cannot be instrumentalized by this . . . If they, the Social Democrats and the Christian Democrats, offer dialogue, they want to integrate us. (interview, May 1982; my translation)

The fear expressed by participants in the self-help movement of instrumentalization and manipulation by skilled tacticians, by the intellectuals operating from within the state bureaucracy was shared by strategists in the Green party:

> Glotz is a problem. The strategy of dialogue by Glotz [pause] . . . I and many others feel very cautious about it . . .[it] is a purely tactical matter, it is really a matter of the SPD attempting to recover lost support, support which had historically enabled the SPD to get into government . . . The real political questions or political goals or criteria for politics are considered by Glotz purely from a tactical viewpoint, so that one does not have the feeling that one is engaged in discussions with some-one who is genuinely curious and wants to change, but rather someone

who is only peering in, in the last resort, and attempting to cream off something for himself. (interview, January 1982; my translation)

According to the alternative daily newspaper, *Die Tageszeitung*, the dialogue of Glotz had 'all the charm of a trap-door'.

This fear of becoming engaged in a discourse articulated by a more powerful opponent is also justified to the extent that government advisers and politicians were very skilled and fluent in expressing themselves, in stressing the need for tolerance, for communication between the state and protest groups and for self-reflexivity. Here are two examples.

> Basically both sides need to change, they must move towards each other. I don't mean that they should therefore give up their own position, but one must find ways whereby both sides can agree with each other to some extent. One shouldn't always say when a compromise has been reached that this is a victory over the other group. That draws people apart. Clearly this path towards compromise is very difficult because for years one has made compromises but always at the expense of the weaker group . . . There must be compromises which do not rob people of their identity. That is decisive. (interview, May 1982; my translation)

> I live in a bourgeois marriage . . . and am not disturbed by the fact that there exist other forms of togetherness elsewhere. I welcome it. But this does not place me under pressure to change my own form of living together . . . I know various strengths and weaknesses of my way of living together and theoretically I know that of others. (interview, May 1982; my translation)[10]

Dilemmas for radical reformists

None the less, new social movements have attracted sympathizers who are also highly skilled communicators and who have an intimate knowledge of the workings of the bureaucracy. New social movements and the Green party have employed social scientists in a manner not dissimilar to established organizations, to provide advice on all major policy issues and on strategies for achieving programmatic goals. The focus here is on the impact of Professor Peter Grottian, a sympathizer of the self-help movement in West Berlin.

An unsuccessful attempt had been made by the Ministry of Education to enter negotiations with some self-help groups, to discuss the possibility of funding them in a bid to gain a better insight into their operation. The groups, reflecting the attitude of suspicion towards politicians such as Glotz, initially rejected these overtures, fearing the loss of autonomy and the creation of divisions within the self-help movement. The collapse of this initiative prompted Grottian to form an organization for the funding of alternative self-help projects. There were two interrelated aims: to seek assistance from the state whilst retaining the autonomy of the groups, and to work towards a united stance among them before making such an approach.

The intervention by Grottian was decisive in persuading a large number of alternative groups to apply for funds from the state and, to some degree, in allowing even a Christian Democratic government to 'infiltrate' alternative self-help projects. Grottian was able to draw on his skill in communicating with both sides and his expert knowledge of the bureaucracy.[11] He argued that the pooling together of their demands and a carefully orchestrated public campaign particularly via the mass media would enhance the political relevance of self-help groups.

This initiative was aided by the fact that the state, even if only for purposes of short-term legitimation, *is* concerned over the lack of 'transparency' of its complex rules, regulations and structures. In West Berlin the Christian Democrats launched a campaign in favour of smaller, more transparent units of organization for the administration of welfare in which the highest levels of state authority would no longer have exclusive control and which, as far as possible, would enjoy a degree of autonomy. Other major parties also supported such measures. Although the state has drawn up criteria to identify 'worthwhile' projects (for instance, their contribution to certain aspects of health care, their capacity to encourage young people to shape their own lives and the rejection of violence as a political tactic) (see CDU Fraktion, 1982), there remains the issue of how to avoid state interference.

The initiative by Grottian was crucial in persuading a large number of groups that state interference could be reduced to a minimum. Grottian proposed that the intermediary organization he had helped to establish within the alternative movement would undertake the task of negotiating the conditions for the distribution of financial help and of submitting applications for funds: this would allow projects to deal with an organization, which though accountable to the state in the last instance, would also be much more sensitive to their needs and modus operandi than the established bureaucracy. He persuaded many that this would 'be better than being pushed around from one bureaucrat to another' (May 1982) but also insisted that they would have to be accountable to the organization for how they used the funds.

Attitudes within the self-help movement towards state intervention have been highly ambivalent – on some occasions they have led to discussions (over possible funding for social welfare projects) with the highest levels of the state apparatus (often via intellectuals who are sympathetic to their aims), on others they have reflected fear of manipulation and incorporation. Foucault's warning against a shallow approach to emancipation and rationality has not gone unheeded. His attempt to undermine notions of the 'whole of society' can be seen as an attack on the 'mindless identification of socialism with interventionism', on the emergence of strategies which would only 'represent a perpetuation of the present' (Minson, 1986: 143, 145).

Eräsaari has drawn on the critique by Foucault and the postmodernists to paint a bleak picture of the 'new social state' which 'institutionalizes selected community help, reshapes citizen expectations and tries to improve civic spirit and community-focused civil society' (1986: 231). He is at least correct in pointing out that the self-help movement has strengthened rather than weakened the power of the social bureaucracy, particularly in the more vulnerable areas such as youth culture and unemployment. Although conservative forces have reinforced the critique by the self-help movement of the inflexibility, inefficiency and inhuman aspects of the modern welfare state (see CDU Fraktion, 1982), it has been demonstrated that self-help groups and their supporters are predominantly middle-class and do not want a reduction in the levels of state welfare (Grunow, 1986: 200, para. 4).

The outcome of these developments is uncertain since they provide both a basis for the expansion of professional power (Eräsaari, 1986) and greater opportunities for challenges to it (Grunow, 1986). It could be argued that

> For many reasons – to be able to follow the discussions of the alternative movements, work with patchwork projects, identify new sociocultural strategies, etc. – critique of the social bureaucracy has already become a major resource of the new social state. Especially when the socialization or connecting work of the social bureaucracies seems in many ways to be an endless process, critical ideas are valuable because the registering of everyday phenomenologies may produce false or illusory results. (Eräsaari, 1986: 239)

Yet there is nothing new in this. The discussion by Bulmer of the Enlightenment approach highlights the willingness by policy makers, mainly in the United States, to encourage research that forces them to question earlier assumptions (1982: 48).

Eräsaari does, however, go one step further in stressing that the final decisions on the basis of data obtained through discussions between self-help groups and professional power are made by the latter (1986: 238) (see also next section). The senior public servant (see above) who was critical of the 'dialogue behind closed doors' was making the same point. It is therefore hardly surprising that most citizens, although they have a fair understanding of notions of choice and consultation, find it difficult to conceptualize control over decision makers (see Papadakis and Taylor-Gooby, 1987).

Eräsaari posits a general trend towards increasingly sophisticated techniques for manipulation, particularly in therapeutic forms of power which encourage people to 'become instruments of power over themselves through themselves' (1986: 239). Self-help is simply a smokescreen for self-manipulation in the interests of the state, for a reduction in state expenditure on welfare programmes. However, he can only suggest an alternative in the most general terms: through a search for 'inviolate' areas of life and through autonomy and decentralization (1986: 239).

The practicality of doing this has not been demonstrated by the self-help movement in West Germany. It has been buffeted between the search for autonomy and the need to secure financial support. Emphasis on the former has led to self-exploitation by participants who work very long hours for low pay; emphasis on the latter has forced projects to turn to the state for support, 'to negotiate with the "devil"' (see Papadakis, 1984: 202).

A major problem facing radical reformists is the general suspicion and fear of the bureaucracy. Any change in this area would require a change in attitudes based on a better understanding by the projects of the complexity of the bureaucratic process, and on greater transparency of these processes. However, initiatives for change will have to come from outside the bureaucracy. Progress in debureaucratization has been limited probably because of the 'absurdity of asking bureaucrats themselves to develop plans for debureaucratization' (Grunow, 1986: 203).

The implications of interventions through dialogue
In an attempt to overcome the rigidities of the civil service, governments have come increasingly to rely on the advice of experts employed on short-term contracts to offer 'neutral' advice to the government and, through qualitative research, to explain the motives of participants in new social movements. These and other initiatives mentioned earlier highlight the ways in which both the state and new social movements attempt to articulate popular perceptions, to develop new strategies and counter-strategies. In the end we find a mixture of successful manipulation and partial implementation of popular aspirations.

Some social scientists have been employed as policy advisers by government departments because they might offer 'neutral' advice. Unlike civil servants who are more likely to offer advice on the basis of individual strategies for career advancement, academics, employed as short-term consultants, are expected to say what they think.

However, until recently such advice has usually relied on quantitative data. The state has successfully used this to secure legitimacy, to provide the necessary 'evidence' to justify particular policies and new initiatives. The rise of the Greens has led to a more rapid introduction of new techniques. The traditional use of quantitative data has proved, on its own, inadequate for these purposes. Quantitative studies commissioned, for instance, by the Office of the Federal Chancellor, had identified the shift in values across all age groups and linked it with declining support for the Social Democrats and increasing support for the Greens. However, the politicians and their professional advisers were at a loss to explain the motivational forces behind these changes. The way was open for the planning division of the Chancellor's Office to commission, for the first time, a full-scale study using qualitative field research.

The research team, in designing a frame for the survey, were influenced by Habermas's concern with the 'life-world', the social milieu of different groups in the population:

> We only took this as a theoretical consideration. Habermas stops when it comes to empirical questions. He says that there is some kind of 'new life-world'. I agree. But how do you measure it? (interview with a member of research team)

The team therefore drew up a range of milieus populated, for instance, by followers of alternative life-styles, traditional working-class families, upwardly mobile workers, hedonists, conservatives and so on. Because they were investigating new issues, they abandoned the traditional approach of classification according to socio-demographic variables. For instance, with respect to sup-porters of the Greens, they argued that the milieu in which they find themselves, rather than their belonging to a particular age cohort, defines their allegiance to a new social movement, their support for new values. In this the researchers were implicitly accepting some of the major assumptions of post-Marxist analyses of social change.

Although most of the data from field research have not filtered through into short-term policy implementation because of the reluctance of the bureaucracy to take it seriously, Federal Chancel-lors have begun to incorporate and rearticulate some of the findings in their attempts to stem the Green tide. They have found that extracts from qualitative interviews are a very useful additional source of information and have cited them in their political speeches. The extracts have been used to add an 'authentic tone' to

otherwise dour political statements. Popular language and perceptions which may present a challenge to established structures are
skilfully filtered into the political process.[12] Data from qualitative
interviews were similarly rearticulated and incorporated into their
speeches in attempts to capture the popular mood.

It should be stressed that supporters and sympathizers of new
social movements and the Green Party have been very willing to
discuss their views and attitudes with researchers working on behalf
of the state.

The personal statements from qualitative interviews have provided
a vital link for Chancellors with the voter. They are, in certain
respects, a far more reliable source of information than that
obtained through established channels of politicians and professional bureaucrats who are more likely to say what is 'expected' of
them to the head of government. In analysing the rearticulation and
incorporation of these data, the way in which they are filtered, one
has to distinguish between the requirements of the government and
those of party general secretaries. For instance the General
Secretary of the CDU, Heiner Geissler, in a similar manner to Peter
Glotz when he was General Secretary of the SPD, has made extensive use of qualitative surveys in formulating party programmes.

The government uses the qualitative material in a similar way to
quantitative data, to secure legitimacy on a day-to-day basis, to
sustain a particular policy or initiative. The rearticulation of popular
discourse is very apparent. The parties, by contrast, have used
qualitative research for long-term planning. The SPD, for instance,
organized a qualitative study into the decline of active supporters
and members. This led to the implementation of a new organizational structure and of new forms of intraparty communication,
including the creation of a personal computer network which
provided local branches with rapid access to information from the
party headquarters in Bonn. The Irsee Programme of the SPD,
particularly the sections on peace, ecology and economic activity,
was heavily influenced by qualitative studies. Researchers from the
institute that carried out the survey were involved in the formulation of the programme which refers to social movements as 'major
partners in Social Democratic policy' (SPD, 1986: 34). There is an
echo here of the 'recursive method' suggested by Giddens which
stresses that structure should not be identified solely with constraint
on human action. Rather, structure 'is both the medium and
outcome of the human activities which it recursively organizes'
(Giddens, 1986: 533).

The cooperation of respondents in these qualitative studies,
including those from new social movements and the Greens, was

achieved with very little difficulty. Some were pleased at being consulted on their opinions and that some attempt might be made to implement them. There was no concern that what they divulged might be rearticulated in order to secure greater legitimacy for either the government or a particular political party. By contrast to the efforts of Touraine in the French anti-nuclear movement, by not overtly seeking to convert respondents the researchers achieved a high measure of success simply by inciting them to express their motives and goals.

There appears to be an absence of resistance to technologies of monitoring and surveillance which incite discourse. In many respects it is hardly surprising, since contemporary social movements themselves rearticulate, filter and incorporate the language of others. The success of the Greens, the impact by their supporters in the alternative self-help movement, can be explained in terms of their more pragmatic and flexible strategies, in terms of their self-limiting radicalism (see Papadakis, 1988).

The difference between the modernist orientation of the Greens and new social movements with a premodern orientation is most evident in responses to a pilot study of right- and left-wing radicalism in West Germany carried out by the SINUS research institute. At first the left-wing radicals, who included strong sympathizers of left-wing terrorist groups, refused to participate in a study commissioned by the government. However, they reasoned that they were already well known to the state security services, that they could tell the interviewer a load of nonsense and falsify the interview and that the inducement of DM 500 would make it worth their while.

A completely different approach was required for supporters of the extreme right. Interviewers often did not reveal who had commissioned the survey and stated, for instance, that they were preparing a paper for a university seminar on German national identity. In addition, female respondents refused to be interviewed by men. Their attitude, according to one interviewer, was essentially feudal. Among them, notions of authority and dominance were much more prevalent. The only way to incite discourse was through disguising the aims of the project. As Arney and Bergen have argued, 'Technologies of domination and control impel silence; technologies of monitoring and surveillance incite discourse' (1984: 170). In this instance, the state was perceived in feudal rather than modernist terms.

There are, of course, severe limits to the influence of social researchers in all these examples. On the one hand they are indispensable intermediaries between the population and large and powerful organizations. They can, to some degree, provide or withhold information. On the other hand, they can easily be hired and fired. The content of their research, the design of their questions, often has to conform to the assumptions and goals of the agency commissioning the study or seeking their advice. Their data, however objective, scientific or authentic, can easily be interpreted to suit purposes of self-legitimation (see Müller-Rommel, 1984).

The problem for Enlightenment Reformism and for Romantic notions of authenticity lies in how to overcome the incipient élitism of their prescriptions for social change. As Silverman, drawing on Foucault, has suggested (this volume), intervention in and rearticulation of discourses by subjects may provide an escape route.

This implies a complementarity of approaches, of emancipatory models and of anti-élitism, so long as they are linked to resistance to the instrumentalization of subjectivity (and support for autonomy) and to careful consideration of the operation of power at the micro level (including an understanding of prevailing institutional structures). The examples in this chapter suggest an uneasy mixture of successful manipulation and partial implementation of popular aspirations through the use of qualitative field research.

In the case of the West German Greens it is the rearticulation, for instance of the theme of nationalism by the peace movement, of widespread discontent with the inflexibility, lack of communication and accountability of the welfare state, of popular concerns with damage to the environment, and of dissatisfaction with the organizational rigidities of modern political parties and other established organizations, that has added to their popular appeal.

The incorporation and rearticulation of these issues in the programmes of major political parties should not be seen as a successful attempt to defuse the impetus of a new political power. New laws for the protection of the environment, greater funding for self-help projects and initiatives for peace and detente, however much they represent an attempt to perpetuate established political structures, may also signal significant improvements or at least a slowing down in the deterioration of the quality of life for most of the population. This success cannot, however, be attributed solely to the progressive emergence of post-industrial, modern, emancipatory discourses. Even if their interventions correlate with the aims of participants in new social movements, social researchers inevitably become part of a technology of normalization. It is for social actors themselves to rearticulate discourses. The capacity of social actors to intervene in, rearticulate and politicize the process of social change is unmistakable.

Notes

1   The term 'new social movements' is subject to diverse interpretations. The development of modern social movements has been linked with the advent of industrialization – with the need for societies to innovate in all spheres of life (see Banks, 1972) and with the dissolution of metasocial guarantees of the social order (including notions of divine law, natural historical evolution and the order of things (Touraine, 1985)). Although these interpretations underlie the meaning of the term 'new social movements' as used in this chapter, we are mainly concerned with those movements that lay strong emphasis on the democratization of society and on a reflexive approach to the creation of identity and meaning (see Cohen, 1985). This includes movements concerned with civil and social rights, alternative life-styles, sexual liberation, ecology, nuclear energy and nuclear weapons, ethnic minorities and so on.

2   The clash, for instance, between a productivist and an ecological model of development is addressed by both groups. However, the former seek to resolve the issue through a change in the political agenda (to a primary focus on measures for environmental protection), whereas the latter, whilst highly conscious of the need to incorporate environmental concerns, retain the primacy of economic growth (see Eder, 1982: 16).

3   Touraine has done this in a very self-conscious manner, drawing upon his experiences to create models for sociological intervention. Others, for instance, Peter Grottian who has offered his expert knowledge to the alternative self-help movement in West Germany, have not attempted to 'theorize' their experiences even though they too have, in essence, intervened in a similar manner (see below).

4   It should be stressed that sympathy for a particular social struggle did not lead the researchers to give up their hypotheses about what constituted the highest level of social conflict. The advantage of this approach lay in creating 'criteria' which could be applied in a range of settings. A further advantage is that it does away with the 'illusion' that the researcher can be detached from material under investigation. There is a parallel here to Foucault's 'methodology' and to the argument that 'the practitioner of interpretive analytics . . . can never stand outside' the phenomena being studied (Dreyfus and Rabinow, 1986: 115).

5   'It is not in the name of personal preferences or ideologies that we announce the visible presence of a new social movement, nor is it as the devoted interpreters of the actors and their ideology, but after an intervention in which we questioned the anti-nuclear struggle at length, placing ourselves far from its practices and its representations, on the summit of a distant social movement' (Touraine, 1983: 180).

6   The group had staged a polemical debate between ecologists and trade unionists which was recorded on video and later played back to the researchers. Touraine, however, interpreted this psychologically, arguing that the group had attempted to purge itself of excessive tensions (Touraine, 1983: 96).

7   The term 'Greens' will be used whenever I refer to both the Green party and new social movements. However, references will also be made to specific social movements such as those oriented toward self-help projects and alternative lifestyles, the peace movement, the ecology movement and so on. Some of the data presented in this section come from an earlier study of the Greens (Papadakis, 1984). I am particularly grateful to several supporters of and activists in the new social movements as well as to several policy advisers working for either state or federal governments for their time and effort towards discussions on the Greens. However, I remain solely responsible for any errors of interpretation or translation.

8   Cohen, in a review of literature on social movements, posits the need for greater synthesis between theories developed by social movements and social theory, between competing social theories, and between macro social theory and theories of social movements (1985: 715–16).

9   Cohen (1985) formulates the problem more in terms of addressing the prevailing institutional structures.

10   However, it would be incorrect to impute purely cynical motives to these statements or to assume collusion between the strategy of dialogue of Glotz and the views of these advisers. Several of them have criticised the failure of Glotz to take practical steps: 'The term dialogue has been misused. It has taken place behind closed doors, but with no practical consequences. I only want such discussions if they lead to something and are not simply programmatic statements. They must have consequences' (interview May 1982; my translation).

11   Grottian had previously carried out several research projects on the bureaucracy in West Germany.

12   There is a parallel to the manner in which medicine, through its discursive practices, filters 'the language of medical paraprofessionals, members of nonmedical professions, and others who present a potential challenge to orthodox medicine' (Arney and Bergen, 1984: 168).

References

Arney, W. and Bergen, B. (1984) *Medicine and the Management of Living*. Chicago: Chicago University Press.
Banks, Joseph (1972) *The Sociology of Social Movements*. London: Macmillan.
Bassnett, Susan (1986) *Feminist Experiences*. London: Allen & Unwin.
Boggs, Carl (1986) *Social Movements and Political Power*. Philadelphia: Temple University Press.
Bouchier, David (1982) 'Review of "The Voice and the Eye" by Alain Touraine', *British Journal of Sociology*, 33: 296–7.
Brand, Karl-Werner (1986) 'New Social Movements as a Metapolitical Challenge', *Thesis Eleven*, 15: 60–8.
Bulmer, Martin (1982) *The Uses of Social Research*. London: Allen & Unwin.
CDU Fraktion (1982) *Grosse Anfrage über alternatives Leben*. Drucksache 9/349 Abgeordnetenhaus von Berlin.
Cohen, Jean (1985) 'Strategy or Identity: New Theoretical Paradigms and Contemporary Social Movements', *Social Research*, 52: 663–716.
D'Amico, Robert (1986) 'Going Relativist', *Telos*, 67: 135–45.
Donzelot, Jacques (1979) *The Policing of Families*. New York: Pantheon.
Dreyfus, Hubert and Rabinow, Paul (1986) 'What is Maturity? Habermas and Foucault on "What is Enlightenment?"', in David Hoy (ed.) *Foucault: A Critical Reader*. Oxford: Basil Blackwell.
Eder, Klaus (1982) 'A New Social Movement?', *Telos*, 52: 5–20.
Eräsaari, Risto (1986) 'The New Social State?' *Acta Sociologica*, 29: 225–41.
Foucault, Michel (1977) *Language, Counter-memory and Practice*. Oxford: Basil Blackwell.
Giddens, Anthony (1986) 'Action, Subjectivity and the Constitution of Meaning', *Social Research*, 53: 529–45.

Glotz, Peter (1979) 'Staat und alternative Bewegungen', in Jürgen Habermas (ed.), *Stichworte zur Geistigen Situation der Zeit*, vol. 2. Frankfurt: Suhrkamp.

Glotz, Peter (1982) *Die Beweglichkeit des Tankers*. Munich: Bertelsmann.

Grunow, Dieter (1986) 'Debureaucratisation and the Self-help Movement', in Else Oyer (ed.), *Comparing Welfare States and their Futures*. London: Gower.

Habermas, Jürgen (1971) *Towards a Rational Society*. London: Heinemann.

Habermas, Jürgen (1981a) 'New Social Movements', *Telos*, 49: 33–7.

Habermas, Jürgen (1981b) *Theorie des Kommunikativen Handelns*, vol. 2. Frankfurt: Suhrkamp.

Habermas, Jürgen (1981c) 'Dialektik der Rationalisierung', *Aesthetik und Kommunikation*, 45/46: 129–61.

Lash, Scott (1985) 'Postmodernity and Desire', *Theory and Society*, 14: 1–34.

Minson, Jeff (1986) 'Strategies for Socialists? Foucault's Conception of Power', in Mike Gane (ed.), *Towards a Critique of Foucault*. London: Routledge & Kegan Paul.

Müller-Rommel, Ferdinand (1984) 'Sozialwissenschaftliche Politik-Beratung: Probleme und Perspektiven', *Aus Politik und Zeitgeschichte*, B 25/84: 26–39.

Papadakis, Elim (1984) *The Green Movement in West Germany*. London: Croom Helm.

Papadakis, Elim (1988) 'Social Movements, Self-limiting Radicalism and the Green Party in West Germany', *Sociology*, 22: 171–92.

Papadakis, Elim and Taylor-Gooby, Peter (1987) 'Consumer Attitudes and Participation in State Welfare', *Political Studies*, 35: 467–81.

Röttgen, Herbert and Rabe, Florian (1978) *Vulkantänze – Linke und alternative Ausgänge*. Munich: Trikont.

Silverman, David (1987) *Communication and Medical Practice*. London: Sage.

SPD (1986) *Irsee Draft of a new SPD Manifesto*. Bonn: SPD.

Thompson, John (1983) 'Rationality and Social Rationalization: An assessment of Habermas's Theory of Communicative Action', *Sociology*, 17: 278–94.

Touraine, Alain (1971) *The Post-industrial Society*. London: Wildwood House.

Touraine, Alain (1981) *The Voice and the Eye*. New York: Cambridge University Press.

Touraine, Alain (1983) *Anti-nuclear Protest*. Cambridge: Cambridge University Press.

Touraine, Alain (1985) 'An Introduction to the Study of Social Movements', *Social Research*, 52: 749–87.

Walzer, Michael (1986) 'The Politics of Michel Foucault', in David Hoy (ed.), *Foucault: A Critical Reader*. Oxford: Basil Blackwell.

Author Index

Subject Index